THE BOY

FROM

BOADUA

One African's Journey of Hunger and Sacrifice in Pursuit of a Dream

PATRICK ASARE

ISBN: 979-8-218-10100-8 (Trade Paper)
Library of Congress Control Number: 2022922654

Printed in the United States of America

Patrick Asare is available for speaking engagements.
Please contact patrickasareauthor@gmail.com

For Papa, Mama, Ernestina, and Patricia

To Art Carey, my wonderful editor.
My sincerest thanks to you for your
candid feedback. It was tremendously
helpful, and I hope you enjoy the
final product.

Patrick

Contents

Photographs

PROLOGUE

The Motivation

"WHY ARE YOU ALWAYS BOTHERING Antoine in class?" I asked Jamal, one of my high school math students.

"He acts White," was Jamal's reply.

"Acts what?" I asked, trying to make sense of his words.

"Acts *White,*" he said again, his voice starting to rise.

"What does that mean?" I was sincerely puzzled.

Most Americans, if only from their exposure to popular culture, would have instantly understood his complaint. I had no cultural context. I was a relative newcomer to America, having traveled here from my native Ghana by way of the Soviet Union.

In the two years I taught in the Buffalo School District, I learned a great deal about America's K-12 public education system and how minority children, in particular, fare in it. Those experiences, absorbed over the course of two more decades, form the core of my present commitment to school reform.

Given the extreme sacrifices I made as a young boy to advance my education, I was astonished to find such large numbers of minority children who made no attempt to learn when they entered my classroom, even though, compared to my village school in Ghana, they had access to much better resources. I, at least, had been lucky. As I observed my students' attitudes toward education, day in and day out, I couldn't help but recall one of my village school classmates, a brilliant, hardworking boy who, despite making enormous efforts to advance his education beyond middle school, was not so lucky. He is now trapped in crushing poverty in the village. Hardly a day goes by when I don't think of him—and his fate.

From other teachers at the school in Buffalo, I learned that the behavior I witnessed was commonplace in many urban American public schools. Haunted by that realization, I set out to try to understand the factors that inspired the children's disruptive behavior and lack of interest in education.

How, I asked myself, had I, an African boy growing up in a village where the prospects for education and betterment were slim to none, succeeded in beating the odds, when all these young people had to do was pay attention, complete their homework, and if they needed help, ask for it? Did they have any idea how utterly hopeless life was in other parts of the world, and how *lucky* they were to be growing up in a place like America?

At that time, I had no idea what I was dealing with—the sheer complexity of factors such as urban culture in America, economic deprivation, parental absenteeism, and racism that combine to make it so difficult for young Black children, especially boys, to make responsible life choices.

Like most young people in Ghana's rural areas in those days, for much of my childhood I pictured America as a heavenly place where neither poverty nor any of the myriad problems we saw all around us existed. From what little history I was taught in elementary and middle school, I knew about slavery and how Blacks in America were treated during that era, but I also knew that slavery had long since been abolished. What I envisioned was an America in which people of all races lived happily and in perfect harmony.

Knowing that the vast majority of my Buffalo School District students came from the poorer sections of the city had made me even more excited about teaching. Education had provided my escape from poverty. That sort of success story was unheard of in my village. Millions of children in those parts of Africa never get the opportunity to pursue even a basic education, ensuring that they will never find their way out of the extreme poverty that plagues the continent. Being a teacher in Buffalo would let me make a difference in some children's lives by helping them obtain the basic education that would empower them to rise above their difficult home environments, just as my teachers in Ghana had done for me. I looked forward to getting up each morning and going into my classroom to fulfill that mission.

Sadly, that bubbly enthusiasm quickly waned. I soon realized that an overwhelming majority of my students cared little about education. Constant disruption of classroom activities by students such as Jamal made teaching practically impossible most days.

The schools in Buffalo had decent classroom furniture, libraries, cafeterias, and other amenities—luxuries unimaginable in my village. The teachers were as dedicated as those who taught me in Ghana. So why were these students squandering such fantastic opportunities?

Since I left teaching over two decades ago, I have spent a lot of time thinking about my experiences in the Buffalo public schools. I have also closely followed the national debate about efforts to reform the K-12 public education system. Over that period, I have gradually learned about the complex set of socio-economic, racial, cultural, and political factors that underlie the dysfunction I witnessed as a teacher.

What if one of my village school classmates had repeatedly targeted me, as Jamal did Antoine, and disrupted all my efforts to learn?

What if the disciplinary problems in my school had made it impossible for the teachers to teach? Could I still have acquired the knowledge to go on to secondary school and beyond?

Was I blessed to have spent my childhood in an impoverished country such as Ghana?

In considering these questions, I began to retrace my steps along that unlikely journey that began from deep inside the African jungle and ultimately brought me to classrooms in Buffalo, New York. This book is not only a narrative of that journey, but also a reflection on issues such as race, socio-economic status, education, culture, the importance of role models, and some of the differences in social structures between Ghana and America that cause similarly situated schools to function differently in those two countries.

Given everything I have learned about American society in my three decades in this country, I am convinced that in some respects, I am lucky to have grown up in Ghana. Thousands of poor American children live in neighborhoods so violent that a safe passage to school is not assured. On top of that are the myriad socio-cultural and other systemic factors that conspire to rob youngsters of normal childhoods. I was fortunate not to have to contend with these challenges while growing up in Ghana.

Life may at times seem hopeless for many minority children in America's K-12 public school system, but that doesn't have to translate into fatalism, as was the case in my Ghanaian village. I lived in the inner city in Buffalo and became quite familiar with the environment there. It wasn't rife with gang violence. Largely, children could ride safely on buses to classrooms where, in theory, they could obtain a decent education. A significant majority of my students in the district could—and should—have taken advantage of the resources the schools offered to better themselves. Something else prevented them from attaining that all-important education. That something was what I set out to find.

Because I wasn't born and raised in this country, I probably will never be able to fully appreciate the entire range of feelings American-born people of color experience during their daily interactions with the broader society. I risk making arguments that either appear insensitive or sound naïve. It is partly for that reason that I waited for more than two decades to write this book. I hope time has given me the perspective to make my conclusions and recommendations worthwhile.

The exceptionally brilliant mind of my village-school classmate was allowed to go to waste by the society he grew up in. I am haunted by that fact. Who knows what he might have become, had further educational opportunities been available? What great things might he have contributed to society?

I am similarly haunted whenever I think about the large number of Black boys who drop out of America's K-12 education system every year, or graduate without proper skills, often with devastating consequences. This country is letting so much talent go to waste. As a naturalized U.S. citizen, I bear some of the resultant cost. That, in part, is what motivates me to do what I can, however small it might be, to improve educational outcomes in America's minority communities.

CHAPTER 1

Growing Up in Ghana

I WAS BORN IN A small village called Boadua, located in southeast Ghana. A decent amount of vegetation surrounded the area, but within the village limits the land was largely bare, except for a couple of large mahogany trees. Only mud houses with thatched roofs dotted the landscape. It felt as if everything around us was brown. The village had no paved roads, other than the main one that linked it to a couple of large towns nearby.

One of my most enduring memories of the place was the overpowering smell of urine that permeated everything. No one had indoor plumbing. Consequently, people were forced to urinate in public spaces. Every few minutes, in broad daylight, someone—man, woman, or child—would duck behind a house or other physical structure to urinate. The smell was particularly pungent during the dry season, between November and May, when the urine would soak into the soil and evaporate in the intense tropical sun.

A public toilet was located about three hundred yards from our house. The two rectangular pit latrines—one for women and the other for men— were separated by a wall. Each latrine was sixty feet long, three feet wide, and forty feet deep and had several wooden squatting slabs laid across the length of the pit. When the slabs wore out, they began to buckle. Whoever was squatting on them could fall into the deep pit and drown in raw sewage. Thankfully, that never happened during my years in the village.

Because of this risk, most people in the village were reluctant to use the public toilet. Others were too lazy to travel there from their corner of the village. A good number did their business in the bushes (because that required a greater degree of privacy) around the village. On windy days, our house was bombarded with unpleasant smells from the public toilet, as well as those that emanated from the nearby bushes. Whenever we ventured into those bushes on our way to the farm or elsewhere, we had to watch out for nasty surprises. We weren't always successful at dodging those "packages."

Even though the village lacked electricity, there was a fair bit of nighttime activity. The animals—chickens, goats, dogs, and cats—that roamed about freely during the day always went to sleep early, but people either congregated in the village square at night to socialize or clustered around wood fires in the open spaces in front of their homes to tell stories. Few people owned clocks or watches, so the vast majority of village folks were roused by the crowing of roosters, bleating of goats and sheep at dawn, or the early-morning call to prayers by the muezzin at the village mosque.

The village environment was typical of developing nations: desolate, with little to offer children. At best, children received a few years of basic education at the small elementary school and then joined their parents as subsistence farmers. Most men had no other options. Women worked as farmers as well, but a few were traders who sold wares such as vegetables and fish at the village market.

Because we didn't have running water, every morning my siblings and I made three or four trips to a river about a mile from the house. We fetched water in large metal buckets and bowls that we carried on our heads and deposited in two large barrels that sat in front of the house. Transporting the water required some well-honed skills: the load was heavy, and it had to be balanced carefully; otherwise the water would splash, causing the bucket or bowl to tumble. This time-consuming chore, among others, had to be completed before school, so on weekdays we woke at dawn.

One morning, my mother banged loudly on the door to the room where my siblings and I slept. Not a single drop of water remained in the two barrels that provided the water for all our household needs.

It was impossible to miss the muezzin's call to prayer, which echoed from loudspeakers in a booming voice that pierced the air. However, on this morning, my siblings and I chose to ignore the call—we had too many chores ahead. We responded quickly to our mother's loud banging; no one could sleep through that.

I picked up my empty bucket and joined my sisters, Esther, Gladys, and Christina, and my brother, Emmanuel, for the walk to the river. I was only eight years old and the youngest member of the team. The bucket I carried was clearly too big for a boy my size, but no one seemed to care. About a third of the journey had to be made through farmland and uncultivated vegetation. During the rainy season, that portion of the narrow pathway was often waterlogged and dangerously muddy. The terrain was treacherous that morning, but we all made it to the river.

The return journey was a different story. About halfway home, my neck felt strained from the weight of the load. As I adjusted my burden, I overlooked a pool of muddy water. I lost my footing and the bucket came crashing down. Now I was covered in water and mud, with nothing to show for my time and effort but an empty bucket. I felt so angry and frustrated.

Esther, who was eleven at the time, was only a couple of yards ahead. When she realized what had happened, she backtracked. I had managed to pick myself up and was holding the empty bucket, wondering what to do next. She stared, waiting for me. Several seconds passed and I still looked indecisive.

"You can't just stand there and feel sorry for yourself!" she shouted angrily.

What? That's all I get? I was about to demand the sympathy I deserved, but she'd already moved on.

"What should I do now?" I asked while she was still in earshot.

"Did your brain fall out of your head, too?" she shouted as she kept walking. "Go back to the river and fetch water to bring home." With that, she rounded a bend in the path. I could no longer see her.

She can't be serious! She expects me to walk without them back to the river? As those thoughts ran through my mind, several women—some carrying babies on their backs along with the heavy loads on their heads— and men passed me. It was clear what had happened to me, but no one seemed to care. Reluctantly, I trudged back to the river. Because traffic along that path was always heavy in the morning, at least I wasn't alone as I retraced my steps.

By the time I reached the river, Emmanuel, Christina, and Gladys had returned. To my surprise, they said nothing; they simply refilled their buckets and started walking back home. They were soon out of sight again, and I was left to negotiate the terrain on my own. By then I was so angry that I decided not to look at anyone as I walked home. I passed my siblings as they were returning for their third fills, but we all acted as if we were strangers.

Although I did not fill my bucket to the top on that second attempt, my neck was stiff by the time I arrived home. My mother asked why my clothes were so muddy. I was shocked to find that none of my siblings had told her what happened. After pouring the water into the barrel, I set the bucket down and recounted the ordeal to her. She told me she was sorry and that I should be more careful next time.

Given the circumstances, I assumed my water-fetching duties were done, so I proceeded to store my bucket.

"What are you doing?" my mother asked.

"My neck is sore. I can't carry another bucket."

"No, no, no, we need more water. You have to make more trips!" she commanded.

Holy Moses! Why can't anyone sympathize even a bit with this poor little boy? I thought to myself. My older siblings were expected to make four trips that morning; three trips would be acceptable in my case. Before school, I still faced other morning chores, along with a bath before breakfast. Way behind schedule, I had no time to waste. I grudgingly picked up the bucket and walked back toward the river, cursing everyone along the way.

I later came to understand that every household in the village faced the same mad scramble. People had to take care of basic needs before moving on to their myriad of other duties for the day; no one had time to offer sympathy to a young boy who had dropped a bucket of water. I needed to toughen up—and fast.

* * *

MOST OF THE PARENTS IN the village, mine included, were illiterate. Education was not a priority, and some parents did not even bother to send their children to school, despite government policy requiring elementary education for every Ghanaian child. Lax enforcement meant that many children were pulled from school to help with farm work. Fortunately, my parents valued education, and my siblings and I were expected to attend school. We worked on the farm weekends and during school vacations.

Children were supposed to be enrolled in kindergarten when they turned five, so that by age six they would be in first grade. However, most parents paid little attention to that milestone. Many children far exceeded the enrollment age before they started school. If one of my father's friends had not intervened, my own start might have been delayed.

Our house was only a few yards away from the elementary school. Every day, from the time I was three years old, I would play with the children in the schoolyard during recess. One day, when I was almost five, my father's friend walked by. He was on his way back from his farm, a basket of produce carried on his head.

"Raise your right arm, bend it over your head, and try to touch your left ear," he told me.

Although confused as to why he was asking me to do this, I did it anyway. The middle finger of my right hand touched my left ear.

"I will ask your father to enroll you in kindergarten," he said, walking away.

Perplexed, I asked the children at the playground what that was about. No one knew. I later learned that most village children had no birth certificates, and their illiterate parents couldn't remember their dates of birth. That made determining when a child was ready to start school a guessing game. Teachers and parents had relied on the right-hand-to-left-ear test for years to determine a child's eligibility for kindergarten.

Because of a classroom shortage, kindergarten classes were held under a large mahogany tree adjacent to the school building. Kindergartners did not need to write and so only needed small chairs. The teacher had a chalkboard, which rested on an easel. The class setup was primitive but effective. We were part of a habitat that included birds nesting overhead and goats and chickens roaming freely. Whenever it rained, class was dismissed. Rainy season fell sometime between July and September during the long school vacation. Even so, we were sent home several times because of rain.

Moving on to first grade was like entering a new, more civilized age. I was in a real classroom with chairs and desks. Although the space was crowded, we did not have to contend with animals and harsh weather. Those were happy times for me. I enjoyed being around other children.

The school itself was a simple building with six classrooms, each equipped with a chalkboard for the teacher and little else. It didn't have a cafeteria, so we were given a ninety-minute lunch break, starting at noon. Everyone walked home to eat before returning for the afternoon session. My siblings and I could not afford to buy lunch and so had to prepare our own at home. That added more stress to the day.

Lunch generally consisted of either boiled plantains or cocoyam and spinach sauce. Preparing the meal required an organized division of labor. One of us made the fire, another peeled the plantains, and someone else prepared the fresh spinach leaves.

We steamed the spinach leaves by placing them on top of the boiling plantain or cocoyam. After a few minutes, we would remove the leaves and grind them in a bowl. Then we would add onions, tomatoes, smoked fish, and finally, pour palm oil atop the entire concoction. It was delicious, but we never had enough time to savor it because of the rush to get back to school on time. We burned our tongues on numerous occasions.

The school had no library. Two textbooks were provided in each primary-level grade for math and English. That was all. Middle school students sometimes received one or two additional textbooks for subjects such as science, geography, and history. Libraries were extremely rare in Ghana in those days and, sadly, that remains the case today. When I was growing up, the closest library was in Accra, the capital city, about seventy miles from Boadua. Almost no one had books at home.

* * *

I was aware during those early years that my family suffered from extreme poverty. All but three of my thirteen siblings were still at home while I was growing up. Ernestina, the oldest, was twenty-five, and the youngest, Matilda, had just been born when I started kindergarten. Esther, three years my elder and the one who preceded me in birth order, was my closest sibling—the one I talked to the most.

My parents struggled to feed us. There was no such thing as birth control in Ghanaian villages at the time. That, coupled with high illiteracy rates, meant that many families had large numbers of children.

On his small farm, my father cultivated several different crops—corn, cassava, plantains, yams, cocoyams, peppers, okra, and tomatoes. My mother mostly stayed home to care for the children. The harvest was primarily used to feed the family, and whatever was left was sold to earn money for our other needs.

Our house was one of a handful in the village with plastered walls and corrugated aluminum roofing. With the tropical sun beating on the roof over many years, it looked as brown as the thatched ones in the village, but it provided better shelter during the rainy season. The house had three small rooms and a long verandah in front. Attached to the house were two other small rooms: one served as a kitchen and the other as a bathroom. The bathroom had no fixtures or plumbing. It was simply a place for bathing. Because there was no tub, after sponging our bodies we would simply pour the water from the bucket to rinse off the lather. The kitchen had no fixtures either, except for two three-legged mounds made from clay. We set our cooking pots on the mounds and placed firewood in the spaces underneath to make cooking fires.

Quite often, the smoke from the cooking fires did not filter out quickly enough through the two small windows in the kitchen, and our eyes would start to burn. At times we were forced to run outside just to breathe. Every family in the village used the same method—although some mounds were built outside in front of the houses—so in the evenings, when every household was making dinner, thick smoke enveloped the entire village.

Each of the three sleeping rooms contained a wooden bed with a straw-filled mattress. My parents had a room to themselves, but there were so many of us occupying the other two that when relatives visited, our parents were forced to share their room with us. The beds in our rooms were reserved for the older siblings, so the younger ones had to make do with either a thin straw mat or a rag on the floor. As the youngest, I often slept on a rag without a pillow. My body ached from sleeping on the hard concrete floor, night after night.

Living conditions in the village were harsh for most people. Young, single men struggled the most. With few employment opportunities available and no social safety net, some inevitably resorted to petty theft, most often of farm produce. Farmers kept constant watch during the harvest season.

I was out running an errand for my mother one hot Saturday afternoon when, from a distance, I saw a large crowd engaged in what appeared to be a brawl.

"What is happening over there?" I asked a woman standing nearby.

"I don't know, but I'm going to find out," she replied.

She started walking hurriedly toward the crowd. Although my mother was waiting impatiently for me to return from the village market, I followed the woman out of curiosity; I wanted to know what the uproar was about.

As we approached, I saw a young man carrying a large basket filled with farm produce. His face was heavily swollen, and he was bleeding profusely from the mouth. He staggered under the weight of the load like Jesus carrying the cross.

"What the hell is happening?" I screamed. I was nine years old and had never seen anything like that.

"He stole produce from someone's farm—it's in that basket," a young boy standing nearby answered.

As I was about to ask another question, two young men rushed toward the accused. One punched him in the face, and the other kicked him in the legs, causing him to fall.

"Jesus Christ!" I screamed and started to cry.

The two men were kicking the alleged thief as he lay on the ground, and others attempted to join in the melee. Before they could get to him, a few women stepped in. I later learned that the beatings had been going on for almost an hour, interrupted at intervals by good Samaritans. Seconds later they would resume.

The nearest police station was three miles away, but because the village had no telephones, the person accused of a crime—almost always male—would first be paraded through the village square and mercilessly beaten. The crowd would then march him the rest of the way to the police station and hand him over to the police for formal judicial proceedings to begin.

Too young to do anything but aware that it was wrong to treat another human being that way, I simply kept crying. The accused was helped back to his feet and the basket placed on his head, but seconds later he was back on the ground from being punched and kicked. I honestly believed he was going to die.

Suddenly, I remembered the errand. I reluctantly left the scene and ran to the market to buy the items my mother needed, all the while praying the accused would live.

"What took you so long?" my mother yelled upon my return.

"I saw a man being beaten to death," I replied, panting heavily from running so hard.

"Who was he fighting with?" she asked, her anger abating a bit.

"Some people accused him of stealing from a farm, and several men joined together to beat him," I told her.

Seeing how upset I was, she did her best to comfort me, telling me that the unfortunate practice was common and unlikely to stop, despite the best efforts of many women and some elderly men. Sadly, I would witness a few more such incidents.

I never understood whether the vigilantes acted out of moral outrage or sadism. I suspected it was the latter because many were rumored to be shady characters themselves.

As the years ticked by, my father realized he could no longer rely on subsistence farming to support our family. He discovered that wholesale merchants were traveling to villages, including ours, to buy lumber for resale in Accra. A couple dropped by our village every other Sunday. My father had some basic carpentry skills, so he set out to make a living from cutting lumber when I was in second grade.

This dangerous, backbreaking work involved felling large trees in remote forests. Ideally, at least two people did the job together, but my father worked alone because he didn't want to disrupt his children's education. He left for work around four in the morning and did not return until dusk.

During each two-week period, he would cut a few hundred pieces of lumber, which he stored in the forest. For some reason, no one in the village tried to steal lumber, so my father never worried about his cache. It may be that the market was limited, or thieves weren't interested because, unlike produce, lumber couldn't be readily consumed.

A day or two before the merchants' arrival, my siblings and I would make multiple trips to carry the lumber back to the village truck stop. My older siblings tied several pieces together, a practice that made the loads quite heavy but reduced the number of trips and allowed us to get the job done in time.

On several occasions, we couldn't transport all the lumber by Saturday night and had to make a couple of trips on Sunday morning before church. We were clearly violating the "Thou shall keep the Sabbath day holy" rule. Not being a churchgoer at the time, my father saw nothing wrong with working Sundays. Knowing how hard he worked, none of us could summon the courage to explain that commandment to him.

My mother attended the village Presbyterian church, and my siblings and I attended Sunday services with her regularly. A few of us even accompanied her to early-morning worship sessions a couple of times a week. There were also Catholic, Salvation Army, and Pentecostal churches in the village. Later, when my father became a Christian, he and Ernestina attended the Pentecostal church a friend convinced him to join.

Demand for lumber fell over time, until it reached a point when my father could no longer find a market for it. A return to subsistence farming did not prove viable. Overuse of farmland in Boadua had led to ever-dwindling crop yields.

My mother always cooked dinner for the family. We didn't have a dining table; instead we placed one large bowl on the ground and we all ate from it. There were a few fast eaters in the group, so we were always on the lookout for cheaters.

"Why are you taking such large bites?" Gladys asked Emmanuel one evening.

"Yes, he's always cheating," Esther remarked.

"He always takes larger bites than everyone, and he eats fast, too," Gladys continued.

I didn't necessarily agree. From what I had observed, Esther and Gladys were no pushovers.

"Why is Mama sitting there so quietly?" Gladys asked, just as I was about to weigh in.

Christina and three other older siblings—Beatrice, Felicia, and Daniel—were locked in their own competition in a separate "eating club" nearby. All eight of us seemed to have called a ceasefire. Everyone stopped eating and looked at Mom. She was sitting in a corner in the kitchen with nothing in front of her.

"Where is your dinner?" Felicia asked.

"There was nothing left for me," she replied.

"So what are you going to eat then?" we asked her.

"I don't know," she replied.

While we had been helping her prepare dinner, we had all heard her say she was extremely hungry. Financially, the family lived from hand to mouth. If all the food for the day was gone, she had no choice but to go hungry.

That realization hit everyone hard. Collectively, we decided to give her part of our dinner, but no matter how much we urged her to take what we offered, she refused.

"It's true that I'm quite hungry, but your portions today were already much smaller than usual," she explained.

It wasn't the first time our portions were unusually small. What we didn't realize was that she had made the choice to forgo dinner many other times. She had always managed to hide it so that we wouldn't feel bad.

After that day, we insisted that she ate dinner, reducing our own portions as necessary. She would pretend to leave something in her bowl, but we knew she never ate nearly enough to satisfy her hunger. On days when food was scarce, we would eat in near total silence. The sadness we felt was palpable.

With no sign of improvement in the family finances, my father had to make a decision. Without formal education, his employment options were limited to farming and low-skilled jobs. He found a piece of fertile farmland to lease in another location about twenty miles from Boadua. Although a relatively short distance away, the land was located in the middle of a jungle, without access to transportation. Commuting was not possible. He would have to relocate the family.

I was in fourth grade, unaware that disaster was about to strike. We would be relocating to an area that was almost uninhabited. Our schooling would come to an abrupt end. Naturally my father was reluctant to make a choice that would have such a negative impact on his children.

While my parents and older siblings struggled with that decision, I continued to live my happy, innocent life, oblivious to what hung in the balance. They agonized over it for a while, until my parents realized they could delay the decision no longer. With so many mouths to feed, the family could not survive on the tiny crop yield from the farm in Boadua. My parents and older siblings began to prepare for the move. I still had no clue what was about to happen.

No sooner had the preparations started than a critical intervention saved the day.

"Papa, I have something to discuss with you and Mama," I overheard Ernestina telling my father one evening. "Can I invite Mama to sit down with us?"

"Sure," my father responded.

I was eager to hear what she had to say. It was highly unusual for my oldest sibling to call a formal sit-down meeting with my parents. They were meeting on the verandah, so I hid behind our bedroom door and eavesdropped.

"I've come up with a plan to keep the family together in Boadua," Ernestina began as soon as my mother pulled up a chair and sat down.

What? Where have they been planning to move us to? I asked myself. Boadua was not a place families left, so Ernestina's words were rather bizarre. That piqued my curiosity even more.

"What's the plan?" my father asked.

"I'm thinking about starting a small business. I'll sell fish and vegetables at the village market. You will continue to work on the farm here. I'm sure that together we can support the family."

I could tell from my parents' reactions that they were excited to hear more.

"There is one problem," Ernestina continued. "Starting this trading business will require capital, and unfortunately I have no money."

"How can you get this idea off the ground then?" my mother asked.

"I'm going to ask a few friends to each lend me a little bit of money," Ernestina responded. "I'm not sure what my friends can provide, but I want to give it a good try. I would hate to see the education of my siblings cut short."

Hearing her last sentence terrified me. *Am I in danger of having my education cut short?* I wondered. Someone had to tell me what was going on.

I burst out of my hiding place and went looking for Emmanuel.

"Do you know anything about the family's plan to move?" I asked him.

"Yes, but I don't know when," he replied. "You didn't know?"

"Obviously not!" I replied with some annoyance. My heartbeat quickened. With a change of this magnitude, why had I been kept in the dark?

No one had formally informed Emmanuel either. Although my parents had discussed the impending move with Ernestina, Beatrice, and a couple of the older siblings, they had asked them to refrain from telling the youngest ones, believing we couldn't keep a secret. My parents didn't want anyone to know their plans until they were finalized. Emmanuel is three years older than Esther, and hence among the youngest, but he had overheard the older siblings' conversations and convinced them to share some details. He had been warned not to tell the rest of us.

Emmanuel was extremely happy to learn about Ernestina's proposal. He'd been worrying about what the move would mean for him. We both found it ironic that, of all people, Ernestina might be the one to save us from having our education halted.

She was about thirty years old at the time. Of the fourteen children in the family, she was the only one who, like my parents, received no formal education. She had been born when times were particularly tough, and it had not occurred to my parents to send their young daughter to school when she turned six. By the time they became aware, it was too late. They always regretted this oversight. As she grew older and saw her younger siblings enjoying school, Ernestina mourned her lack of education, but she never dwelt on her misfortune.

A few months later, Ernestina had managed to scrape together a little money by borrowing tiny amounts from a few friends in the village. She went to work right away, and for a brief period, it appeared that the family could be kept together in Boadua.

Our hopes were soon dashed. Even with Ernestina's support, the family struggled financially. We consumed a fair amount of her inventory. With the farm yielding little, and the heavy burden of providing for such a large family falling almost entirely on Ernestina, the small amount of seed money was almost gone. Something else had to be done.

My father, rather painfully, decided that he would leave us in the care of our mother and move to the jungle alone. He hoped to grow and harvest enough food from the new farm to supplement Ernestina's profits. The price of remaining in Boadua was that we would not see our father for extended periods of time. It was a sad day for the family when he left.

From that point onward, my brothers and I spent our school vacations—and some weekends—helping my father on the new farm. He came home occasionally to visit, but he spent much of the rest of his life away from the family.

My father, photo taken in Boadua

A typical Ghanaian village (stock photo)

My sister Ernestina at the Market

My brother Emmanuel

My sister Esther

CHAPTER 2

Scales and Lashes

THE LIFELINE THROWN BY ERNESTINA came with added responsibilities for the rest of us. Every other day, she purchased a couple of large cartons of frozen fish from a wholesaler in a nearby town. She'd then smoke the fish at home before taking them to the market to sell. After school, we would walk three miles to carry the cartons of fish—on our heads—from the warehouse back to the house. We would also carry home the firewood needed for the oven, collecting it from a nearby forest or purchasing it at the village market.

"Wake up, boys and girls!" our mother shouted from the verandah one morning as she banged loudly on the door of our room. "You have fish to scale before you fetch water from the river and do your other chores. If you don't hurry up, you're going to be late for school."

It was just past three in the morning. We had gotten only five hours of sleep. Esther, Emmanuel, and I had carried cartons of fish from the warehouse until late the previous night, while our other siblings had stayed up later than usual doing their chores as well.

We got up quickly, retrieved the three cartons of fish, and opened them. All were frozen solid, and every single one had to be scaled. Ernestina sold a variety of fish, such as tilapia, catfish, red snapper, mudfish, and mackerel. On this occasion, the warehouse had only red snapper in stock.

"I will help with the scaling," Mother said, when she realized the magnitude of the task.

We worked as fast as we could. Inside each carton was a microcosm of a Siberian winter. Within minutes, our fingers were numb. Scaling red snapper is a risky operation because of the sharpness of its needles, and the numbness made that morning's task even more dangerous. Only much later in the morning did my fingers return to normal.

We also helped Ernestina smoke the fish. Afterward, we would carry some of the smoked fish and vegetables to the market. Often, even before we began school, we were completely exhausted.

If Ernestina needed to travel to nearby towns to buy supplies or was busy at home, I would carry wares to the market and sell them until she arrived. In Ghanaian culture, it is almost taboo for boys or men to sell goods at the market.

In our family, there was little concern for separation of duties. The men did many tasks traditionally reserved for women. I felt embarrassed having to sell wares at the market. Fortunately, my male schoolmates did not tease me. Having no reason to be at the market, they never saw me there.

* * *

WHEN I WAS GROWING UP in Ghana in the 1960s and '70s, teaching was one of the few white-collar professions in the country. Teachers had a high social status, and as a result they commanded respect that kept them in control of their classrooms.

The rules in place in the elementary and middle schools I attended in Boadua were not much different from those in America's urban public schools today. We were expected to do our homework, get to school on time, keep quiet in class unless called upon by a teacher, and respect our teachers and classmates. Almost always, students obeyed the rules. They understood that if they didn't, punishment would be immediate.

Corporal punishment was permitted at that time. In my schools, every teacher had a cane handy. The number of cane lashes—typically administered on the backside—depended on the rule violated. Punishments took place in front of the entire class as fair warning to the others.

I was too young in those days to judge whether any of those punishments were justified. However, given what I know now, some of the teachers probably abused their power. In most societies, even criminal acts are occasionally excused based on mitigating factors. We could not comply fully with certain school rules for perfectly understandable reasons. That did not matter. We were punished anyway.

Getting to school on time was particularly difficult, given our many morning chores. Some students had to wake up at dawn, work on their parents' farms, or carry produce back to the house, all before school. Some farms were located far from the village. By the time such children returned home, they would have only a brief period to take a bath and get something to eat, and no matter how hard they tried, they couldn't make it to school on time.

In our geographic area, there were a couple of smaller villages with no schools. Children from those villages had to walk three miles each way. There was no other means of transportation. The teachers made no allowances for such students. Whoever came to school late received six cane lashes. It was the standard punishment. I had a taste of it on a few occasions.

All students were required to attend a daily morning assembly held outside on the school grounds. It began with the national anthem, followed by the headmaster's announcements. The assembly was the absolute worst place to receive punishment because the entire student body witnessed it.

One morning, I had been running around frantically trying to finish my chores and wound up being late. I had slipped and fallen (again) during one of my trips to the river; that had set me back twenty minutes. I could hear the national anthem as I ran to school, but it was over by the time I arrived. The headmaster was just about to begin his announcements, so I tried to sneak into the line of classmates. I didn't make it.

"Come over here, Patrick!" one of the teachers yelled.

My heart sank. That teacher was widely considered one of the meanest. Big and tall, he was known to give the worst cane lashes.

"You know you're not supposed to be late for the national anthem, right?"

"Yes, sir," I replied, my entire body trembling. All eyes were focused on me. "I tried to get to school on time, but I fell—"

I could not complete the sentence because, as I was speaking, he picked up his cane and yanked me toward him. He gave me six strong lashes. In those few seconds, I experienced intense pain and utter humiliation. The lashes left welts all over my backside.

Dear Lord, please inflict the worst possible curse on this man, I prayed. I was ten years old, and as a Christian, I knew those thoughts were sinful, but in the moment I felt fully justified.

At the end of the school day, additional chores awaited most children. Completing homework was not a top priority because illiterate parents deemed other things more important. That meant there simply was not enough time. Certainly a few neglected their homework out of laziness, but they were the exceptions.

Fearing the lashes, most children did whatever they could to avoid breaking rules. Only rarely did the teachers show any mercy.

While these rigid rules may have seemed unfair in retrospect, they were probably necessary. Any leniency might have been seen as a license to show up late to school, for example. If tardiness became rampant, the entire social order would break down, and the school could no longer function properly.

Within Ghana's education system at the time, teachers did not seem to be aware that different children had different abilities and could not learn at the same pace. Various practices unjustly discriminated against students who were not gifted academically, as well as slow learners.

We all dreaded the mental drills required in math class. Typically, a teacher dictated a list of ten questions. He or she paused between each one for a minute or so to allow students to write down their answers. Although the questions were often simple, involving memorized multiplication tables or basic arithmetic, some required a bit of calculation. None of this was made easier by our frantic morning routines, which left us stressed and exhausted. These rapid-fire questions were universally detested.

It had been one of those mornings when my mother had yelled at us like a drill sergeant to wake up at three in the morning to scale fish, meaning that I had worked non-stop for almost five hours by the time I arrived at school. I was not late, but I was dead tired.

"Take out your paper and pencils," our fourth-grade teacher commanded as soon as we walked into the classroom after assembly. We all knew what was coming.

"Fifteen times seven; fourteen times nine; seven times thirteen."

As he read the questions, it felt as if he was allowing less time than usual. The next five questions were simple word problems, and he finished off with two more multiplication table questions.

I should have breezed through that morning's drill. The teacher had alerted us to the multiplication tables he would be testing us on, and I had studied them the previous night. However, exhaustion kept me from responding to those first three questions quickly enough. Worse, as I struggled to remember the answers, my attention was diverted from the teacher's dictation and I missed the next couple of word problems. There were strict rules against asking teachers to repeat questions during those drills. That morning proved disastrous for me.

Sometimes, instead of grading the tests later, a teacher would walk around the classroom immediately after the drill to inspect student answers.

Students received cane lashes for any wrong answers. On this morning, I didn't have to wait long to learn my fate.

"You didn't study for this drill, did you?" he asked, as he looked at the nearly blank sheet of paper in front of me.

"I did study, sir," I replied sheepishly.

"Don't you lie to me!" he shouted.

"Please, sir, I studied—I just messed up." I knew that explanations were pointless in this zero-tolerance society, so I left it at that.

"You are way better than this. Go and stand in front of the class!"

He knew I was a good, generally conscientious student, but he was not prepared to listen to any excuses. Six other students were also indicted for poor performance that morning and were sent to join me in front of the class. I got only three correct answers and was thus sentenced to receive seven cane lashes. "Injustice" was instantly served.

I was tempted to ask God to curse him, but I resisted; I knew he meant well. It wasn't the last time I had to suffer that injustice. My situation at home never changed. I was always at risk.

Another even more abominable practice was the public shaming of students with low class rankings. In those days, schools in Ghana administered comprehensive end-of-term exams in all subjects. Class rankings were based solely on those exam results. On the last day of each school term, the headmaster and teachers assembled the entire student body for an end-of-term ceremony. They were held on the same grounds as the daily morning assemblies.

Teachers took turns calling the names of their students in order of class rank. As each student's name was called, he or she walked up to a stage in front of the assembly. Although I had witnessed a few already, one day the full extent of the unfairness of the practice struck home. That epiphany came to me in the third grade from what I witnessed at the end of the first term.

"The overall best student in the class for this term is Paul Asante," the sixth-grade teacher announced. "In second position is George Manu." For the next several minutes, he read the names of the remaining twenty-eight students in his class. As the number of people waiting to be called grew smaller and smaller, I observed palpable apprehension on their faces.

"The last student in this class for this term is Alberta Amakye," the teacher concluded.

As the young girl walked toward her classmates in front of the assembly, she burst into tears. By the time she joined them on stage, she was inconsolable. It was the first time I saw someone cry like that at an end-of-term ceremony. Following tradition, the audience clapped for the class ... but I did not. I could not take my eyes off the crying girl.

Why would they embarrass her like that? I asked myself. The cruelty was compounded by the presence of parents and siblings, as well as other members of the community. Worse, students almost always went to those ceremonies not knowing their rank. Ceremonies took place right after exams, when most teachers would have scrambled to finish grading their students' papers and tabulating their scores. There was simply not enough time to let students know their rankings before that "public execution."

At the time, none of us had ever heard of the right to privacy. Even if we had known that publicizing students' academic records was wrong, I doubt we could or would have done anything about it. Teachers and school administrators wielded so much power that their decisions were rarely challenged.

After that experience, whenever I attended those ceremonies, I worried about the feelings of the lower-ranked students and the negative psychological impact of outing them. Perhaps the teachers believed that a public shaming would motivate these students to work harder. I doubt that was the case. Instead, discouragement probably led them to drop out of school.

That, sadly, is what happened with Alberta. Although she was three years my senior in elementary school, the small size of our village meant that I knew a lot about what went on in other classes. Also, that first episode made me particularly interested in her situation. I heard that she was absent a lot during the next term. Toward the end, she stopped attending school altogether. She had dropped out by the time the next ceremony was held. Apparently, she didn't want to be subjected to that public humiliation a second time.

Another problem with our education system was that in those days in Ghana, few avenues existed for non-academic pursuits. A less-than-average student could receive cane lashes on a daily basis for performing poorly on mental math drills, no matter how hard he or she tried, then end up being humiliated in front of the entire community at the end of a school term. Perhaps, given the opportunity, that same poor child might have excelled as a musician or athlete.

Fear, unquestionably, can be a powerful motivator. It is what drove us as students in Ghana to sacrifice so much sleep and wake up at dawn every day, so we could finish our chores and get to school on time. No matter what, we somehow found a way to complete our homework.

One morning I awoke in sheer terror. Ernestina had received a large order for smoked red snapper from a family organizing a traditional wedding ceremony in the village. Whenever we scaled red snapper, we washed the fish afterward before we smoked them. Because we had four large cartons of red snapper to work on, we needed extra water. That meant that the previous day after school, we had to make additional trips to fetch water, then go to the warehouse to carry the cartons of fish home. It was so late by the time we finished that I completely forgot to do one homework assignment before bed.

"Wake up!" the familiar voice called out. Knowing the magnitude of the task ahead, we didn't hesitate to get up as we normally did.

I suddenly remembered. "Jesus, I forgot to do one of my homework assignments!" I shouted as soon as I stepped out of the room. "Can I please finish my homework before I scale the fish?" I asked my mother.

"No! Don't you realize how much work there is to do?"

"Please, Mama, if I don't finish it, I will receive cane lashes at school."

"Do you think saving yourself from cane lashes is more important than your family's survival?" she retorted, irritated that I was wasting precious time. I backed down.

The standard punishment for failing to do homework was ten cane lashes. It was a foolish mistake and incredibly rare. I was in a bind, but I was determined to avoid that certain punishment through any means possible.

I hurriedly retrieved the paper on which I had written my homework. Everyone was already busy scaling the fish.

"Where are you, Osei?" my mother shouted. While I was growing up, my parents and Ernestina always called me by my middle name—Osei. The rest of my siblings called me by my first name.

"Just a minute," I said.

When I sat down with the paper on my lap, she looked at me with annoyance. "And what exactly is that paper for?" she asked.

"It's my homework."

"Are you crazy? Don't tell me you're going to be doing homework here!" she screamed.

"Don't worry, I'm going to scale the fish as fast as I can and hopefully get a few minutes to finish this homework before school," I reassured her. That calmed her down a bit.

My siblings were all working furiously, but they kept glancing at me during that exchange. I wasn't sure whose side they were on. Apart from Ernestina, they all knew what fate awaited me if I showed up in school with an incomplete homework assignment, so I hoped they would show some sympathy. None was forthcoming, as far as I could tell.

I put my head down and started scaling as fast as I could. The fish were frozen, as always, so my fingers quickly numbed. With the speed I was working, I was at risk of serious injury. However, I needed to get ahead enough so a few minutes would be left to finish the homework. After the scaling, we still had all the other morning chores to finish. Things did not look good.

Every few seconds, I glanced quickly at the paper on my lap. I was doing as much homework in my head as I could. If I was lucky enough to get a few minutes to spare, I could scribble down the answers quickly.

"Can you stop that nonsense and focus on the work?" my mother shouted angrily when she caught me taking one of those glances.

Now that I was in her crosshairs, I realized I was better off completing the scaling and seizing those precious minutes from some other task.

As soon as we completed the "fish factory" work, I picked up my bucket and ran toward the river. Normally, I waited for at least a couple of siblings, but under the circumstances, there was no time to waste. After all, I was a fifth grader, a big boy, and I could handle the solo journey. Within an hour, I had completed my three required trips. Suddenly I saw a ray of hope. I just had to bathe, do the homework quickly, grab a bite of food, and go to school.

"Where are you, Osei?" I heard my mother ask, just as I was about to pick up the bucket of water and enter the bathroom.

"I'm going to take a bath," I replied.

"Come here first. I need you."

What? She is going to have me do something again? I ran over, anxious to find out why she was calling me.

"Please carry this to the market for Ernestina." She pointed to a large basket filled to the brim with vegetables—eggplants, onions, peppers, and okra.

"Can I please take my bath so I can do my homework?" I implored her.

"Osei, I already told you, Ernestina's business is far more important than your homework. That homework isn't going to buy food for you to eat, is it?"

I couldn't argue with that. She helped me put the basket on my head, and I was off to the market.

I wanted to run but the basket was too heavy. On my way back, I sprinted as fast as I could. Esther and Gladys were in the bathroom, so I hurriedly took my bucket of water and went into the makeshift bathroom my father had built on the side of the house. It was just a small enclosure, fenced with aluminum sheets. The bathroom inside the house was inadequate for heavy morning traffic, when so many of us had to take baths at almost the same time.

After scaling fish, we had to scrub ourselves thoroughly, because the scales were all over us—in our hair, on our arms, and on our feet. This morning there was no time to be thorough.

"Can I have the towel, please?" I shouted at the top of my lungs.

"Your sisters are still in the bathroom, and they are using it," my mother responded.

"Can you get it for me, please?" I was frantic.

"Esther says she is using it now; you will get it in a couple of minutes," my mother said.

Oh, my God! What kind of family have I been born into? Is life supposed to be this complicated? I stood there naked, shivering, and annoyed.

Towels were luxury items in the village, expensive and in short supply. When a family managed to acquire one, usually from traveling merchants, it was handled with great care. Our family only had one now. When my father had relocated, he'd taken the other with him.

By the time my mother threw the towel over the fence to me, only ten minutes remained before morning assembly. I hurriedly dried myself and put on my uniform. I picked up the homework paper—it had fish scales all over it that I had to shake off—and, within two minutes, I had written down my answers. It felt like magic! That mental work, done while taking those quick glances at the paper, did the trick. I didn't have time to eat, but that was fine with me; I preferred hunger to the pain of receiving ten cane lashes. I made it to morning assembly with seconds to spare. Heaving a huge sigh of relief, I belted out the national anthem alongside my classmates.

The fear was ever present in my village schools, as was the knowledge that the teachers had absolute authority to administer punishment. Teachers and school administrators enjoyed so much respect that it was unthinkable for any student to openly disobey a teacher's instructions. That combination of fear and respect helped create an effective learning environment in schools that otherwise had little in terms of resources.

In retrospect, I cannot condone the draconian measures the teachers took to enforce their rules, or the public shaming of less gifted students. However, these were different times, and none of us could afford to feel sorry for ourselves. Life was too hard, and self-pity would have made it harder. In an ideal, more enlightened world, there would have been more compassion.

Even within this fear-based academic atmosphere, school was a refuge of sorts. I could be with friends and engage in normal children's activities. Almost all the children in my school were at the same socio-economic level because most families in Boadua were similarly poor. However, I envied the kids who didn't have as much work to do at home. Most children came from smaller families and so did not have to fetch as much water in the morning, for example. Waking up that early to prepare and smoke fish was also unique to our family. The other fish sellers at the village market ran much smaller operations.

Home was not the only place where we were expected to do chores. We did not have janitors at school, so students took turns cleaning the classrooms and school grounds. We did weekly rotations, sweeping the floors and dusting classroom furniture. Apart from the cleaning duties, students also cut the grass on the field where we played soccer and other sports. When it was time to cut grass, everyone brought machetes from home. The field was quite large, and the entire student body took part.

As for sports, there weren't many options. It was either soccer or track and field. I was never good enough to get on either team. Nevertheless, I had a passion for soccer and played whenever I could. All the boys loved soccer, so every one of them was out on the field during recess. Shoes being scarce in the village, we played barefoot.

Soccer balls were beyond our means. The school owned a couple, but they were used only when we competed with other schools. For recreation, we relied on old, worn-out balls that had been discarded. For us, those were luxury items. We kept a pump nearby while playing, because every few minutes the ball would deflate.

* * *

At the end of the afternoon school session, my siblings and I would help our mother prepare dinner. She usually started the process before we arrived. Dinner choices were limited. Except for a handful of days during the year, we had *fufu*, a staple of the Akan tribe in Ghana. *Fufu* is made from boiled cassava and plantains, pounded and mixed together to form a dumpling. It is served with soup poured on top of the dumpling in a bowl.

Most people in Ghana eat *fufu* with their fingers. That is how we ate it at home.

Preparing *fufu* for our large family was a laborious process. We had to peel large quantities of cassava and plantains, which we boiled in a large aluminum pot. The pieces of cassava and plantain were then placed, one at a time, in a mortar and pounded into a dumpling with a pestle. The pestles we used were about five feet tall and had brushed ends. My mother would sit on a stool and place the cassava and plantains in the mortar. Two children, each with a pestle and working from a standing position, would pound them into a dumpling. As we pounded, my mother would knead the mixture with her fingers to make sure the texture was consistent.

The placement of the cassava and plantains in the mortar, and the pounding and kneading, had to be perfectly coordinated; otherwise we would hit our mother's fingers with the pestles. Since we had done this every day for years, we had almost perfected the art. The risk was minimal but by no means zero.

I had gone into my parents' room one evening to retrieve something for my mother, when I heard a scream. I ran over to see what had happened. It was our worst nightmare: her right hand was dangling by her side, and one of her fingers bled profusely. Emmanuel and Esther were on pounding duty that evening, and Emmanuel had accidentally hit her finger with his pestle.

"Can you call a taxi right away?" she asked, breathing heavily.

Emmanuel and Esther were rooted in place, seemingly in shock. Without waiting for further instructions, I ran to the taxi stop at the village square. I was struggling to speak when I arrived, so I started waving frantically.

"What's the matter?" asked one of the drivers, a worried look on his face.

"My mother is badly hurt. She needs to go to the hospital right away," I yelled.

He opened the front passenger side door for me, jumped into his seat, and drove as fast as the narrow pot-holed, unpaved road leading to our house would allow. By the time we got there, my mother looked as if she were about to faint. She had lost a lot of blood. My older siblings, who had rushed to the kitchen as I was running to get the taxi, had unsuccessfully tried to stop the bleeding by wrapping her right palm in pieces of cloth.

We all helped our mother into the taxi, and Gladys and Felicia accompanied her to the hospital, which was in another town two miles away. Although we had been hungry when we returned from school and it was well past dinnertime, we couldn't eat while she was at the hospital. No one had an appetite.

We waited anxiously for another couple of hours before they returned. I was relieved to see that she looked much better. Her finger had been stitched, and her right hand was heavily bandaged.

"Did you eat already?" she asked immediately.

"No," we replied.

She seemed surprised. "You haven't eaten since this afternoon, and you must be very hungry, so what is stopping you?" she asked, gravely concerned.

"We've all been extremely worried," Christina said. "We couldn't possibly eat without knowing what was going on at the hospital."

"Okay," she said, "get in the kitchen and eat. It's late."

It was close to nine o'clock. Reluctantly, we marched into the kitchen, got the food ready, and sat down to eat. Emmanuel and Esther had clearly not fully recovered from the psychological trauma, but our mother encouraged them to eat too. That was probably the only time I remember having leftover food. Our appetites simply never returned that evening. Given our mother's hand injury, she could not eat the fufu, so Felicia fed her soup.

One vivid memory from childhood is my mother's attention to detail. There were weekly rotations of duties for us, and one of them was dishwashing. We had a lot of pans, plates, and bowls, so typically two people were assigned to wash dishes during the week. Whenever we brought washed dishes to her, our mother would inspect them for food stains. If she found one on any plate, cup, or pan, she would demand to know who had cleaned that particular item. Invariably, the offender would get a hard knock on the head. Sometimes she would deliver the blow with the bowl or pan.

The knocks and hits were never violent—just strong enough to send the right message. We all learned quickly that it was foolish to show her any washed item with even the smallest stain. There were no child protective services in Ghana, so there was never any danger her children would be taken away from her for abuse.

My mother was always kind and protected us. She was also tough as nails when she needed to be. It wasn't easy to raise five boys and nine girls almost single-handedly.

CHAPTER 3

An Extraordinary Man in the Jungle

THERE ARE PEOPLE WHO, REGARDLESS of the obstacles in their lives, still have the inner strength to keep going. I was extremely lucky to have such a rare individual in my life: my father. He had tremendous courage, worked tirelessly, and willingly made unbelievable sacrifices that carried significant risks to his personal safety for the sake of those he loved.

My father was said to have been born in 1910. His illiterate parents could not make and keep such records. He later learned from relatives that he was born around the time of a major earthquake in Ghana. That put the year at 1910 and managed to give him a sense of the timing.

Both his parents died when he was still quite young. He was sent away thereafter to live with an uncle who was a hard worker and a strict disciplinarian. His uncle did not send him to school; instead, he put him to work on his farm and taught him carpentry.

My father left his uncle's house and set out on his own sometime in his twenties. He lived in a couple of small towns, doing odd carpentry jobs and tending to small farms, until he met my mother. She, similarly, had no formal education. Her own parents had died when she was still young. After my father and mother married, they settled in Boadua.

* * *

SHORTLY AFTER MY FATHER MOVED from Boadua to the jungle to begin his new farm, my older brothers started visiting him during breaks from school. It took several months before I made my first visit. I was about ten years old then, and in the company of my older brothers Richard (twenty-six), Daniel (twenty-four), and Emmanuel (seventeen). They knew what to expect, having been to the farm a few times already, but no one had described the journey and the place itself to me. I was about to receive the biggest shock of my young life.

The farm, which the family still owns, is located about seven miles from the village of Okumaning. A couple of passenger vehicles carried traders to Okumaning twice a week—on Tuesdays and Fridays—to buy produce that farmers in nearby villages brought to market there to sell. Any travel to Okumaning had to be conducted on one of those two days.

We made this visit on a Friday. The truck ride on the dusty, potholed road was the bumpiest I have ever experienced. My brothers said little. The somber looks on their faces told me the trip would be unpleasant. I didn't ask any questions, not being in a talkative mood myself. I knew that the truck stop at Okumaning was the farthest we could travel by vehicle. The rest of the journey would be on foot. I pictured a short walk from that truck stop.

On their previous visits, my brothers had taken supplies to my father. That day, we were carrying kerosene, cooking oil, salt, soap, sugar, smoked fish, and a few other items. Everything was packed in boxes, which we would carry on our heads.

Heavy loads required a cushion to protect the scalp. Typically, we rolled old pieces of cloth into cylindrical shapes and placed them on our heads. The weight of the load and the carrying distance determined how thick the cushion—and hence the size of the cloth—needed to be. At home this unscientific calculation was done on the spot to save time.

My first hint that something awful was about to happen was the sizes of the pieces of cloth each of my brothers had brought. Because I was clueless about the nature of the journey, mine was relatively tiny. Everyone looked at me and just shook their heads. It was obvious that I could not get any decent cushion from that small piece of cloth, so they kindly took some of the items from my box and added them to theirs to lighten my load. Even with that, I had a fair amount to carry.

At Okumaning we got something to eat before setting off on the final leg of our journey. The first mile or so was not too bad. We had a relatively clear pathway through light vegetation. After that, we traveled slowly on a narrow pathway through dense forest. The trail was not always clearly defined, which meant determining where to go was pure guesswork.

I couldn't keep up with my brothers and fell yards behind them every few minutes. Knowing they couldn't allow too much space between us, they kept stopping to let me catch up. I was several yards behind when I came to a spot where the pathway was unclear. I couldn't tell which way they had gone; I was stumped. I panicked.

We had already been walking for what seemed like an eternity, and my load felt heavier than any bucket of water or basketful of produce I had ever carried. My neck was stiff, and even calling out to them for help was difficult.

"Hello! Where are you?" I summoned all the strength I could muster. "I'm lost—you need to come back and get me." Nobody heard my calls, so I just stood there, utterly terrified.

As they'd grown tired, they had become distracted and forgotten I was with them. It was Emmanuel, himself a little behind Richard and Daniel, who suddenly realized I was nowhere in sight. In a panic, he called out to them, and they retraced their steps. They had to zigzag quite a bit because of the density of the forest.

"We're so sorry," Richard said when they found me ten minutes later.

It was the first time anyone had apologized to me for anything. The combination of emotions—fear, relief, and tiredness—made me start to cry.

"Let's put down our loads and rest for a few minutes," Richard suggested.

"That's a great idea," Daniel said.

They placed their loads on the ground and took mine as well. We sat there quietly for about five minutes; then Richard said it was time to go.

Although they slowed their pace considerably, I still couldn't keep up. I was a couple of yards behind again when I came upon a small stream. We had already crossed several—of varying depths—but in each case, the water was relatively clear. I had to tread carefully when the water was deeper, but overall, the crossings had not been a problem. This stream was totally different. It was too murky to gauge the depth of the water.

"Hello! I don't know how I'm going to cross this stream. Can somebody help?" I yelled. They were all within earshot, so Daniel walked back to the opposite edge.

"It's quite deep and slippery at the bottom. Be careful," he said.

"Okay," I replied nervously. I slowly lowered my right foot into the water, planted it firmly, and attempted to drag my left foot into it. "Oh my God!" I screamed, as I almost slipped and fell into the water. Luckily, I regained my footing. Moving gingerly, I managed to rejoin them.

Soon after my encounter with that stream, we confronted our next obstacle: a large tree trunk. The top was at chin level, so I couldn't scale it, even without the load on my head. My brothers were taller, but they couldn't scale that trunk easily either. There was no way around it. The forest looked impenetrable.

We all stood there for a few seconds, loads still on our heads. I couldn't tell from their faces if they had encountered this particular trunk on their previous journeys.

"We have to put down our loads and scale this trunk one at a time," Richard declared.

It was a welcome break because my neck was as stiff as a rock. Freed of his load, Daniel started to climb over the trunk. He struggled mightily, slipping a couple of times, but finally made it to the other side. Richard and Emmanuel handed the loads over the trunk to him. Emmanuel went next.

"What should I do?" I asked Richard. I wasn't sure how I was going to scale the trunk. I was too small.

"I'm going to help you," he replied.

He lifted me up and set me on top of the trunk. Daniel pulled me down to the other side. After Richard scaled it, we resumed the journey.

Two hours later, we came to the scariest part. A major river ran through the forest, and we had to cross it in order to continue. It was twenty yards wide and several yards deep. The remoteness of the area and sparse population meant there was no bridge.

The people who lived in the forest beyond the river had improvised. They'd felled a large tree to build a rudimentary bridge long enough to touch both banks of the river.

How exactly are we going to cross this river? I asked myself. I had always been afraid of water. I had heard stories of people who had drowned while swimming in the river in Boadua. I couldn't swim, and neither could anyone in my family. Whenever I went to fetch water, I took care not to step more than a few inches into the river, lest I be swept away by the current.

This tree trunk, suspended across the river, appeared to be the bridge to the other side. I prayed for someone to tell me that we would be crossing in some safer way.

"You all have to be very careful crossing this river," Richard said.

"How exactly are we going to do it?" I asked with a high degree of trepidation.

"We have to walk on the tree trunk."

"What? I can't do that! I don't know how to swim, and neither do you. If I fall into the river, I will die."

"Patrick," he said, "there is no other way. You just have to be careful."

36

The trunk was thirty feet above the river. Emmanuel and Daniel were both silent, their nervousness written on their faces. My knees started to wobble and buckle, and my entire body shook uncontrollably. *This must surely be my last day on earth,* I thought.

The worst part of the ordeal was that we would be crossing the river with our loads on our heads.

Richard crossed it first. I watched as he took excruciatingly slow steps, placing one foot in front of the other while balancing the load on his head. It took an eternity for him to reach the other side. *There is no way I'm going to participate in this insanity,* I said to myself. Then Emmanuel made it to the other side. Was this a nightmare or reality?

"It's your turn," Daniel told me.

"I can't do it! Why put a young boy like me through such an ordeal?" I argued, holding my ground and starting to cry again. Meanwhile everyone waited patiently. They were giving me all the time I needed to compose myself.

After finally acknowledging that I had reached the point of no return, I braced myself and took the first step. There were long pauses between each subsequent step. I was intently focused on the "bridge" all along, but at the midpoint, I made the near-fatal mistake of looking down at the water. I grew dizzy. The gravity of that mistake quickly dawned on me. Any small misstep would send me tumbling into the river. It was like walking on a tightrope while trying to balance a heavy load on my head.

Miraculously, I made it across. Almost immediately, the trembling of my body intensified. My near-death experience was severe enough to warrant psychological counseling.

"How much farther do we have to go?" I asked after Daniel finally made it across.

"We're only halfway there," Richard replied.

"What? Is this really necessary? Isn't there a better way to find the food we need?"

The ten-year-old philosopher was at it again. No one was in the mood to debate, so they simply resumed walking. They were already a few yards ahead when I finally realized I needed to stop feeling sorry for myself.

By the time we reached the farm, it was early evening. We had been walking for five hours. Under normal circumstances, we would have arrived sooner, but there had been too many obstacles in the dense forest that required careful navigation.

Our father was nowhere to be found. In those days, when we needed to call out to someone in that type of environment, we made howling sounds like a wolf that has strayed from its pack. The loudness of our howling was dictated by the density of the forest.

Richard's first few attempts failed. He was too tired to raise his voice enough. Daniel and Emmanuel also took turns. Finally our father heard the signal and howled in response. It took him several minutes to reach us. I couldn't believe that the simple two-room mud hut we stood next to was his actual living quarters.

It was. I was dumbfounded. What on earth was he doing in a place like that? He had built this structure all by himself, using soil dug up from his farm. I have never stopped wondering how a person could leave his family, move to a remote, uninhabited forest, and live there by himself the way my father did.

The forest was virgin and dense. Some of the trees were more than one hundred feet high. The place was filled with a variety of birds and wild animals, including deer, foxes, and porcupines. Every few minutes, a monkey swung through the air, jumping from one tree branch to another. It seemed like a nature-lover's paradise, but we had not come as tourists. The family captain had sailed into this "green ocean" to keep his sinking ship afloat. He had four support sailors on this day to help him in his mission. Our support would be temporary, however. We had only a few days' break from school.

An hour after we arrived, the sun began to set. Minutes later, we were completely enveloped in darkness. Our kerosene lantern was not equal to the job. We all clustered around it, because moving even a few feet away felt like falling into an abyss. Around nine o'clock, as we prepared for bed, the entire place fell silent. All the animal and bird noises ceased. The atmosphere was perfectly serene.

We placed straw mats on the dirt floor while I wondered how on earth I was going to relax enough to sleep. I was afraid monkeys or other wild animals would enter the open hut and attack us. Although I was incredibly tired and needed the rest, fear kept me awake for much of the night. I lay there quietly, listening for sounds of approaching animals.

Nothing happened. I awoke in the morning feeling relieved. My feet were extremely sore from all the walking, but it was time to begin the day.

Because our father was starting his farm from scratch, he did not have any crops to harvest. At the time of our visit, he had just cleared a piece of land and was preparing it for planting. Every few days, he trekked two miles through the jungle to a nearby village to buy cassava, plantains, and other raw ingredients for meals. After breakfast, Emmanuel and I were sent to buy more cassava and plantains, while my father and the rest left to work on the farm.

After we returned, we rejoined the three of them. Although I was used to working on farms, I quickly realized this was a different nut to crack. The vegetation was thicker and much more difficult to clear. We had to expend considerable physical effort with our machetes to get the job done. For several hours, we cleared brush and cut up the branches from trees my father had felled.

The work was nonstop. We knew the way our father operated, so although we grew tired, we kept going as long as he did. In the early afternoon, he let us take a break. We returned to the hut to get a drink of water and eat leftover plantains with spinach sauce for lunch. After an hour's rest, we went back to the farm. By then, I was finding it increasingly difficult to even swing my arm.

Because we spoke little as we worked, I kept glancing at my brothers to see how they were faring. Not much better than I. My father, on the other hand, was the Energizer Bunny, keeping up a steady pace. After several more minutes—by then I was just going through the motions—I said a few prayers, and soon thereafter the call finally came for us to quit for the day.

Back at the hut, it was time to cook dinner. Emmanuel and I were sent to fetch water from a small stream nearby. It was so shallow that we had fill the buckets by collecting water in cups. In the dry season, we later discovered, the stream often dried up completely, forcing us to travel a mile and a half through the forest to a larger river. On this occasion, although it was the middle of the dry season, we were able to collect some water from the stream. It was brownish in color, but it would suffice.

The water was probably unsafe to drink. All kinds of soil sediments and other foreign material had been washed into the stream, and at the very least, we should have boiled it, but we never bothered. There was little time for such "low-priority" tasks. The river water we fetched in Boadua wasn't much better. Especially during the rainy seasons, it was often brown and likely contained even more foreign material, since it flowed through heavily populated areas. We never bothered to treat or boil that water, and we drank it for years. I'm not sure how I am still alive.

After a week on the farm, it was time to return to Boadua to resume school. During the next several months, all four of us made a few more short visits to bring supplies and help out. Richard and Daniel were already out of the house and had come for short stays. They left Boadua not long afterward, and from that point onward, Emmanuel and I formed the two-man support crew.

* * *

I HONESTLY DID NOT BELIEVE my father would live on the farm for long. Although I was relatively young, I had a sense of the precarious nature of that environment. I kept hoping and expecting that he would give up and return to Boadua. At the time, I thought anything would be preferable. But then, one school vacation after another came and went, without any sign of him changing course. I ultimately realized this was how the remainder of my childhood would be.

We made that dreaded journey from Boadua to the farm in the same fashion numerous times in the subsequent years. I never got used to it. For long vacations in particular, I had nightmarish thoughts of spending three months in such a remote location, completely isolated from the rest of the world.

The work was extremely laborious. A typical day started at six in the morning. Emmanuel and my father would head out to the farm, while I prepared either boiled plantains or yams. I always picked the freshest spinach leaves that had sprouted overnight right off the cocoyam stalk and steamed them for the sauce. The plantains and yams were also freshly harvested. Because nothing was grown with fertilizers or pesticides, it was organic food at its purest. Without realizing it, I was probably eating some of the healthiest food in the world. Whole Foods would charge top dollar for produce such as this.

When breakfast was ready, I would howl to Emmanuel and my father. I had by then become an expert at howling and could summon them with just one or two tries. After breakfast, the actual workday would begin. We normally worked four hours, took a half-hour lunch break, and then worked for another four hours until it was time to prepare dinner. We only broke this routine on Sundays and days when we carried produce to sell at the market.

In his third year in the forest, my father started a cocoa farm. He kept expanding his operations until he had several acres of cocoa plants. To get a good bean yield every year, the brush on the cocoa farm had to be regularly cleared. That became one of our main jobs. We used machetes to clear brush from morning until evening over the course of several weeks.

My father had incredible stamina. I never could understand how he could work that hard for several hours, nonstop, at such a punishing pace.

By the middle of the afternoon, I was usually worn out; he looked as fresh as he had when the day began. He could never sit still. After the day's shift, when we were back at the hut preparing meals, he frequently returned to the field. In his mind there was always work to be done.

* * *

THE FARM WAS INFESTED WITH a variety of poisonous snakes, including cape cobras, carpet vipers, black mambas, and boomslangs. We saw at least a couple almost every day as we cleared brush. There was always the risk that a snake would attack and bite. We usually saw them in time to kill them before they had the chance. At times we would come close, almost stepping on one, the brush being so thick in some areas.

Whenever we saw one close by, we ran for our lives. As we ran, we often tripped on tree limbs and other obstacles. I was never sure which carried more risk—running away in a panic or confronting the snakes.

One hot afternoon, we were clearing brush when I saw vibrations in the vegetation about two feet in front of me. This movement signaled us to the presence of a rodent or a snake. The rodents were generally harmless, so we left them alone. I paused to see if I could determine what exactly was under the brush.

The vegetation stood still for a few seconds, but just as I was about to resume clearing, I saw the head of what appeared to be a large snake. Emmanuel was about five yards away. Despite being older, he was much more frightened of snakes, and he was already angry with me for raising too many false alarms that sent him running away unnecessarily, thus putting his life at risk. I wanted to be absolutely sure before alerting him.

"Run!" I screamed, sprinting as if shot from a cannon. A giant black cobra was flipping its tongue about wildly under the brush.

"What is it?" Emmanuel asked as we tore out of there.

"A giant black cobra!" I yelled.

After we had both reached a safe distance, we brainstormed ways to kill it. Leaving it alone was not an option. We would have to abandon that entire section of the farm for months on the chance that it still lurked out there. Whenever we saw a snake on the farm, we did whatever we could to kill it. Our father had returned to the hut to fix his machete, having minutes earlier struck a large rock and damaged the blade.

"We need long, solid branches," I said.

"You know where it is so you're going to have to take the lead,"

Emmanuel suggested. He was embarrassed to admit being afraid to confront the snake.

"Don't worry about that. Just get a branch and let's go," I yelled.

We ripped out two large branches from a nearby oak tree and crept cautiously toward the area where I had seen the snake. We spoke in hushed tones to avoid alerting it to our advance. Because it might have moved, the danger zone had broadened considerably. We stood silently, about three yards away from the spot, and watched for any sign of movement. Within seconds, I saw the vibrations again, meaning that it hadn't moved. Our branches were about five feet long.

"I'm going to move a little closer and strike it," I told Emmanuel.

"Okay, I'll be on the other side to corner it in case it tries to get away," he offered. He shifted to a spot diagonal to me.

Bam! I made the first strike.

"Watch out! It's moving toward us!" Emmanuel screamed as he started to run away.

"Come back, we need to finish it!" I commanded, striking again.

The cobra was now flipping around dangerously as if on the attack. Understanding the urgency of the moment, Emmanuel sprinted toward the cobra, coming at it from an opposite angle. We both struck it repeatedly with our branches before subduing it and ultimately finishing it off. By the time we finished the job, we were breathing heavily.

We learned early on that in that environment it was either kill or be killed. In the case of snakebite, there would be no way to get to a hospital in time to prevent death by venom.

The situation was made even more dangerous by our lack of appropriate clothing and footwear. Buying them required money we did not have. We normally wore shorts and open-toed sandals made from discarded car tires. With no socks, our legs and feet were totally exposed. The snakes had plenty of skin to bite.

If a snake was especially close, we would use the machete to cut off the head, striking rapidly because snakes are swift and pose the most danger when wounded. We had to finish the job quickly before they could fight back. Whenever we were lucky enough to spot them while they were still a few feet away, we would use a long tree branch.

Doing all that difficult manual labor was hard enough without being constantly on guard. Some of the more poisonous snakes lived in the cocoa trees. While we were bent over, clearing the brush and looking out for snakes on the ground, something could land on us from above.

A few weeks after Emmanuel and I killed that giant cobra, we encountered another snake while clearing brush.

"Get out of there!" Emmanuel yelled. He had already started to run, so I took off after him.

"Did you see something?" I asked as we ran.

"Yes! A snake on the cocoa tree you were under!"

That afternoon our father was only a few yards away, so he knew immediately what was going on. Though also afraid of snakes, his fear was not nearly as severe, and he had one of his cocoa-harvesting tools nearby. It was a ten-foot-long pole with a hooked metal blade at the end.

"Show me where it is," he said, when he came over to where we had taken refuge.

"Over there on that cocoa tree," Emmanuel answered, pointing from that safe distance. Our father walked carefully toward the tree.

"There it is! It's a boomslang," he explained. "A deadly snake. Move away!" That was our cue. Emmanuel ran for dear life again, and I quickly followed suit.

From the distance, we could see our father playing cat-and-mouse with the boomslang. It was trying desperately to escape, moving from branch to branch. Finally, we saw him yank the boomslang hard from a branch. It fell to the ground in two pieces. The sharp blade had sliced it in two but not killed it. The head still posed a great danger; our father ripped out a branch from one of the cocoa trees and struck it repeatedly until it died.

Over time, Emmanuel's fear of snakes made him paranoid. Whenever we worked on the farm, he would constantly cast an eye about for anything crawling around—either on the ground or in the trees. It got to a point where my father and I didn't even bother to look for snakes. We were confident that if there were ever any danger, Emmanuel would surely know. That was the case on this occasion. I was extremely lucky. Without him there, who knows what might have happened? The boomslang had been dangling dangerously on a branch directly above me, and according to Emmanuel, it was poised to drop onto my back.

We were living in a perilous environment, in grave danger almost every minute. Somehow, we managed to stay alive, day after day.

* * *

ONE NIGHT DURING A VISIT to the farm, the extreme danger of my father being alone in the jungle became especially real to me. I had stepped away into the darkness, just a couple of yards outside the hut, to retrieve something. I did not carry the lantern because it was being used elsewhere. Almost immediately, I felt a sharp sting on my right foot. The pain was excruciating. I let out a loud scream, and my father and Emmanuel rushed out with the lantern. I thought I had been bitten by a snake, which meant death would be imminent.

My father saw the culprit immediately—a giant black scorpion. I was relieved. I had no idea how poisonous scorpions were and was comforted that it was not a snake.

Within minutes my foot was grossly swollen. I felt an intense burning sensation and a severe itch all over my foot. I needed urgent medical attention. I obviously could not walk on that swollen and painful foot, and there was no means of transport. If I had any hope of getting to a hospital, it would have to be two days later, on a market day. Even then, I would need to walk those seven miles from the farm to Okumaning.

Fortunately, my father knew of an herbal remedy. Taking the lantern, he rushed into the forest, returning a few minutes later with a bunch of leaves. He mashed them in his hands and applied the plaster to my foot. Within seconds, I felt some relief from the sharp burning sensation. He then wrapped the leaves on top of my foot with a piece of cloth. The swelling subsided within a couple of days and I was able to resume normal activities.

On that occasion, I was lucky to have both my father and Emmanuel nearby. Their quick intervention saved me. After that experience, I worried constantly about my father being alone on the farm.

What if a scorpion had stung him in the middle of the night when he was alone? Could he have walked on a painful, swollen foot into the forest to collect the leaves himself? What if, instead of a scorpion, it was a snake? What would his chance of survival be? What if a severe injury left him immobile?

CHAPTER 4

Harvests and Arbitrations

WE NORMALLY HARVESTED COCOA DURING the long vacation from school.
At that time, the cocoa pods would turn a yellowish-orange color, which
meant they were ripe and ready to be harvested. We cut down the pods
from the cocoa tree stems and branches with machetes, one at a time. After
everything had been harvested, we would pick up the pods and carry them
in baskets to an open area. The harvesting and collection of the pods took
anywhere from three to five days, depending on the yield in a given year.
By the time we were done, we had gathered several thousand pods into one
big pile.

We then cut the pods open to extract the beans. Usually other farmers
and their families helped us finish the job in one day. That was important
because the beans had to be stored in one pile and covered with leaves for
three days to allow fermentation to occur. We returned the favor when the
other farmers completed their harvests.

After the three-day fermentation period, we placed the beans on wooden
beds to dry them in the sun. It typically took a week to dry the beans
completely. Then we would bag and carry them to the government-owned
purchasing center at Okumaning to sell. Each year, we had several bags
of cocoa beans to carry. It took multiple trips over the period of a week to
transport everything from the farm to Okumaning.

Additionally, Emmanuel and I carried heavy baskets filled with
plantains, corn, and other produce to sell at the market. Rainy season almost
always overlapped with harvesting season, so on the way to market, we
walked for long stretches on muddy, slippery forest pathways.

Because the farmland was incredibly fertile, the crop yield was so abundant that we could never carry everything to market. Each year, we watched beautiful bunches of plantain and bananas, fruits and vegetables such as oranges, avocados, and tomatoes, and other produce such as yams and cocoyams simply rot on trees and in the ground. Meanwhile, in Boadua, less than twenty miles away, families were going hungry because my father's farm was inaccessible.

Emmanuel and I sometimes couldn't bear to watch produce go to waste. On a few occasions, the temptation to carry everything became so great that we bit off much more than we could chew.

One of our worst such experiences occurred early one Friday morning as we were carrying produce to market. It was still dark when we left the hut. Emmanuel and I were supposed to carry bags of dried cocoa beans to a depot at Okumaning, but late the previous evening we realized we had run low on kerosene for our lantern, as well as salt and fish. My father asked Emmanuel to carry a basket filled with plantains instead. The cocoa would not be purchased until the end of harvesting season, so we would sell the plantains to obtain the cash we needed for necessities.

We needed a decent amount of money for the supplies, and there were many beautiful green plantains ready to be harvested that day; therefore, Emmanuel filled his basket to the brim with plantains. It turned out to be a calamitous mistake.

His load was so heavy that it slowed him down considerably. I kept worrying that he had gotten lost in the forest. I would wait for him to catch up. Within minutes he lagged behind again. As much as we all hated to see those beautiful plantains left to rot, my father and I had agreed that the load was too heavy and had tried to warn him.

I was several yards ahead when I heard wailing. At first, I couldn't tell what it was, so I stood very still to listen. The sound grew louder, and I turned to find that it was Emmanuel. Tears streamed down his cheeks.

"What happened?" I asked him in a panic.

"Help me get my basket down, I need to rest," he said, still wailing.

I set my load on the ground and helped him bring down the basket. His neck was so bent that I thought he would collapse.

"Throw away some of these friggin' plantains!" I implored him.

"I can't! I've carried them this far—I won't waste energy like that."

"Okay, let's rest for a few minutes and see what happens."

Conditions along the path were particularly bad that morning. It had rained continuously for three days, and water was pooling everywhere.

In some areas, the mud was knee-deep, and we could never judge its depth by simply looking. We had to step in it. We proceeded carefully, taking frequent detours to avoid dangerous spots and vast pools of water. Poisonous snakes lurked among the vegetation.

"Let's go," Emmanuel said after a ten-minute rest. His neck looked a lot better.

"Are you sure you want to carry this whole basket again? I think you should lighten the load a bit. Maybe we can store some of the plantains here and pick them up on our way back." I tried hard to convince him, but he wouldn't budge.

"We won't get enough money for the supplies if I leave some here. Plus, I don't want to do double work by carrying them back to the farm."

"Okay, let's see how things go," I said, relenting.

I helped him with his basket before struggling to get the bag of cocoa on my head by myself. It was quite heavy, and my father had helped me the first time.

"I think I broke my leg!" I heard him scream, a few minutes after we resumed walking. I rushed toward him.

"What happened?" I asked as I threw the bag of cocoa onto the ground and ran to him.

He was lying prostrate, covered in mud. Broken pieces of plantain were everywhere.

"I stepped into a pool of muddy water that was quite deep. I felt a twist in my leg, and I think I broke it." He started to wail again.

Oh boy! What am I going to do now? I just stood there, scared to death. We were alone in this deep jungle in the early morning. It was possible no one would come along our path all day. If indeed Emmanuel had a broken leg, we were in deep trouble.

I wouldn't be able to carry him back to the farm—or better yet to Okumaning, from where he could be transported to a hospital. We were close to the midway point. Either option required a long walk.

Could I leave him here and run back to the farm to fetch my father? What if he faints while I'm gone? I started to cry. As soon as he heard me crying, he sat upright and felt his leg.

"I think I might be okay," he said. "I felt a sharp pain in my leg when I fell but it doesn't hurt badly anymore."

Dear Lord, please heal his leg so we can get out of this jungle, I prayed quietly. As we both sat there in silence, a million thoughts ran through my head. The more I considered the options, the more complicated the situation appeared to be.

"Let's just get up and go," Emmanuel said suddenly.

"Go where?" I asked.

"To the market," he replied.

"Are you sure you can walk?"

After a brief pause, he said he could.

"Can you help me load the plantains into the basket?" he asked.

"Don't be silly! They're all broken—nobody will buy them."

"No, quite a few pieces are intact. We can sell those. Remember, we need kerosene and other important items," he argued.

We collected several plantains that were in good shape and placed them in the basket. I stopped him when it was about half full. I was in no mood for more accidents.

The market was about to close when we finally made it to Okumaning. Most of the produce buyers had already wrapped up for the day, but we found one woman still open for business. We asked her if she was interested in buying the plantains.

"Sure, let me see what you have," she replied. Emmanuel and I set our loads on the ground. "What happened to these plantains?" she asked. "They're all muddy."

Emmanuel gave her a quick account of what had transpired.

"I'm so sorry to hear that," she said. "As you can see, the market is closing and I'm getting ready to leave so I don't have a lot of time for this. I can give you three *cedis* for the plantains."

"No way! She can't be serious," I protested. I picked up the basket and started walking away, angry at the woman's callousness. *We've been through hell and she has not a shred of sympathy for us*, I thought.

"What are you doing, Patrick?" Emmanuel asked, perplexed.

"No way am I going to sell that basketful of beautiful plantains for three *cedis*!" I replied with indignation.

"Come back—we need to sell! We're out of kerosene. You want to sleep in darkness for an entire week in that jungle?"

That got my attention. I turned around and approached the two of them, forcing a fake smile to diffuse the situation.

"I will buy these plantains only because of your sensible brother," she said, extremely annoyed.

What? She's calling me stupid on top of cheating us?

"Come on, can't you take a joke?" Although it was a lie, I hoped it

48

would soothe her anger and encourage her to offer us more money for the plantains. She didn't fall for it.

"Here," she said, offering the three *cedis* to Emmanuel.

"You greedy bastard," I said under my breath. I was extremely angry. If we had arrived when the market was in full session, that quantity of plantains would have fetched at least ten *cedis*. She took advantage of our desperation. With what she paid us, we could buy only a half-gallon of kerosene. That week we had to do without the other items.

It being several hours past our expected return time, our father was worried sick. After a while he set out for Okumaning. We left the market late in the afternoon and were still two hours from the farm when we crossed paths.

"What took you so long?" he asked, looking very worried.

Fortunately, Emmanuel had a minor sprained ankle. The pain had subsided by the time we reached the market, so on the return journey he was fine. Our father was so relieved that his worst fears had not been realized. We arrived at the farm just before sunset.

* * *

WHENEVER WE SPENT OUR VACATIONS on the farm, I counted the days until the next school term, when I could finally escape from that oppressive isolation. The night before each departure from the farm seemed especially long, eager as I was to return to civilization.

A different emotion took over when it was finally time to depart. As soon as Emmanuel and I bid my father goodbye and took the first few steps of the return journey, loaded with produce to take to Boadua, tears filled my eyes. The happiness of the previous twenty-four hours gave way to sadness.

I never discussed my feelings and concerns with Emmanuel. If he had similar fears, I'd be even more distressed. I wanted badly to preserve the illusion that my father would be safe in the jungle.

As much as I hated life on the farm, the prospect of leaving my father alone for such long stretches in that dangerous place was terribly upsetting. He would have to spend all those frightening nights in the jungle by himself then prepare his own breakfast, work hard all day, and return to the hut to cook his own dinner. Each week, he would carry produce all by himself to sell at the Okumaning market to buy the supplies he needed. Even at that young age, I understood that it was too heavy a burden for one human being to bear.

My father never saw my tears. I was always out of his sight before they began to flow. If he had, he would have assured me everything would be all right. Not that I'd be convinced.

Usually, those feelings of sadness carried over into the first few days of my return to Boadua. My father visited the family regularly, but only for brief periods. He couldn't be away from the farm for long.

Did he really feel he needed to go to such extremes to fulfill his obligations as a father? This is the question I still ask myself. Then I did not fully appreciate the magnitude of his sacrifice. If anything, I resented him for choosing a path that made much of my childhood so difficult and unhappy.

Despite the bad hands life had dealt him, my father never indulged in self-pity. He had incredible optimism and believed that any individual, regardless of circumstances, has the power to do positive things in life. Given the cultural environment in Boadua at the time, he could easily have taken the easy road because expectations were generally low.

There were many other fathers in the village—with similarly large families and their associated problems—who made little effort to support their families. They believed in destiny—that the situation was beyond their control. My father took extraordinary measures to keep his family intact. He wanted every one of his children to have the chance to reach their potential.

My father was also highly intelligent, and it is a shame that he never had the opportunity to attend school. He used to say that if he had been educated, he would have become a lawyer. He had a great sense of humor, an incredibly sharp and analytical mind, and unquestionable integrity and objectivity. For many years, he acted as the de facto village judge. Whenever people had marital problems, disputes, or simply needed advice, they would seek his counsel.

The verandah in front of our house frequently served as a courtroom. Whenever my father was at home on one of his brief visits, a few families would stop by in search of resolutions to their problems.

Disputes occasionally centered around sharecropping. Quite a few families owned farmland in Boadua and would lease parcels to others. The typical arrangement was for a lessee to take a third of the crops harvested, with the remaining two-thirds going to the landowner. There were frequent allegations of cheating. Usually, the landowner would accuse the lessee of taking more than his share, but it could be the other way around. The aggrieved party would petition my father, who would then summon both sides. More often than not, both parties left the arbitration satisfied.

My siblings and I were bored by those agricultural matters, and only listened in if we had nothing better to do with our scant spare time. The disputes that commanded a front-row seat were related to marital affairs. Sometimes I did eavesdrop, along with the girls—Esther was almost always present. My brothers were all older and too serious-minded to pay attention.

One evening, we were in the kitchen helping to prepare dinner when we overheard a woman telling our father that her husband had agreed to appear before him the following evening for a mediation session. Polygamy is prevalent in Ghanaian villages, and the woman was the first of her husband's four wives. We had heard so many stories about that man and his wives that we knew it would be a blockbuster session. The older girls, who had heard many similar stories over the years, seemed less excited. Esther and I immediately booked our seats.

At exactly seven the next evening, we hid behind the door of our bedroom. Homework and chores could wait. Shortly thereafter, the wife took her seat, followed a minute or so later by her husband.

My father started the session by presenting the "facts of the case." Because the wife was the complainant, he asked her to speak first.

"I would like to know from my husband why he is favoring his third and fourth wives at my expense," began the wife. "He rarely sleeps with me nowadays and often doesn't come home to eat the dinner I make for him."

"Is that true?" asked my father, looking at the husband, who was a taxi driver. "And if so, what do you have to say about that?"

"She's not telling the truth," replied the husband. "I don't spend any more time at my other wives' places than I do at her house. It's true that I don't always eat her dinner. I often buy something to eat outside, because by the time I pick up my last passengers, it's early evening and I'm hungry."

"You're the one not telling the truth!" argued the wife. "You're in those women's homes almost every evening, and I know that because I have friends who see you going there and tell me."

"Who are those lying friends of yours?" asked the husband in an angry tone.

"My friends are not liars—you're the liar!" she shouted.

"You can't talk to me like that! You know that in Akan culture a woman has to respect her husband. Maybe your attitude is the root of your supposed marital problems."

"Please refrain from speaking in disrespectful tones to each other," pleaded my father. "If you keep this up, we won't get anywhere. I know you both want your marriage to work, so let's do our best to resolve this issue peacefully."

"Let me tell you what I think the problem is," said the wife, addressing her husband. "You think because they are younger, they are more attractive. I have bigger and nicer breasts than both of them, and my ass is bigger and better too!"

"What do you think? Does she have better 'assets' than they do?" asked my father, laughing heartily. He had a way of injecting humor into critical moments in mediations, when he sensed tensions were rising.

Esther and I started to giggle. No one knew we were eavesdropping, so we had to be careful.

"I guess she's right," the husband said, laughing.

"There you go. Case closed!" said my father, still laughing.

The session continued for a while. My father stepped in frequently to prevent matters from turning acrimonious. In the end, the husband admitted that he hadn't been spending enough time with his first wife and was also not giving her as much money as before. He promised his wife—and my father—that he would do better going forward. As soon as the session ended, Esther and I snuck out.

Through those types of sessions, we got to hear so many salacious stories that Esther and I became the go-to guys in school. When some of the other children wanted to confirm rumors they were hearing around the village about people's sex lives, they came to us. If only there had been tabloids in the village looking to buy our stories ….

Another of my father's impressive gifts was his unique ability to speak all the major dialects of Ghana. Apart from the six nationally recognized dialects used to conduct official business, there were many others he could also speak flawlessly. I don't know how he learned them, but it was fascinating to see him switch effortlessly from one to another. He appeared to pick up a language after only a bit of exposure. English was used infrequently in the rural areas, so he never had an opportunity to learn it. Still, he had a good bit of English vocabulary and could put a few short sentences together in some settings.

My father was a tremendous role model, thanks to his wisdom and practical way of thinking. In his view, nothing good happened in life without hard work and sacrifice. He did not believe in superstitions. In a part of the world where superstitious beliefs are so widespread and form such an integral part of everyday life, his approach, to me, was truly remarkable. My father was my greatest teacher and the best influence on my life. He never said much during all those years I was with him. However, just being around him, watching how he operated and the way he conducted himself, was an education in itself. I am grateful for all the opportunities I had to spend time with him and observe his hard work, determination, and optimism.

CHAPTER 5

The Audacity!

"SIR, CAN I PLEASE HAVE that wrapping paper after you're finished?" I asked the gentleman who had just bought roasted plantains from the street-side food vendor in the village square.

"What did you say?" he asked, a puzzled look on his face.

"I asked if you could give me the wrapping paper for your plantains after you're done eating," I repeated.

"What are you going to use it for?"

"I want to read what's on it."

He looked at me as if I were the weirdest person he had ever encountered.

"Here." He handed the piece of paper to me. He took a few steps, turned around to look at me once more, and shook his head.

I was eleven years old at the time. Almost immediately after I started elementary school, I had a sense that I liked looking at things written on paper. Illiteracy was rampant in Boadua, so it was unusual to see anyone reading anything. That made my love of reading an alien concept in the village. Given that there was no library, and the couple of textbooks provided at school were mostly kept there and used only during class, there were hardly any books around. Even if we had been allowed to take them home, the dry textbooks could not feed the insatiable appetite for reading that, inexplicably, I had developed as a young boy.

Among the prepared foods sold by the mostly female vendors who served the village square were cornmeal dumplings (called *kenkey* in Ghana) served with hot pepper sauce and fried fish; cooked rice served with stew; roasted or fried plantains; and cornmeal porridge, which most people ate with bread. Because dinnerware was rare in the village, moist foods were usually served on leaves (some as large as sheets of printing paper) of a West African species of *asplenium nidus* (a fern). Dry foods such as roasted plantain or bread were wrapped in scraps of old newspaper. Most food vendors placed long, rectangular benches by their stands for customers to sit on and eat their meals. After eating, most customers dropped their wrapping papers on the ground. The food vendors would pick up the trash at closing.

One day, purely by accident, I picked up one of those discarded newspaper scraps in the village square and read it. I learned right away that this was a great way to obtain reading material. Whenever I had a few minutes to spare in the evenings, I would lie in ambush by the food stands, waiting for people to finish eating so I could pick up the scraps of paper they discarded. After a while, I began asking them politely to give me the paper wrapper. Some days I didn't have time to wait and would return home empty-handed. Sometimes I got lucky and accumulated a few pieces in a single night.

Some customers were curious as to why I was making those requests. They thought I might try to resell those newspaper scraps to other vendors for cash. Most people were in a hurry and would simply hand over their scraps and leave.

One day, while reading one of those scraps, I came across an article about Achimota Secondary School, an elite boarding school founded by the British in Accra during the colonial period. According to the article, the school had educated almost all of Ghana's most influential people. Many of its graduates had gone on to study at Oxford and Cambridge Universities in England, returning to serve as presidents, ministers, and leading academics.

The article made an instant impression on me. It seemed to suggest a direct link between attending the school and becoming a person of prominence in Ghana. I decided there and then that I wanted to study at Achimota, and ultimately at Oxford or Cambridge, so that I too could become an influential person in Ghana.

I was too naïve to realize that my newfound ambition was not only absurd, but also completely mad. This was, after all, a school that catered to children of the ultra-wealthy and Ghana's small elite social class. It was the Ghanaian equivalent of Eton College, the British boarding school located near Windsor Castle on the outskirts of London. Completely oblivious of the futility of my pursuit, I set out on a mission to gain admission to Achimota.

All along, I had known that reading those old newspaper scraps was never going to be completely satisfying. Not having the full newspaper, I often missed parts of articles. Even if an article happened to be fully contained on one page, I might not get to read it all. Vendors rarely used entire sheets. If only a fraction of a sheet was used, I could miss large sections of an interesting article. Those limitations prompted me to think about buying the newspaper instead.

Every morning my siblings and I each received a few coins from Ernestina to buy breakfast. It was only enough to buy a small meal; that was all she could afford without bankrupting her fledgling business. Having no other source of income, I resolved to use that breakfast money to buy the newspaper every day. What money remained was not enough to buy a meal, which meant I would have gone to school hungry. Not yet prepared to do without breakfast, I continued to rely on the scraps of old newspapers for a while.

Reading the article about Achimota had, however, intensified my curiosity. I worried that I was missing numerous similarly interesting and valuable articles. I became increasingly eager to read the entire newspaper.

There being no televisions in Boadua at the time, I could only learn about the world outside our remote village through the newspaper. I woke up one morning, went to the small village post office where the newspapers were sold, and handed over my breakfast money in exchange for a newspaper. It was the best decision I ever made.

The few pennies I had left were not enough to buy food. From saving those pennies, I could buy breakfast only once a week.

Given the number of physically demanding chores I had to complete each morning, skipping breakfast was a terrible idea. On days that we had to wake up at three in the morning to scale fish before fetching water from the river, my stomach would start to growl as soon as I arrived at school. Sometimes it growled so loudly that everyone would turn to look at me. Making matters worse, at recess I would go out and play soccer with my friends. It hadn't occurred to me that I needed to avoid strenuous activity in order to conserve what little energy I had.

Should I just give up on this newspaper-buying idea? I asked myself whenever my stomach growled painfully in school. When I tried to return to the old regimen, however, I realized I had reached a point of no return. I had no idea what addiction was, but I was suffering from a severe form of it. There is such a thing as addiction to reading, after all.

I don't remember what triggered my interest in reading at such an early age. It was a rather unnatural habit for any child in that village. No parents ever read to their children—mostly because they were illiterate—and none of my older siblings spoke to me about reading. Whatever that trigger was, it became the force that changed the entire trajectory of my life.

Without the newspaper, I would never have considered secondary school. The most likely outcome for me—as it was for the other fifty-nine children I started school with in Boadua—would have been a middle school education, followed by subsistence farming for the remainder of my life.

My siblings and I often bought *kenkey* (without the fried fish because we didn't have enough money), rice and stew, or *kokonte*—another food staple in Ghana—for breakfast. *Kokonte* is made from dried cassava that is milled and then boiled in hot water to form a dumpling. It is similar to *fufu* in texture but brownish in color. Most often it is served with peanut soup.

Kokonte and *kenkey* are not ideal breakfast foods, especially for children who will be sitting in classrooms, trying to learn. They are heavy fare that will put even the most wide-awake person to sleep. Any nutritionist (there were none in the village) observing us eating those foods in the morning before school would have been horrified. In spite of that, *kokonte* seemed to be everyone's top choice—my siblings and I, and most children in the village. In our family, we burned so many calories doing our morning chores that *kokonte* and *kenkey* were probably not bad choices.

Only one woman sold *kokonte* in the village square. She prepared the dumpling at her stand each morning, stirring it with a large wooden ladle, in a giant aluminum bowl sitting on a fire, while the pot of peanut soup boiled vigorously in another large aluminum bowl by her side. The demand for *kokonte* was high, and a huge crowd gathered around the woman every morning. Because every student was trying to buy a bowl of *kokonte* and hurriedly eat it to avoid being late for morning assembly, there was always pushing and shoving. It was quite a sight—so many children with outstretched hands trying to get their empty bowls to the woman to be served. In the melee, the vendor often got hit in the face and head with empty bowls.

Equally fascinating was the sight of so many children shoveling down *kokonte* and boiling-hot peanut soup with their fingers. It looked like an eating contest. Often, by the time they were done, some children would come dangerously close to being late for school. They wouldn't even bother washing their hands in the large bowl of water that sat near the vendor.

Instead, they simply wiped their soup-covered fingers on their uniforms before dashing off to morning assembly.

Using my money to buy the newspaper meant skipping that excitement each morning. *Kokonte* and peanut soup, most Ghanaians will attest, is incredibly delicious. Denying myself that pleasure was an unimaginable sacrifice; somehow, I had the fortitude to stay away from the party week after week.

The intense, constant hunger took its toll, and I began to look gaunt. There were days when I felt so weak and dizzy that I couldn't concentrate in class. On such days, I would make simple mistakes on the morning mental drills and wind up receiving cane lashes on top of the already terrible hunger. What I was doing to myself made no sense, but my young brain couldn't figure that out. I was placing myself in grave danger.

"You're so stupid!" Esther shouted angrily at me one evening. Although she was looking straight at me, I initially didn't realize I was the target of her insult.

"What did I do wrong?" I asked.

"Instead of using your breakfast money to buy food, you buy newspapers. If you keep doing that, you'll die!"

Why was she so angry? Totally perplexed, I decided to walk away and mind my own business. I knew that people died when they grew old, but I couldn't see the connection between reading a newspaper and dying. *What does she know about death anyway?* I asked myself.

Esther was the only family member who knew what I was doing. Neither my parents nor any of my older siblings ever asked me about it. Esther had been worrying about my gaunt appearance for a while. She genuinely felt that something terrible was going to happen to me if she didn't speak up.

Her words frightened me and got me thinking. *This is indeed too much to bear. Maybe it makes sense to just stop buying the newspaper after all?* Throughout the next day, I was preoccupied with the question of what to do next.

Once again, I found myself unable to kick the addiction. After agonizing for a few more days, I decided to continue buying the paper. Esther tried a few more times during the next several weeks to persuade me to give up what she saw as a dangerous habit, but I ignored her. Fortunately, she did not take the matter up with my parents. They would have intervened, and I'm not sure I could have disobeyed them, had they told me to stop.

Luckily, we had an orange tree behind the kitchen in our house, and that tree became my savior for parts of the year. When oranges were in season, I at least had something to satisfy my hunger in the mornings. Because the elementary school was only a few yards from our house, I would run home during recess, pick up a knife from the kitchen, and hurriedly climb the tree—in my school uniform. I would perch precariously on one of the branches, pick several oranges, and slice them to eat. The oranges were delicious and filling, but the whole process was extremely risky. I had only minutes to spare (returning late from recess would mean receiving cane lashes), and I was scrambling up a tree with a sharp knife in my pocket. It was an accident waiting to happen.

One morning something terrible did occur. Growing up, I slept in the same bedroom where Ernestina used to sleep. Altogether, there were five of us in the room each night. I noticed that after she returned from the market each day, she kept her money in a pouch and left it in a drawer in the room. On days when the chores were particularly strenuous, I took a few pennies from the pouch so I could add to my savings to buy food. I only did so occasionally.

I made sure no one was in the room when I took the money. I was able to get away with it for a while, but on that fateful morning, I was caught with my hand in the "cookie jar." Ernestina walked in the moment I opened the pouch, clearly seeing what I was up to.

I put the pouch back in the drawer and bowed my head, completely ashamed. I was frozen in place for a couple of minutes, expecting her to yell at me—or worse. To my utter surprise, her lips did not move. She acted as if she hadn't seen anything, picked up what she came into the room for, and left. I stood there for a few more minutes and then exited the room.

Dazed and dejected, I picked up my stuff and left for school. Throughout the day, I thought how it would have been better if she had slapped me right there on the spot. I would have taken my punishment and moved on, as best as I could. Instead, I kept reliving that moment with increasing anxiety.

I returned home that evening prepared to face justice. Again, I encountered complete silence. I hadn't told anyone what had happened and wasn't sure if Ernestina had either. Another day went by. It was pure torture, and I had no idea what to do with myself by the end of the second day. *Maybe she didn't see what I was doing after all? If she did, what is she thinking? Is she trying to come up with the worst punishment she can think of?*

On the evening of the third day, after we had eaten dinner and I had completed my evening chores, my mother called me in for a private talk.

Since she had never done this before, I knew immediately what was in store.

"Can you tell me what happened in the room two days ago?" she began.

I tried to speak but my lips felt so heavy, I couldn't get the words out.

"I want to know what you were doing with Ernestina's pouch in your hands that morning," she said again after a few seconds.

"I took a few pennies to buy food because I was extremely hungry," I confessed, looking at the floor and speaking slowly.

"She gives you money every morning to buy food, so why did you need extra pennies? Don't you know that if you do that, her business will collapse, and we will all have to leave Boadua and go live in the jungle with Papa? Don't ever do that again, do you understand?"

"Yes, Mama," I replied. With that, she dismissed me.

My mother was well aware how hungry we were at school, because the food we were able to buy with our breakfast money was insufficient. She had no idea that my transgression resulted from an entirely different motivation.

I was utterly surprised by the unexpectedly calm reaction of both Ernestina and my mother to such an incident. My father was a strict disciplinarian, and my school had a strict disciplinary code. If either of those parties had found out, I would have been in serious trouble.

To this day, I remain convinced that neither my mother nor Ernestina mentioned that incident to anyone else in the family. In the thousands of conversations I have had with my siblings over the years, the subject has never been raised. Of all my siblings, Ernestina is the quietest and the most introspective. The character she showed in that moment, and in the ensuing days, is just one example of her modus operandi. She is a saint-like figure in the family and highly revered by all.

At home, I was always a good, hardworking kid. Because of that, I guess my mother and Ernestina decided to give me the benefit of the doubt. In essence, they gave me a second chance. The vitally important lesson I learned from that humiliation is this: maintaining a good reputation—at all times—is wise, because you never know when you might need to cash in on some accumulated goodwill.

Another equally important lesson was that a leader's authority often derives from the level of respect he or she commands. I respected my mother and Ernestina so much that I never wanted to disappoint them again. It was the last time I ever stole anything. If they had handled the situation differently—had given me some form of harsh, physical punishment—I am quite sure the incident wouldn't have had the same impact.

* * *

WHEN I WAS GROWING UP, children in Ghana generally completed ten years of elementary and middle school, followed by seven years at the secondary level, after which students had to pass rigorous examinations to qualify for the university. The typical student began university at almost twenty-three years old. Most towns and villages had elementary and middle schools that were free. Secondary schools were not. Located mostly in the district and regional capitals, they were predominantly boarding schools that charged tuition, room, and board. In many Ghanaian villages, no one knew anything about secondary school. While my family remained oblivious to my new goal, I was determined to do whatever was necessary to advance my education by gaining entrance to secondary school.

We had three kerosene-powered lanterns for lighting at home. Often, one or two were out of service because the glass shades had broken. We couldn't buy replacement shades in the village, so we had to wait until someone could travel to a larger town and buy them for us.

In addition to those three, we had a makeshift lantern, crudely constructed using a cylindrical empty milk container about the size of a twelve-ounce evaporated-milk can. A narrow, cylindrical exhaust pipe was mounted on top. Through the pipe, we dropped a wick (made from a rolled piece of old cloth) into the kerosene-filled chamber of the milk can, leaving a quarter inch of wick sticking out. We used a match to set it aflame. I often relied on its dim light for my homework and reading.

The smoke that billowed from that makeshift lantern (called *bobo* and used in many village households) was as thick and dark as exhaust from an old diesel truck. Using the *bobo* to study was a nightmare. The smell of kerosene and smoke could be overpowering. Worse, the dim light caused severe eye strain. Even when all three lanterns were available, they were in service for "more important" tasks, meaning I couldn't use them until everyone was asleep. I inhaled significant amounts of kerosene fumes and smoke over many years from studying with the *bobo*.

Because of my many chores, I struggled to find time to read the newspaper every day. I would read sections at school in spare minutes here and there and then stay up late into the night to finish it and do my homework. By the time I went to bed, it was so late that only a few hours remained until Mama woke us at dawn to start another day filled with nonstop work.

According to the article about Achimota, competition for places at the school was fierce. The school's students not only came from wealthy homes but were also some of the best and brightest in the nation. In most cases, their parents and other relatives were alumni who could guide them through the admissions process.

I read that an applicant had to speak and write English exceptionally well to stand any chance of gaining admission to the school. That requirement placed me at a disadvantage. We learned English in school and, largely, all instruction was conducted in English (because Ghana had been a British colony). However, the English we spoke at school was rudimentary. Few people outside of school in Boadua spoke any English. Needless to say, I was unlikely to become fluent.

Most students at Achimota came from the cities. There, they attended private schools with strong English language programs. Their English teachers were often native speakers, and being the children of diplomats and expatriate workers who mostly communicated in English at home, they had an advantage there as well. I had to find a way to catch up.

The benefits of reading the newspaper, which was in English, had already begun to show in my work at school. Every week we were assigned to write an essay on various topics. My essays were earning greater and greater praise and were often read aloud in class as examples for other students to emulate. I knew better than to be carried away by this positive response, because the standards of the village were low. I was nowhere close to being good enough to compete with students in the Achimota applicant pool.

Even if I cannot become a fluent speaker, improving my writing ability might be a good way to compensate, it dawned on me one day. *If I do well enough on the writing portion of the test, it might make up for my other deficiencies.*

My newspaper reading was often hampered by my limited vocabulary. The school had a couple of dictionaries, but we were not allowed to take them home. I realized I had to buy a dictionary for my personal use. That meant saving those leftover pennies from my breakfast money until I had enough. It took a few months to save what I needed. During that time, I went entire weeks without eating breakfast.

As it was with most things, dictionaries were not sold in Boadua, so I had to give the money to a merchant who came to the village periodically.

He bought the dictionary in Accra and delivered it to me on his next visit, along with a notebook for recording unfamiliar words and their meanings.

The dictionary proved extremely helpful. Before long, I had almost filled the notebook with new words and their meanings. I began to carry it wherever I went, trying to memorize its contents. After the first one was full, I ordered a second. I learned words such as *flabbergasted, mortified, confound, august* (as in "majestic"), *allude,* and *conflagration,* paying particular attention to the context. That enabled me to sprinkle some of my class essays with words I knew would impress my teachers.

With my improved vocabulary, reading the newspaper became much more enjoyable. In the process, I was learning not only about the rest of Ghana but also about other parts of the world. I had heard numerous biblical stories about Israel from church sermons, so I found articles about the Arab-Israeli conflict particularly interesting. Reading about events in other countries made me even more determined to leave the village to explore that wider world that had begun to fascinate me so much.

Other than the intense reading, there was much more I had to do if I had any hope of becoming a student at Achimota. I would need to excel at the math and general knowledge components of the admission test, widely known as *common entrance*. In addition to what was taught in their mostly private schools, my competition had access to test study materials I did not. All I had were my school textbooks. The lessons in my school were entirely focused on the end-of-term exams, so I needed to look elsewhere to prepare for the external secondary school admission test.

I found out that the test administrator sold copies of past examination booklets that most applicants used as supplementary preparatory material. Once again, I was forced to save my leftover pennies for a few months. I eventually obtained a few copies of old test booklets.

Working with those booklets proved enormously helpful. They gave me a feel for the types of questions I would encounter on the test. More importantly, reading those questions and finding answers broadened my knowledge beyond anything possible with only village school resources at hand.

If I had known from the outset how difficult it would be to gain admission to Achimota, I almost certainly would not have considered trying. Even a strong performance on the entrance examination did not guarantee admission. As I later learned, it was the only secondary school in Ghana with a two-step admission process. Students who had scored high enough on the *common entrance* to qualify were offered provisional admission. They then had to endure a rigorous interview process. Only those who also passed the interview were admitted.

My mother and my siblings must have seen that I was studying unusually hard during the year leading up to the exam, but no one asked me why. Academic matters were of little interest in the village. Because my parents didn't know much about education anyway, I didn't bother to tell them what I was doing.

During those months, I learned how much determination to achieve a cherished goal can drive a person. Greatest of the numerous obstacles I faced was finding a quiet place to study. Our house simply did not have private spaces where I could hide and study.

"Can you folks keep your voices down?" I yelled one night in frustration, as I was trying to take a practice test using one of those old test booklets.

"We're telling stories. How dare you tell us to keep our voices down!" yelled Esther, always the smart aleck.

"Will you shut up?!" I yelled even louder. "I'm trying to do something important, and you guys keep disturbing me." Seeing how my yelling annoyed her, I tried to appeal to her common sense.

"Why is what you're doing more important than the stories we're telling?" she asked, raising her closed fist with the right thumb pointing at me—the Ghanaian equivalent of giving someone the middle finger.

I was tempted to say something nasty, but I didn't. Esther could be quite vindictive, so I was careful not to escalate the situation, fearing she would do something to ruin that entire study session for me. And my mother was close by. I didn't want to get in trouble.

Usually, we all sat outside in the open, in front of the verandah, to tell stories at night. On this day, it was raining and everyone congregated on the verandah. I was sitting in one corner, close to where Esther, Charlotte, and Matilda (Charlotte was born after me, followed by Matilda) were sitting. That was the only place I could find, because people were already asleep in the bedrooms. In the end, I had to stop the test and wait until they finished telling stories and went to sleep.

If only I'd had access to a library. The school was close by, but there was no light there. I had no choice but to wait until late at night when everyone was asleep.

"Can I please have the lantern to study?" I asked my mother another night. I had been using the *bobo* for about an hour, and I could no longer see. It felt as if I had gone blind from squinting for so long. On top of that, my eyes were burning from the thick smoke pouring out of the *bobo*. I had tried to place the *bobo* a few inches farther away to reduce the amount of smoke I was inhaling, but then the light was inadequate.

"You know we cannot have the *bobo* in the rooms, don't you?" she asked.

"Yes, but I'm trying to finish my homework and readings so I can go to sleep a little early. We have to wake up at three o'clock to scale fish," I added to strengthen my argument.

"I know that, but I'm sorry, you'll have to wait till we are done using the lantern," she replied.

That battle was clearly lost, so I gave up. We were strictly forbidden to use the *bobo* in the bedrooms. That night, I waited for over an hour before receiving the lantern.

When it was finally time to take the *common entrance*, I felt that I had prepared enough to get a decent score. To say it had been a hard slog was a massive understatement. The nearest test center was in Asamankese, twenty miles from Boadua. I had never traveled anywhere alone, so this was going to be quite an adventure.

"I'm traveling to Asamankese early Saturday morning," I told my mother two days before the test date.

"What?" she asked as if she hadn't heard me.

"I'm traveling to Asamankese on Saturday," I repeated.

"To do what?" she inquired.

"I'm going to take a test," I replied.

"You take your tests in school, so why do you have to travel all the way to Asamankese this time? Are your teachers taking you there?"

"No, Mama, this is not a school test. I'm going by myself," I informed her.

"You're too young to travel to Asamankese alone," she protested.

I was twelve years old then; she had a point. I managed to assuage her fears. She asked no further questions about the test itself, mostly because she didn't know what to ask.

Knowing I would need to eat a decent breakfast on the day of the exam, I had diligently saved my leftover pennies for a couple of weeks. I woke up at dawn on the test date, boarded a passenger vehicle, and traveled to Asamankese. It was still quite early when I arrived, so I had plenty of time to get breakfast.

In those days, Ghana had nine administrative regions. The regions were further subdivided into districts. Boadua and Asamankese were both in the Eastern Region, and Asamankese was the capital of one of the region's districts.

The test center was located on the campus of Asamankese Secondary School, on the outskirts of town. I had never seen the types of structures I saw on the campus that morning. They were large, two-story buildings and freshly painted. The campus had beautifully manicured lawns, and because many of the grounds were paved, the place was not as dusty as the village. It being early Saturday morning, most of the students were still asleep in their dormitories, and the campus was quiet.

Is this what secondary school is like? Does the Achimota campus look like this? I asked myself. *If I do well enough on this test, I could be leaving the village next year to go and live in a place like this.*

A guard at the school entrance had directed me to the test center. Immediately upon arrival at the center, I began to feel nervous. I was used to taking exams in school at the end of each term, and those were always stressful. The environment at the test center felt a lot more intimidating. It was a large hall with nice desks and chairs neatly arranged in rows. The room could accommodate up to two hundred people, and it was almost full, with other candidates and the proctors already present. Seeing so many unfamiliar faces, each with a tense expression, made me even more nervous. *Could any of these people be applying to Achimota as well?*

Once the test began, however, I quickly regained my composure. The exam was a lot more manageable than I had anticipated. All my hard work had paid off. Afterward I felt that I had done reasonably well.

It still hadn't dawned on me that the goal I had set for myself was crazy. I had also done myself a huge favor by not telling anyone in Boadua I was applying to Achimota. My teachers would have considered it too much of a stretch and advised me to target a lower-tier school, if indeed I thought my family could afford to send me to secondary school at all. Affordability was also an issue I'd never considered. All I knew was that I desperately wanted to attend Achimota.

After the exam, I waited nervously to learn my fate. I received the results about six weeks later and was extremely happy to discover I had done even better than I expected. It was a good first step. The next couple of weeks would be even more nerve-racking. Most secondary schools made their decisions within two weeks after the release of the *common entrance* results.

During that period, anxiety left me strangely quiet. My mother and some of my siblings noticed the change in my mood and wondered what was wrong. I told them everything was fine.

Esther, unquestionably the nosiest of my siblings, had asked me once why I was always studying so hard. Three years my senior in middle school, she didn't remember having to work so hard when she was in my grade. I told her I was preparing to apply to secondary school.

"What's that?" she asked.

I wasn't surprised that she had never heard of secondary school. Seeing that she wasn't overly interested in the details, I kept things brief. She knew that I had gone to Asamankese to take the exam, but she couldn't make the connection between that and the change in my mood.

Mail was not delivered to homes in the village. There were no street addresses. The postmaster would sort the mail every few days, and then he would send word to recipients to come to the post office.

I had just arrived home from school one afternoon and was getting ready to help with dinner preparation, when a young boy came by to tell me that the postmaster wanted me to come to the post office to collect a letter. Since I rarely got letters and had already received the *common entrance* results, I suspected that it might be a letter from Achimota. *If indeed it was, would it be a yes or no?* I sprinted like a hare to the post office.

"How are you?" the postmaster asked. I bought newspapers from him every morning and he knew me quite well.

"I'm well, thank you," I replied, my voice quavering.

"Good to hear. You received a letter—let me bring it out for you." He had absolutely no idea what he was about to hand me.

Sure enough, the letter had the Achimota School seal. I struggled to open it because my hands were shaking terribly. With my eyes half-closed, I took a quick look at the first line and saw the beautiful words I had been waiting for.

Congratulations! You have been conditionally admitted to Achimota Secondary School.

My heart must have skipped several beats in those next few minutes. I quickly read the remainder of the relatively short letter. Because the admission was provisional, there weren't a lot of details. It contained the date of my interview and not much else.

The letter emphasized that the interview was as important as the test scores, and that failure to do well could result in denial of admission. I had always been nervous about that part of the process and this confirmed my fears. Given the fierce competition, there were no guarantees I would get in.

However, this was a big achievement, and I had to celebrate.

The postmaster didn't witness my excitement because I walked a few yards away before opening the letter. After reading the letter again to make sure I hadn't dreamed it, I sprinted home, screaming wildly and waving the letter in the air. Those antics attracted a lot of onlookers.

"Where have you been, Osei?" my mother asked. "Come in here and help!" She waved me into the kitchen.

"Wait! Wait! Mama! You cannot believe the news I just received," I said to her, panting heavily from that hard run.

"What news?" she asked, perplexed. I hadn't shared my *common entrance* results with anyone and neither my mother nor my siblings knew I had been expecting a letter.

"I have received conditional acceptance to Achimota Secondary School," I informed her.

"And what, exactly, is that?" She looked even more perplexed.

Unable to contain my excitement, I ran out of the kitchen into the neighborhood, screaming and jumping about with joy.

"What is going on with that boy?" one woman asked.

"He has been accepted to Achimota Secondary School," replied Esther. "What is Achimota?"

Before Esther could reply, the woman simply shrugged and went back to whatever she was doing. The rest of the bewildered crowd also quietly dispersed. They clearly didn't understand being so excited by something like that.

I didn't sleep the entire night. No matter how much I had tried to explain to my mother and my siblings how big an achievement it was to be accepted to that elite institution, no one was impressed. I was shocked and disappointed that no one at home wanted to help me celebrate the occasion.

"I got accepted to Achimota!" I ran into the classroom immediately after morning assembly and broke the news to my teacher.

"You what?" he asked, mystified. I was shy and never talked much in school, so the excitement in my eyes startled him.

"I was accepted to Achimota Secondary School," I repeated. I handed the letter to him, not expecting him to believe me without proof. He read the letter and was stunned.

"What? Where? How? How did this all happen?" In his shock, he fumbled around for words.

Before I could answer, he bolted out of the classroom and went into the headmaster's office. He called me over to join them, then invited the other teachers for a quick meeting in the office. Within a couple of minutes, the entire staff had gathered there, abandoning their classes, which were supposed to be starting at that time. All activities in the school had effectively halted.

My teacher read the letter aloud and immediately passed it around for the headmaster and other teachers to see for themselves. I could see every jaw drop as the reality of my achievement began to sink in. There was absolute silence for several seconds. The teachers kept looking at each other as if stunned by the magnitude of the news.

"Patrick, can you tell us how this all came about?" the headmaster asked, after he eventually regained his composure.

I began to lay out the series of events that led to my discovery of Achimota and the motivation to apply to the school. As I told the story, the teachers were transfixed. They stood still as statues. By the time I finished the narrative, we had been in the office for more than half an hour. The students, who had been sitting quietly in their classrooms, had begun to wonder whether something had gone seriously wrong in the school.

"That was quite audacious!" one of the teachers exclaimed, after I finished explaining.

The other teachers seemed to have regained consciousness as well, and questions began to fly at me from all directions. As the back and forth continued, the headmaster suddenly remembered that school was supposed to be in session.

"Please go to your classrooms to start your lessons, but let's regroup with Patrick to talk some more after the school day," he told the teachers.

The teachers patted me on the back and congratulated me as they left. I walked back into the classroom with my teacher, noting the curious looks on the faces of my classmates.

"Do you know what Achimota Secondary School is?" my teacher asked the class. Not a single hand went up. The only student who would know was absent from school that day. "Do you know what secondary school is?" he inquired. Again, not a single hand was raised.

Realizing that he would have to create an entire syllabus to explain what had occurred, he simply told them I had done something miraculous. He asked the class to give me a standing ovation. They duly obliged, not knowing exactly what they were applauding.

CHAPTER 6

The Interview

AT THE END OF THE day, the rapid-fire questions from the teachers and headmaster resumed and continued for more than an hour. It started to look as if the meeting would take all afternoon, but the headmaster stepped in, saying that my family would be worried. I was quite late getting home to begin my after-school chores, and I would have been in trouble with my mother had my teacher not accompanied me.

I was in Form 3 (the last-but-one year of middle school) at the time and Mr. Vincent Kpatakpa was my teacher. He was an older gentleman, probably in his early sixties. I consider him one of the best teachers I have had in my educational life. Though he was feared by many because he was strict, I liked him a great deal. He was highly dedicated to his work; plus, he could be quite funny.

"Good afternoon, ma'am," Mr. Kpatakpa said to my mother.

"Good afternoon, sir," she responded.

"You should be extremely proud of your son," he told my mother. She looked at him and smiled.

Though an entire day had gone by, my mother hadn't realized what her son had achieved. Mr. Kpatakpa knew she did not understand, but unlike my classmates, he had to take the time to explain. My parents would need to become deeply involved in the process from that point forward. My mother was preparing dinner, so Mr. Kpatakpa promised to return later in the evening for a sit-down meeting.

Coincidentally, my father was returning from his farm in Okumaning the following day for one of his periodic visits. My mother suggested postponing the meeting to enable my father to participate. Mr. Kpatakpa thought that was a great idea.

"You should be extremely proud of your son," Mr. Kpatakpa told my parents, repeating the same line from the previous evening. "What he has achieved is more than miraculous."

My parents listened quietly while he told them about Achimota Secondary School—and the near-certain impossibility of any child from Boadua gaining admission there. He went on to say that, in reality, it was completely impossible; he had qualified his statement only because I had somehow managed to overcome the odds.

My parents' eyes began to light up. Mr. Kpatakpa did a fantastic job laying it out so that even the most clueless person would understand the significance of the achievement. Because, he told them, the admission wasn't final yet, we could start serious planning only if I passed the interview and was formally admitted. That meant there wasn't a whole lot more to discuss that evening. My parents asked only a couple of basic questions.

"I will accompany Patrick to the interview in Accra," Mr. Kpatakpa offered in closing.

"Thank you!" my parents said.

"We wouldn't find our way if we had to take him," my father added.

* * *

"The interview is in only two weeks, so we have to start preparing now," Mr. Kpatakpa told me as soon as I arrived in class the following morning. I had no clue what an admission interview entailed. "I'm going to think about possible questions you might face, and together we will prepare answers for them. As I told your parents, I will meet with you for one hour after school each day between now and the interview."

"Thank you, Mr. Kpatakpa," I responded.

In the first session later that afternoon, Mr. Kpatakpa walked me through the basic mechanics of a formal interview.

"When you are called into the room, politely greet the interviewers and remain standing until they ask you to sit down. After that, listen carefully to all the questions, maintain eye contact with the person asking, and speak clearly when answering."

He conducted mock interviews with me during each session over the course of those two weeks. We covered all the basics, such as where I came from, my parents' occupations, why I had applied to Achimota, and whether

I had applied to any other schools. Toward the end, he asked me more difficult questions, such as what I wanted to become in the future and why. I had answered so many questions by the end of that two-week period that my head was spinning.

* * *

ON THE DAY OF THE interview, we left Boadua at four in the morning, traveling by bus to Accra. It was my first trip to Accra, so I was excited. However, soon after the bus left Boadua, I started to worry. We had prepared thoroughly for the interview, but I found my nerves taking over. The anxiety persisted for the entire journey. Mr. Kpatakpa noticed my harried state and tried to keep me engaged in conversation to soothe my uneasiness. The seventy-mile trip lasted three hours. The road was bad in some areas and the bus stopped a couple of times along the way to drop off passengers and pick up others.

It was seven thirty when we arrived at the campus. The place was unlike anything I had seen or read about. I had been impressed by the campus of Asamankese Secondary, but this was on a much higher level. The campus sat in the middle of Achimota Forest, a national forest reserve, at the northern edge of Accra. The grounds were leafy and the atmosphere serene. It was simply gorgeous.

I could tell right away that I was totally different from all the other applicants. The other children had arrived with their parents in fancy cars and were neatly dressed. It was the first time in my life that I wore anything resembling dress shoes, but my pair was a cheap knockoff.

All the interviewees and their families were gathered in a large hall outside the interview room. As we waited, I kept looking at the other children for signs of nerves. I couldn't detect any, and that made me even more nervous. From their calm demeanors, I concluded I was the only unprepared one. Some of the parents were even joking with their children. *Do these people have nothing to lose? How could they be taking something of this magnitude so lightly?* I kept asking myself.

"Let's step outside for a minute," Mr. Kpatakpa told me.

What? Has he seen something bad? I followed him.

"Do you remember everything we practiced?" he asked, after we found a quiet spot.

"Yes, I do," I replied.

"Remember, the first impression is the most important; make sure you greet the interviewers politely when you step into the room and don't sit until you're told to do so."

"Thank you, Mr. Kpatakpa, I will make sure I remember those protocols."

I started to sense a little nervousness in his voice. He had become so personally invested in this pursuit that the pressure had begun to get to him, too.

We had been sitting down for less than five minutes after returning to the waiting area when he asked me to step outside with him again.

"Do you remember the part about maintaining eye contact with the interviewers and speaking clearly when answering questions?" he asked.

"Yes, I do," I replied again.

"Oh, one more thing. If you don't understand a question, say 'I beg your pardon, sir (or madam, if it's a woman), can you please repeat that?' and thank him or her after you get clarification."

"Thank you, I will remember that," I replied.

During the hour-or-so wait in the hall, Mr. Kpatakpa conducted four more mini-coaching sessions. They were highly useful because, due to my nervousness, I seemed to have forgotten much of what I had learned.

I finally heard my name called. "Patrick Osei Asare."

"Good luck," Mr. Kpatakpa whispered as I got up to walk to the interview room.

"Thank you," I said.

A young lady ushered me in. The atmosphere in the interview room turned out to be a lot more intimidating than what I had felt outside. I stood in front of a panel of eight men and women seated behind a majestic table— long, rectangular, and made of rich brown wood with a gleaming top. Hanging on the walls of the equally majestic room were several large oil paintings. In my newspaper readings, I had learned about famous painters such as Michelangelo, Picasso, Rembrandt, and van Gogh. *Were any of these possibly made by one of those famous painters?* I wondered.

The men were in suits and ties, and the women wore fancy dresses. These were clearly people of high stature in society, the kind I had read about in the newspaper. I immediately froze, my mind a blank. I stood still for a few seconds, with my head down, trying to recollect the advice Mr. Kpatakpa had given me only minutes earlier.

Suddenly, I looked up at the panel and saw broad smiles on everyone's faces. The smiles helped calm my nerves. They all responded to my unduly delayed "polite greeting," still wearing those broad smiles, and then they asked me to sit down.

"How are you doing this morning?" asked the woman in the middle, the lead panelist. I later learned that she was the chairperson of the school's board of trustees. There were two other trustees on the panel. The headmaster of Achimota was also there, and the remaining panelists were teachers and administrators.

"I'm doing well, thank you, madam," I replied.

"Please state your full name for the panel," the lead panelist asked next.

"Patrick Osei Asare."

"Where do you live, and what school do you attend?" she continued.

"I live in Boadua, where I attend the local Presbyterian middle school."

The panelists exchanged glances when I mentioned Boadua. Clearly, none of them had ever heard of the place. The village was too small to be on any map of Ghana.

"Where exactly is Boadua located?" the headmaster asked.

"It's near Akwatia," I said.

"Oh, that diamond-mining area?" another panelist asked.

"Yes, sir," I replied.

Akwatia is a well-known town in Ghana because a British-owned diamond-mining company in Ghana was headquartered there for many years. Most of the initial questions were basic and easy to answer, so after a few minutes, I relaxed considerably.

"How did you find out about Achimota Secondary School?" the headmaster asked me.

"I read about it in the newspaper two years ago," I replied.

"What newspaper?" the lead panelist followed up.

"The *Daily Graphic*," I replied. It is the national daily newspaper in Ghana.

"Are students required to read the newspaper in your school?" the headmaster asked.

"No, sir," I replied. "I started reading it on my own and kept up the practice because it allowed me to learn about national events and other places in the world." I saw a lot of nodding going on across the table.

"So, tell us why you decided to apply to Achimota," the headmaster asked next.

"The article I read talked about the great education this school provides. I learned that many past Ghanaian prime ministers, ministers, diplomats, and other prominent people attended this school—and later went to Oxford and Cambridge," I responded.

My answer seemed to have frozen the panelists in their seats. They all sat there in silence for several seconds, exchanging glances.

"Would you like to become a prime minister or diplomat in the future?" one of the panelists finally asked.

"Yes, sir," I replied.

They all looked at one another again, as if this was the most ridiculous thing they had ever heard. The broad smiles returned to their faces.

"You are quite an impressive young boy," the lead panelist said. "We have tremendously enjoyed talking to you today, and we hope to see you again soon. You may leave now."

"Thank you, ladies and gentlemen, for this opportunity," I said, repeating verbatim what Mr. Kpatakpa had coached me to say. The panelists called the young lady to usher me out.

"How did it go?" Mr. Kpatakpa asked eagerly as soon as I walked into the hall.

"I think it went well," I said.

We went outside, and for the next fifteen minutes he kept firing questions at me, trying to ascertain the mood in the room and how the entire interview had unfolded. Based on what I told him, he expressed confidence that I would pass the interview.

Earlier that morning, we had taken a taxi to the campus from the Achimota Junction bus stop on the main road to Accra, so we needed to find a taxi from the campus to take us back to the junction. From there, we would make our way to the city center to catch another bus to Boadua. Just as we were about to leave the interview waiting area, a man in a fancy suit approached and asked where we had traveled from. Mr. Kpatakpa told him we were from Boadua.

"Where is that?" the man asked.

"It's a small village near Akwatia," Mr. Kpatakpa replied, just as I had told the panelists.

"How long of a drive is it from here?" the man inquired further.

"We came by bus and it took a little over three hours. We're catching a taxi to go back to Accra so we can take another bus for the return journey," Mr. Kpatakpa answered.

"Is your car in the shop?" the man asked.

What is he asking? I wondered. In my mind, a shop was a place or store where you went to buy basic items. I didn't understand how a car could be in a shop.

"No, I don't own a car," Mr. Kpatakpa replied.

That surprised the man, who assumed that anyone bringing his child to an Achimota interview must own a car.

"If you'd like, I will take you to the junction and then you can make your way from there," the man offered.

"That would be great," Mr. Kpatakpa answered.

We walked with him and his son, who had just completed his own interview, to his parking spot.

"How was your interview, young man?" the man asked me as soon as he started driving.

"Er, it went quite well, thank you," I replied hesitantly.

I momentarily failed to hear his question because I was blown away by the utter beauty of the interior of the "thing" we were sitting in. I was used to traveling in taxis and buses with rusted bodies, worn seats, and dust-filled interiors. This was something from another planet. It had four wheels and was structured somewhat like the taxis in Boadua, but I couldn't tell exactly what this thing was. It was shiny black, with an absolutely gorgeous interior. *What world do these people here live in?* I asked myself.

The man was a renowned professor at the University of Ghana at Legon, the most prestigious university in the country at the time. He had attended Achimota and later graduated from Cambridge University in England. *Is this what I could become in the future if I pass this interview?* I wondered.

The Legon campus was only a couple of miles away from the Achimota campus—in the opposite direction to where he was driving us. He was fascinated to hear that Mr. Kpatakpa was my teacher and that he, not my parents, had brought me to the interview. As it turned out, we were the only people at the interview that day who had traveled by mass transportation. I sat in deep, meditative silence, only listening in periodically to the conversation of the two adults and marveling at the man's son and the clothes he wore.

"I wish you well," the man told me as he dropped us off at the Achimota Junction.

"Thank you, sir," I said.

"What was that?" I asked Mr. Kpatakpa immediately after they drove off.

"What was what?"

"The thing that the man was driving. Was that a car?"

"Of course!" Mr. Kpatakpa replied.

"What type of car?" I asked.

"A Mercedes-Benz. It's incredibly expensive, the type of car only rich people drive. You'll probably never see one in Boadua."

I had many more questions concerning this so-called car, but we had to hurry to the station to catch one of those dilapidated, prehistoric buses that would take us back to the village.

It was already dark by the time we arrived. Mr. Kpatakpa accompanied me back home. My father had returned to Boadua a day before the interview to make sure I had everything I needed. As soon as we walked into the house, the entire family congregated to hear our account of the trip.

"I think Patrick did a wonderful job in the interview," Mr. Kpatakpa told them. He provided a brief summary of the day's events and once again said they should be immensely proud of me.

"Patrick, can you tell us what Accra looks like?" Esther implored.

"We saw little of the city itself, because most of our time was spent on the Achimota campus," I told her.

"But Mr. Kpatakpa said you went to the bus station to take the bus," Charlotte jumped in. "You must have seen some of the people there and what they looked like."

"I was so fixated on the interview and the campus that I actually didn't pay much attention to anything else," I explained. "I can tell you a lot more about Achimota and what a beautiful place it is."

"No one cares about stupid Achimota! Accra is the capital of Ghana, so that is what we all care about," Esther muttered in frustration.

My parents, after listening to Mr. Kpatakpa's summary, asked a few basic follow-up questions about the interview. My siblings only wanted to hear about Accra—most of them had never been there. I was terribly disappointed not to be able to really share with my family the wonderful things I had learned on the campus.

* * *

ABOUT TWO WEEKS AFTER THE interview, I returned home from school one day to find a letter from Achimota. The letter was certified, so the postmaster had brought it to the house. Just as with the previous one, my hands shook uncontrollably as I opened it. I kept my eyes closed for a minute and prayed before unfolding the letter.

Congratulations! Your admission to Achimota Secondary School is now official, read the first sentence.

I couldn't believe my eyes. The dream was now a reality, and all my hard work and sacrifice had been richly rewarded. I ran outside once again, jumping and screaming even louder this time.

Surprisingly, no one came to the scene on that occasion. To the neighbors, I was that lunatic boy screaming for no good reason again.

"Mr. Kpatakpa, Mr. Kpatakpa, I passed the interview!" I screamed with joy, after arriving at his house minutes later. I had again sprinted like a hare.

"We did it! You did it! Congratulations, I'm so proud of you!" he shouted in his elation, giving me a bear hug. We hurried back to my house.

"Your son did it! He is a little magician," he said to my mother. "This entire village should be incredibly proud of him." Mr. Kpatakpa couldn't contain his excitement. He spent a couple of hours in the house, talking with my mother and me, and the rest of my siblings, about all the possibilities that lay ahead.

I immediately began to prepare for what I thought would be the start of my journey toward an Oxford or Cambridge education. My father had returned to his farm a few days earlier but was scheduled to visit the family in Boadua again that weekend, so I didn't have to wait long.

"Papa, I passed the interview—here is the letter!" I handed it to him as soon as I walked into the house from school that afternoon. I had been carrying it with me ever since I received it. My father couldn't read, a fact that, in my excitement, I had forgotten.

"I am utterly happy for you, and we are all enormously proud of your achievement!" he said. Since I first received the conditional acceptance letter, Mr. Kpatakpa and the rest of the teachers at the school had spoken with my parents so often about Achimota that my father now understood the full significance of the moment.

The letter contained a list of the things I would have to buy for my first year at the school. It was fairly lengthy, including a number of optional items. Just the basics—uniforms, shoes, luggage, and bedding—would require a large sum of money. For a poor family like ours, it was insane to think my parents could afford to send me to such an expensive school.

I was well aware how poor we were and should have considered the affordability factor all along. Completely consumed by that burning desire to attend Achimota, I had been blind to everything else. I had managed to get myself onto the moon, but now I had to come back down to earth and deal with the real world.

My father sighed deeply after I finished reading the list to him. His cheerful demeanor turned gloomy, and he fell silent. Of immediate concern was the twenty-five-*cedi* deposit needed to reserve my seat in the incoming class. That deposit was the equivalent of about fifteen U.S. dollars at the time. Not a large sum, but for a family like ours, it was significant.

Due to the number of applicants on the waiting list, a quick response was required. We would need a miracle to make it all happen, but I hoped my family would somehow come up with the deposit. We could worry about the money for the hefty tuition, room, and board later. My father asked me to give him time to think about it and discuss the matter with my mother.

A couple of days later, my parents called me into their room. From their grim looks, I feared the worst. After a brief period of silence, my father dropped the bombshell.

"We have thought long and hard, and considered every possibility, but the family cannot afford to send you to secondary school. Regrettably, you're going to have to give up your dream of attending Achimota Secondary School."

What? Did I hear that right? I asked myself. I could see the pain in my father's eyes. My mother sat quietly, looking down much of the time as if in shame. Because she'd been at home the whole time, she had heard even more than my father from my teachers about my accomplishment. She knew what was at stake. She was probably wondering how on earth they were going to explain to my teachers that they were asking me to throw away such an opportunity.

It took several seconds for my father's words to register. Then I burst into tears, knowing for the first time an absolute emptiness in my soul. I had worked awfully hard and denied myself many things in order to achieve that dream. It had all been for nothing.

I had never heard of such a thing as a scholarship. In the village, we were in the dark about many things. Though I had learned a lot about secondary school and university, strangely, I had never read anything about how people financed their education. All I knew was that secondary schools charged tuition, and that families had to pay.

My parents made several fruitless attempts to console me. I felt confused and numb. I got up quietly and left, keeping silent for the remainder of the evening.

I could not sleep even a few minutes that night, and the next morning I felt extremely tired and dejected. Everyone was up by the time I came out of the room. My siblings were engaged in their morning routines, and they must have been told to leave me alone because everyone was uncharacteristically quiet. Even the normally loquacious Esther had turned into a meditating monk.

For the first time in many years, I did not buy the newspaper that morning. I thought about skipping school but decided against it.

"What's wrong? Did something happen to you?" Mr. Kpatakpa asked, gravely concerned. I appeared unusually tired and disheveled when I walked into school that morning. "Come with me to the headmaster's office and let's talk." I followed him quietly, my face somber. "Tell me what's wrong," he said as soon as he closed the door.

"My parents told me last night that they cannot come up with the money to pay the deposit. They say there is no way they can pay the tuition either, if I enroll at Achimota. I'm going to have to give up the opportunity." Tears streamed down my face.

"No way, we cannot let that happen!" he exclaimed. He hurriedly left the room and asked the headmaster, who was in one of the classrooms at the time, to join us in the office.

"Patrick's parents told him they cannot afford the tuition to secondary school. He won't be going to Achimota after all," he informed the headmaster.

"No way!" he exclaimed.

"Calm down, Patrick," they both told me.

"We will come to your house tonight to speak with your parents and try to come up with a plan," Mr. Kpatakpa added.

The two of them met privately with my parents for more than two hours that night. Before they left, my father called me into the room.

"Osei, as you know, we have been talking with your teachers about your secondary school issue," he began. "We have considered every possibility but have not been able to come up with a workable solution."

As he spoke, the glum faces of Mr. Kpatakpa and the headmaster confirmed my worst fears.

Among the options was for the teachers to contribute small amounts out of their salaries each month to supplement whatever my family could come up with. That plan wasn't feasible because my family had *nothing* to contribute. We didn't even have enough money to buy food on a daily basis, so my mother often went to bed hungry. The idea that such a family could come up with money for secondary school tuition was unrealistic. The burden would fall entirely on the teachers, who were paid so little that they themselves struggled to feed their families.

A few days after that fateful meeting, my father wanted another chance to discuss the decision. I had recovered enough to sit down and chat with him.

"Osei, it was extremely difficult for your mother and me to ask you to give up the Achimota dream," he began. "We explored every possible option. Letting such an opportunity go to waste will haunt me forever. My own life would have been quite different if I had found support to obtain a basic education when I was young.

"Life can be cruel," he went on. "However, it is vitally important to stay positive at all times and try to make the best of every situation. If you do, everything else will take care of itself."

"Thank you for your advice, Papa," I said, adding, "I promise I will continue to work hard."

Knowing my father's character and having watched how he conducted his life, I was convinced that if he said he couldn't do something, it must be beyond his capability. There were no programs we knew of that would offer a student loan to at least get me started. The writing was on the wall. I grudgingly opened my eyes, read it, and began the slow mental process of adjusting to that reality.

* * *

IT WAS EXTREMELY DIFFICULT FOR me to return to school for the remaining few weeks of that school year. One more year of elementary school remained—which I would have skipped if I had gone to Achimota. I had lost all interest in school and had no idea what path my life would follow next.

During those gloomy days, Mr. Kpatakpa spoke to me frequently. He did his best to keep me engaged in school, but even he realized that the situation was too difficult for a child my age to deal with. At home, my mother, in her usual gentle and kindhearted way, did her best to cheer me up. She let me know that she and my father were both hurting as much as I was, but that, somehow, we would all find a way to master our emotions.

By the time school reopened for that final year, I had recovered sufficiently and was ready to return. Life, for me, would never be normal again, but at least I could function a little better than I did during the final weeks of the previous year.

A few weeks after the new school year began, my wounds were

painfully reopened. I had completely forgotten to return the response form to Achimota. The acceptance deadline had long passed so I assumed it was all over. To my surprise, I returned from school one afternoon to find another letter from Achimota. It was already two weeks into the new academic year, but according to the letter, my seat was still being held.

This reminder cast me into another deep well of sadness. My father had returned to the farm, and everyone else seemed to have moved on because, as far as they were concerned, the matter was settled. I kept the letter and did not respond.

After another couple of weeks, the school sent a second reminder. Again, I did not respond. A third letter arrived two weeks later. It advised me in a friendly tone that it was the final opportunity for me to confirm my intent to enroll; otherwise the seat would be offered to someone on the waiting list.

Looking back, I should have written to the school after I received the second or third letter to explain why I couldn't accept their offer. I still deeply regret that failure. Based on everything I later learned, Achimota did not offer financial aid in those days, so letting them know about my family's poverty would have made no difference. I should at least have extended the courtesy, since they bent over backward—by sending multiple reminders—to accommodate me. It was an unfortunate lapse in judgment, though understandable given the devastation I had suffered.

I had a sense that the school authorities were eager for me to be a part of that year's class and therefore gave me as many opportunities as possible. It was probably the first time someone with my socio-economic background had dared to apply. Alas, it was not to be. Some lucky child eventually benefited at my expense. It was the last time I heard from the school.

During the entire first term of that final year in middle school, I was distracted and unable to shake a constant, haunted feeling. I kept playing back pictures of all those children I had seen at the interview, imagining the lives of the lucky students on that elite campus. There was possibly a future prime minister of Ghana among them. Many would hold high positions in future governments, and others would become diplomats, top professors, businessmen, and scientists. Some would go on to Cambridge and Oxford and become world-renowned in their fields of study.

Based on my test scores and interview performance, I could compete with those children academically, but I had no choice but to settle for a much different life in the jungle because of my family circumstances. It was a painful realization that just working hard and doing all the right things is not enough to get you where you want, and deserve, to be. Maybe I was destined to remain in the village. However, I had "seen" too much to accept that fate.

CHAPTER 7

Embracing Competition

SPORTS COACHES TELL THEIR TEAMS to play to the referee's whistle. In a soccer game, a player who stops chasing after a ball on the assumption that an infraction has occurred, or that the ball has gone out of play, can squander a potential scoring opportunity. Only a game referee has the authority to determine when play should stop, so until a player hears that whistle, he or she must keep on playing. Competitive sports games are filled with surprises. Teams not expected to win can wind up victorious. A team that is trailing badly can miraculously turn things around and win. And then there are some teams that simply refuse to lose.

This idea of never quitting during a soccer game occurred to me in the last year of middle school. A couple of months into the year, I realized that I was profoundly bored. For the first time in many years, I had no goals; everything I did seemed utterly meaningless. Soccer was the only thing that appealed to me at that time, so I played as often as I could.

Each grade in the school had two teams that competed against each other. These two teams also competed with those from the grades immediately below and above them. As an offensive player over the years, I set myself a target of scoring at least one goal in every competitive game. I was deeply disappointed whenever I fell short, particularly after the games we lost. That constant need to score goals meant that I had to chase after every loose ball. This was indeed the message that every coach I played for emphasized: never quit until you hear the referee's whistle. I took that message to heart.

Apart from playing soccer at school, I loved to watch professional matches on television. Those games were broadcast live on Sunday afternoons, so after church I would run three miles to Akwatia, where one of the diamond mining company employees owned a television. On match days, he set his television on a stand in the front yard of his apartment, where a large crowd gathered to watch. Chores made it impossible for me to attend every week. Whenever I did, I snuck out of the house, which meant being absent during dinner preparation. I risked incurring my mother's wrath. But she was surprisingly accommodating, perhaps because I accumulated enough goodwill during the week. I rarely suffered much more than a rebuke.

Playing regularly and watching games had made me quite knowledgeable about soccer. As time went on, I pondered how the sport could be a metaphor for life; both were full of surprises. It occurred to me that, as far as secondary school went, I should stay in the game in case a surprise awaited. Even if my chances of winning were slim.

I had put away all the materials I'd used for test preparation, convinced I wouldn't need them anymore. Those musings about soccer prompted me to retrieve them. Until I heard the final whistle, I was going to keep chasing after every seemingly hopeless ball.

To attend secondary school at the end of that final year, I would have to take the entrance exam again—test scores were only good for a year. I had no reason to believe that my family's financial situation would improve enough by the end of that year to enable my parents to pay the secondary school tuition. So studying for the exam felt like a pointless exercise. However, in addition to playing soccer, my studies offered relief from my unbearable boredom. I needed to compete, and I found a friend to help drive my academic ambitions.

* * *

SOME EVENTS IN OUR LIVES that first appear to be misfortunes later prove to be blessings. At the beginning of third grade, something seemingly terrible occurred. I could find nothing positive about it at the time. Only after many years did I come to realize it was one of the best things that had ever happened to me.

In the first and second grades at my village elementary school, I was the best student in my class. My teachers praised me often, and I figured I could simply sit back and enjoy the ride for the rest of elementary school. Just as that dangerous complacency was about to set in, my standing as top student was jeopardized.

There were two separate classes in each grade, with about thirty students per class. In third grade, the teachers decided to reshuffle the students. As a result I was placed in the same class as Francis—the best student in the other class. Within a few weeks, I realized I had been the best student not because I was particularly good academically, but because I lacked competition.

Francis had a gifted mind—one of the best, in fact, that I have ever come across anywhere in all my world travels. He excelled in every subject, and things seemed to come effortlessly to him. His brilliance made him the center of attention. Like any normal eight-year-old, I resented Francis for commanding the attention I used to receive. Tall for his age, Francis was also well built. He was quite gregarious, with a great sense of humor. Consequently, every student in the class gravitated toward him. Even at that young age, he had a presence about him.

I was too young at the time to understand the benefit of competition, but I resolved to do whatever I had to in order to regain my lost status—and the attention that came with it. I quickly learned that it would not be easy. Francis was too good. To succeed in dislodging him, I would have to really apply myself.

Francis' family was not as large as mine. He had only two siblings. His father, unlike mine, had some basic education and worked as a security guard for the diamond mining company in Akwatia. Their resources were not as stretched as my family's. Francis almost always had enough to eat. Having fewer chores, he had more time to study. Still, even if our personal situations had been similar, I doubt it would have made much difference in our class rankings.

Francis and I remained classmates for the remainder of elementary and middle school. Initially, I couldn't tell whether he cared about the class ranking or not. He was full of confidence and probably knew that his position would never be in jeopardy. As I expected, he took the top spot in the end-of-term exams throughout much of elementary school. On the rare occasions that I managed to dislodge him, he fought back like a tiger the next term to reclaim what he considered his rightful position. Only then did he appear to put any effort into studying; normally, his demeanor was relaxed. That's when I realized he was a fiercely competitive person who indeed cared about his class rank.

It was in middle school that I started reading the newspaper. I usually brought it to school, where I had more time and space. Not long after that, Francis also started to buy the newspaper and bring it to school. From that point on, the two of us competed to see who would finish the entire paper first.

Both of us loved to play soccer, but that race to finish the paper sometimes kept us from recess, which was the only time we got to play. Over time, we found ways to fit both soccer and reading into those tight time slots. We were unwittingly developing valuable time-management skills.

"Did you read that article in today's paper about the former American president who resigned and has been pardoned by the new president?" Francis asked me one day during recess.

"Yes, I did," I replied.

"What's his name, Nixon?" he asked.

"Yes, Nixon."

"Do you know what they mean by 'pardoned'?" he inquired.

"Yes, I looked it up in the dictionary. He did something bad and was about to be sent to prison; the new president decided to forgive him so he wouldn't go to prison." Francis didn't have a dictionary and occasionally borrowed mine. "How could a president be sent to prison, by the way?" I wondered aloud.

"I have no idea. Maybe they weren't serious about that," he replied.

Although the article did include some details about the Watergate scandal that had engulfed the Nixon administration prior to his resignation, they were well beyond the scope of our comprehension. Ghana was under military rule at the time, with a president who seemed omnipotent. At twelve years old, we were both just beginning to become politically aware and had been following the political upheavals in Ghana and the rest of Africa with keen interest. To us it was unfathomable that anyone in Ghana could ask the all-powerful military leader to leave office and possibly imprison him afterward. That is why we were baffled by the events unfolding in America.

We naturally discussed sports-related articles most of the time because of our mutual passion for soccer. However, political events—both in Ghana and elsewhere—were also big topics of conversation. Being the only students who read the paper, we gradually developed a close friendship through that exchange of stories and ideas. After a while, we were aware of our friendly competition. Eventually it became fun for us, and we spoke openly about it.

Over time, I began to see the benefits of our rivalry. My reading-comprehension and writing skills, as well as my concentration, had improved. In subjects like math and science, I could grasp concepts a lot quicker than before.

Francis and I had been engaged in that intense but friendly competition for several years before I came across that eye-opening newspaper article about Achimota. To have any chance of beating him to the top spot in the class, I had always been forced to push myself to the limit. In so doing, I had developed an incredible work ethic that served me well during my preparation for the secondary school entrance exam. At that young age, I had already seen the benefit of competition.

It is astonishing to me now that someone with Francis' fine mind would not pursue any education beyond middle school. His father had only a middle school education. Like most of the other parents in the village, he didn't have any higher expectations for his son, although he knew how brilliant the boy was.

Unlike me, Francis was a realist. When I was about to apply to secondary school, I asked him whether he was interested. He told me he'd never considered it. His not-unreasonable answer disappointed me. Although his father had a steady job, Francis didn't think he could afford secondary school tuition. I tried to convince him to apply anyway.

Finally he agreed. Unfortunately, I couldn't study with him as often as I had hoped. Even if there had been places where we could study together, we couldn't have taken advantage of them because I was almost always occupied by chores.

In spite of those limitations, I found it helpful to discuss sample questions with Francis at every opportunity, and to simply talk with him about the application process. For him, it was merely an intellectual exercise. However, once he agreed to take the test, he clearly approached it with seriousness.

I regretted not being able to persuade Francis to apply to Achimota. He told me that if he wasn't going to go anywhere anyway, he saw no good reason to waste the time and effort required for the Achimota application. Instead he selected a second-tier school also located in Accra. I took some consolation from that. If by chance we both made it, we would be in the same city and could continue our friendship.

Francis easily passed the entrance exam. His scores were slightly better than mine, which meant that most likely he would have also gained admission to Achimota. That realization didn't seem to bother him, however. No secondary schools in Ghana offered merit-based scholarships in those days, so he harbored no hopes of getting into any school, even with those excellent test scores. He told me he would show the results to his parents and let me know what happened.

The school that Francis selected did not conduct interviews as part of the admission process, so he received an unconditional acceptance. While I was nervously preparing for my interview, he could have already started preparing for secondary school. I envied him and began to question whether I had made the right decision by gambling on Achimota. If I failed the interview, and somehow Francis ended up going to secondary school, I risked finding myself back in middle school and not having him around for that entire year.

Not wanting to entertain such a scary prospect, I suppressed it quickly. Also, I knew deep down that my choice wasn't a mistake. I would not be happy in any other school. For me it was Achimota or nothing.

Francis's parents did indeed dismiss his announcement to them out of hand. They knew it wasn't remotely possible for them to send their son to secondary school, so any conversation about it would be pointless. Having never entertained high hopes, Francis took their reaction in stride and simply moved on.

In those weeks after I received the devastating news that my parents couldn't afford to send me to Achimota—a time when I was barely able to function—I once again found myself envying Francis. I wished I could think like him. Apart from being a brilliant person, he exhibited an admirable level of maturity. He was one of those people who could maintain their composure even under pressure. His presence and encouragement during that very trying period in my life helped restore some of the sanity I had lost.

* * *

Unbeknownst to everyone except Francis, I quietly prepared and took the secondary school entrance exam again toward the end of the second term in my final year of middle school.

"Why don't you take the exam with me?" I asked him.

"For what?" he replied. "Nothing has changed. My parents still can't afford the fees. It would be a pointless exercise. And by the way, why do you want to go through all that again? Have your parents promised to send you next year if you gain admission?"

"I haven't spoken to anyone at home about it, so there are no such promises. I want to try again just in case." I couldn't stop hoping for a miracle.

I made several more attempts to convince Francis to take the exam, but he didn't budge.

"What are you planning to do after middle school?" I asked him a few weeks later.

"I have no idea," he replied.

There were no good options for him or any child growing up in Boadua. Jobs at the diamond mining company where his father worked were incredibly hard to get. Francis would more likely have to lease a small piece of land and start subsistence farming. I at least had my father's farm to fall back on, but I wanted something better. *Nothing has changed financially in my family either, but I'm going to keep chasing after my secondary school dream,* I told myself.

I was pleasantly surprised when I received my results. They were even better than the year before. I was thirteen years old then and already past Achimota's age limit of twelve, so for my first choice I selected a second-tier school located in Akim Oda, one of the district capitals in Ghana's Eastern region. I selected Oda for three reasons. One, it was the best secondary school in that area at the time. Two, it was relatively close to Boadua—only about thirty miles away. Three, Gladys had just started teaching at an elementary school in that town, so I would have a relative nearby.

Given my scores, I had no doubt that I would be accepted. The acceptance letter arrived sometime in the middle of my final term. This time it was a low-key affair, without any jumping for joy, because I hesitated to call attention to my news. The prior year's experience had been painful for everyone; it was better not to put myself, and everyone else, through it again. I read the letter, reviewed the forms, and tucked the packet away. That school was less expensive, but that was unlikely to make any difference.

The day after the middle school final examination, I fully appreciated the misery that awaited me for the rest of my life. I woke up that morning with nowhere to go and nothing to look forward to. No next year of school lay ahead. And, because school was the only place I could indulge in my other passion, soccer, I faced a life of complete emptiness.

My next destination, in all likelihood, would be my father's farm in the jungle, a scary and unpleasant place. I had worked hard and sacrificed so much to avoid working there. Now I could not escape that fate, and I probably should have accepted it sooner.

For a few weeks after the school year ended, my parents asked no questions about my plans. I suspected they were giving me time to rest and gather my thoughts. I spent those weeks mostly walking aimlessly around the village. Francis and many of our classmates were still around, so sometimes I hung out with them. Nothing could put my mind at ease; the fear of spending the rest of my life in that scary jungle was ever-present.

* * *

"MAMA WANTS YOU TO COME home right away," Matilda said. I had been out walking by myself that afternoon.

"Why?" I asked.

"Some people have come looking for you."

"Are you sure it's me she wants?" I tried to clarify.

"Yes, she mentioned your name."

Confused, I turned around and walked slowly toward the house, thinking, *I don't know anyone outside this village; that can't be right.*

Two men sat on the verandah, talking to my mother. Their expensive clothing indicated their high status. They did not look like any of my parents' distant relatives who visited occasionally. My father was on his farm, so my mother was the only adult at home.

"This is Patrick," she said as I walked up.

"Hello, Patrick, how are you?" one of the men said.

"I'm well, thank you," I replied.

Who are these people? My mind raced to process what was happening.

"Bring a chair and sit down," my mother said. "They want to talk to you."

After I sat down, one of the men said, "My name is Samuel Abosi. I'm the assistant headmaster of Oda Secondary School."

"I'm Kevin Korankye, one of the teachers," the other one stated. My heartbeat quickened considerably as they made their introductions.

"We're here to speak to you about your application to the school," Mr. Abosi said.

I was almost dizzy, unsure if I heard him correctly. *Why would the assistant headmaster of a secondary school travel all the way to my village to speak with me about my application?* I wondered. I had seen the competition to get into secondary school from my prior experience at the Achimota interview. School officials did not go around visiting applicants' homes. Was this a prank?

"Your sister Gladys is a good friend of ours," Mr. Abosi began. He did all the talking for the next several minutes. "We went into town last week and stopped by her apartment for a brief visit. During our conversation, I asked Gladys whether she happened to know an applicant to the school from Boadua whose last name matched hers. We knew that Gladys was from Boadua, but Asare is a fairly common name. Gladys asked the first name of the applicant, and it was only after we told her that she realized it was indeed her brother."

Mr. Korankye chimed in, "We were both overjoyed to hear that the applicant everyone was raving about was the brother of our good friend."

"I told Gladys that you had obtained one of the highest *common entrance* scores ever seen in the school's history," Mr. Abosi continued. "We couldn't wait to meet you at the beginning of the school year. Gladys was visibly confused because she didn't know that you had applied to secondary school this year. She proceeded to tell us your Achimota story, saying it was unlikely you'd be able to enroll at Oda this year either. That news prompted us to cut the visit short and drive straight back to campus."

According to Mr. Abosi, the two of them went to see the headmaster, who quickly called a couple of administrative office personnel into a meeting to discuss my application. He wanted to see if there was anything the school could do to make my enrollment possible. At that meeting, they collectively reviewed my application, together with all the other information in my file. The solution they were looking for came from a piece of information I had provided, purely by accident, in my application.

I had listed my father's occupation as "cocoa farmer." Normally, I simply wrote "farmer" when completing forms. The Cocoa Marketing Board (CMB), the government agency in charge of purchasing cocoa from farmers, happened to have a scholarship program for children of cocoa farmers that I qualified for. Most cocoa farmers, including my father, didn't know about the program. The vast majority lived in villages where people rarely had access to such information. Worse, even if farmers knew about it, they would seldom be able to take advantage of it. Hardly any children from such families attempted to go to secondary school.

"Do you know anything about the CMB scholarship?" Mr. Abosi asked me.

So far my mother and I had done nothing but listen intently. *Is this just some weird dream or what?* I kept wondering.

"No, I don't," I replied.

"We assumed as much, so we brought you the forms. You need to send them in as soon as possible, because the CMB normally requires them well in advance of the school year to allow sufficient time for processing." He handed them over.

Akim Oda is located in one of the major cocoa-producing regions of Ghana so the CMB had a heavy presence there. As a result, the school administrators were quite familiar with that scholarship program.

"Thank you very much!" I said as I accepted the forms. My hands were trembling, and my head was spinning. It felt as if I were riding a giant roller coaster.

"How on earth did you manage to get admitted to Achimota from this village?" Mr. Korankye asked.

"If you don't mind, can you please tell us how it all happened?" Mr. Abosi added.

I sat still for a few seconds before regaining my composure enough to recount the series of events that led to that miraculous outcome.

"What a story!" they said in unison after I'd finished.

"You *are* quite a remarkable young boy!" Mr. Korankye said.

"He's beyond remarkable!" Mr. Abosi added.

"Before we leave, do you have any questions for us?" Mr. Abosi asked.

"No, sir," I replied. "Thank you again."

"You're very welcome," he said. "We look forward to seeing you on campus in a few weeks' time."

"And thank you for hosting us," Mr. Abosi told my mother. "It's nice to meet both you and Patrick. Again, he is a remarkable boy, and you should be really proud of him." The two men conversed with her for a few minutes on general topics before taking their leave.

Is this really going to allow me to attend secondary school? I wondered, still feeling dazed as I looked at the forms. I had witnessed many miraculous endings in soccer games, but nothing like this.

"I'm so happy for you, Osei!" my mother exclaimed. "I've been so worried about you since you completed your final middle school exams. I'm really grateful to God for opening this path for you. We're all going to pray hard for this dream of yours to come true."

"Thank you, Mama, I'll be praying hard, too," I replied.

It was difficult to contain my excitement. I knew I shouldn't get too far ahead of myself. Despite that significant development, there was no guarantee I would actually make it to secondary school. The amount of money required to buy the long list of personal items required could still pose a problem. The scholarship, even if I obtained it, would only cover tuition, room, and board. My family would still have to cover many other expenses. I could not take that for granted. Any celebration at this point was premature.

I traveled to the jungle the following morning to tell my father the news. It was mid-afternoon when I arrived, and he was working on the farm.

"There's something I need to tell you right away," I said.

It was the first time I saw my father look nervous. Whenever we went to the farm, we waited till he had finished his work for the day and eaten dinner before relating any news about the family or other important developments at Boadua. He was afraid something serious had happened to someone in the family for me to want to talk to him right away. He hurriedly walked back with me to the hut.

"Don't worry, it's good news," I said. "Two men from Oda Secondary School came to the house yesterday and said I could likely get a scholarship to attend secondary school."

He appeared puzzled. "What do you mean? Didn't you tell me last year that if you couldn't go to Achimota and you wanted to reapply for secondary school, you'd have to take the *common entrance* again?"

"Yes. I took the exam again and applied to the school the gentlemen came from."

"You what? Did anyone at home know about this?" he asked incredulously.

"No, I didn't tell anyone. I was too bored, so I just decided to retake the exam."

"What's a scholarship?" he asked.

"It means the government will pay my expenses at secondary school."

"Do you really think this is possible?" my father asked.

"I don't know for sure. They sounded quite convincing, so I'm hopeful."

"It would be a huge relief for me," he said. "I've been haunted by what happened last year. I really hope that something positive comes out of this." His eyes shimmered with happy tears.

We returned to Boadua the next morning. Later that evening, he convened a meeting with my mother and Ernestina to discuss next steps.

"I'm going to do whatever I can to help," Ernestina promised.

"Osei, I want you to write letters to Gladys and your older siblings to inform them that everyone will be expected to contribute, regardless of how little income they make," my father added.

"I'll do that right away," I said.

Fortunately, my scholarship application was approved quickly. It was a terrible shame that not much effort had been put into publicizing the CMB program. I probably could have attended Achimota on that scholarship if I had known about it the previous year.

My family managed to scrape together just enough money for the bare essentials I needed to take to school. I bought a mattress, bed sheets, luggage, a pair of shoes, some clothing, and toiletries. The scholarship also covered the cost of stationery and school uniforms—items that all students purchased from the school bookstore. I could finally relax, knowing that I now had some control over my destiny.

The scholarship was conditional on my keeping up my academic performance. I had been told that secondary school would be a lot harder than middle school, but that did not worry me. *So long as I'm in good health, nothing will happen to make me lose that precious scholarship. If I have to work like a donkey, day and night, I'm fully prepared to do it,* I told myself. The strong work ethic I had learned from my father, and through the competition with Francis, would always be there for me to draw on.

In those last few days before I left home to start secondary school, I thought a lot about Francis. I kept wondering what miracles might have occurred for him if he had just taken the entrance exam.

CHAPTER 8

Out of My League

GLADYS ACCOMPANIED ME TO CAMPUS on a Saturday afternoon, two days before classes were scheduled to begin. The campus was located in a heavily wooded area about three miles away from the town, so we traveled there on a bus. First we went to the administration building to register.

"Welcome! You're the student everyone has been talking about," the gentleman at the counter said, a broad smile on his face.

"Thank you," I replied sheepishly.

"We're so glad to have you here! Here's a map of the campus. You're going to be in Red House," he said after I filled out the registration forms. "The four boys' dormitories are color-coded. We have Red, Blue, Green, and Yellow Houses."

Having visited her friends there a few times, Gladys was familiar with the campus and had no trouble finding Red House. *All these buildings are white, so why do they give them color names?* I wondered as we approached the dormitories. Every building on campus was painted white and the dormitories all looked alike. No color coding or signage. In those early days, freshmen had to learn the campus layout quickly to find their way back to the dormitories.

The two girls' dormitories were located about ten yards away from the boys'. Unlike the boys', the girls' dormitories had real names—Agnes and Victoria Houses. That didn't help; the buildings looked similar and the names weren't anywhere on the buildings.

"I'm so happy for you, Patrick," Gladys said as we stood in front of Red House.

"I'm speechless. I can't believe that I've actually made it to secondary school."

"Take good care of yourself. I'll be back next week to see how you're doing."

"Thank you for all your help," I told her.

I learned later that the boys' dormitories, apart from the color-coded designations, were also named after some national historical figures. Red House was Attafuah, Blue was Frempong-Manso, Green was Danquah, and Yellow was Ahenkorah. Students often used the local names, but the color-coded nomenclature was more common in formal settings.

Unlike in Boadua, spaces in and around the campus were paved, so there was no dust. The lawns were neatly manicured. All six dormitories were two-story, rectangular white buildings. Each floor had one large room with twelve metal bunk beds. Attached to the large room on each floor was a bathroom with six showers and six toilet stalls, as well as a storage room. I had been assigned to the second floor, occupied by a mix of freshmen and upper-class students. Even without introductions, I could tell who the freshmen were—from the apprehension on their faces. I'm sure I had that look, too.

The interior walls were also painted white. Apart from the bunk beds and student suitcases, there was nothing else in the room. Each student was permitted one suitcase in the room for everyday essentials. Additional luggage had to be kept in the storage room to minimize clutter. Everything was neatly arranged.

"What's your name?" one of the upper-class students asked.

"I'm Patrick," I replied.

"Welcome to Red House," he said. "Where are you from?"

"Boadua," I responded.

"Where's that?" he asked, confused.

"It's near Akwatia," I replied. Everyone in the room looked at me curiously.

"Here's your bed." He pointed to the top shelf of a bunk bed in the middle of the room. There were a couple of other unoccupied beds, but the rest were neatly made. I took out my mattress and bed sheets.

"Let me help you," the upper-class student said when he saw how I struggled. Since I had slept on straw mats my whole life, I had never made a bed before.

After we finished making the bed, I heard a strange sound emanating from a corner of the campus. *What was that?* I wondered. I looked around the room, and the freshmen seemed equally baffled. It sounded like beating drums, and it continued for a couple of minutes. *Why would anyone beat drums in this place?*

"Everyone get ready and let's go—it's dinner time," another upper-class student said.

There were no clocks in the dormitories and few students wore watches. Thus, drums summoned students to school-wide gatherings on weekends and after-class hours. During class hours, designated students rang hand-held bells to signal class-changeover times. The two large drums were housed in a wooden shed situated on a small hill at the northern edge of the campus. A designated student beat the drums whenever it was time for students to gather on campus.

The beating of drums commonly occurred during traditional festivals in Ghanaian villages and towns. At such events, chiefs and kings and elderly men and women danced to the rhythm of the drums. It was highly unusual to hear those sounds in other settings, which is why we were so perplexed.

We filed out of the room and followed the upper-class students to the dining hall. It was a large room with sixty rectangular tables and two benches per table. Each table seated ten students. The dishes were served in two large cylindrical aluminum bowls and placed in the middle of the table. A couple of students—typically from the upper classes—served portions onto each student's plate. Dinner that day was rice and beef stew. *This smells delicious!* I thought, as the aroma filled the air.

Because meat was quite expensive in Ghana at the time, Ghanaian families rarely ate it. In my family, it was typically once a year—for Christmas dinner. Rice was also a luxury in my family because it was more expensive than plantains and cassava. To have rice and meat on my first day in secondary school was a real treat.

When my plate was handed to me, I quickly ran into technical difficulties. In Boadua, we ate almost everything with our fingers. Here, there was a complete set of cutlery on the table that we were required to use. I had never used a knife and fork. I hesitated, waiting for other students at the table to start eating so I could watch how they used the cutlery. Lunch at Gladys' apartment had been my only meal that day and I was quite hungry. To my dismay, no one was in a hurry. The students were more interested in learning what their friends had done over the summer. *How am I going to eat this food?* I wondered.

After several minutes, I realized I'd have to find another way to get the crash course I needed. I looked around at the tables nearby. A few feet away, a couple of students were eating, so I craned my neck to see how they did it. I managed to acquire enough knowledge to get started.

"Put down your cutlery, dinner is over," the upper-class student on duty announced.

What! I can't eat any more of this delicious meal? I had eaten only a third. Grudgingly, I lay down the knife and fork. After hearing a few announcements, we were told to return to the dormitories. I didn't say a word to anyone at the table that evening, and I felt utterly miserable as I left the dining hall.

This is really nice! I thought as I lay on my bed. I had never slept on a foam mattress, and it felt really comfortable. I should have slept soundly, but I was so hungry that I tossed and turned.

At seven thirty the next morning, the drums beat again.

"Wake up!" an upperclassman shouted. "Make your beds and get ready for breakfast."

Maybe I should ask someone at the table to teach me how to use the cutlery when we get there, I thought.

"Okay, let's go," the upperclassman said when we heard the sounds of the drums again half an hour later. I walked nervously with the group to the dining hall.

To my relief, we had tea for breakfast that day. The table was laid with bread rolls and a couple of spreads—peanut butter and margarine. Because eating this meal didn't require much technical expertise, I was able to get through breakfast without major problems. For me, it was another luxurious repast. Tea, bread, and margarine were all foods that we hardly ever ate at home; they were things rich people ate.

The entire student body ate breakfast, lunch, and dinner together at the same time each day. I was never able to summon the courage to ask for lessons in using cutlery; I was too embarrassed to reveal my rawness. It took surreptitious observation—over several days—for me to manage it.

Classes began Monday—my third day on campus. There were two classroom buildings facing each other. Each had two stories, with three classrooms on each floor. First-year students were grouped into three separate classes with twenty-five students each, and we occupied the ground floor of one building. The chairs and desks were arranged neatly in three columns. The classroom walls were painted white, and two large windows let in so much sunshine that it always felt as if we were sitting outdoors. Other than the teacher's desk and chalkboard, there wasn't much else in the room. Despite the scant furnishings, the rooms looked quite nice.

"Hello, Patrick, it's nice to see you!" Mr. Abosi said. I had gone to his office to thank him on that first day of classes for his visit to Boadua that made my enrollment possible. "Come with me and let me introduce you to the headmaster."

"John, this is Patrick," he said.

"Hello, Patrick, it's very nice to finally meet you. Welcome to the school," the headmaster said.

"Thank you all so much for helping to make my secondary school dream come true," I said.

"It's our pleasure, and we know you'll enjoy your time here," the headmaster said in response.

There was a set curriculum for the first- to third-year students. In the fourth year, students elected to be either on a science or liberal arts track. During that first term, I took algebra, English grammar and literature, French, physics, biology, chemistry, history, geography, and music.

The workload was heavy but manageable. I had always been a quiet, shy kid, but I became even quieter because I felt intimidated in this new environment. I hardly spoke a word in class in those initial weeks. Quite a few of the students had attended private schools, and they were mostly from cities and big towns. I assumed they came from well-to-do families. More self-confident than everyone else, they did much of the talking in class. The rest of us kept a low profile.

The first person who tried to get me to speak in class was the English teacher, Ms. Kontoh. She was a petite woman, in her mid-forties at the time, and was well-liked on campus because of her gentle nature. Whenever she asked a question, she would call on someone from the group of students who had raised their hands. If no hands went up, she picked someone at random. My hand was always down, but whenever she called me, I had the right answer.

"Wait, Patrick, I'd like to ask you something," she said to me after class one day as the students were walking out. "Why don't you ever raise your hand? You always seem to know the answer—is it shyness?"

"Yes," I admitted.

"You shouldn't be. You're a brilliant student; you shouldn't be afraid to speak up."

"Thank you. I'll make sure to raise my hand next time if I know the answer."

"I'm glad to hear that. Please do."

From then on, I did make an effort to raise my hand to answer questions—only occasionally because I continued to be intimidated by my urbane-looking classmates.

During the third week of school, I realized that two boys and one girl in my class, and another boy in my dormitory who was a second-year student, had been missing for a few days. I kept wondering where they'd gone. Having no friends yet, I couldn't ask anyone. A couple of days later, I heard that those students had been sent home because they had not paid their tuition and other bills for supplies from the school bookstore. They could not return until their debts had been paid.

Hearing about students being barred from campus for non-payment of bills scared me to death. I knew even in those initial few weeks that I was hanging on by a thread. When I left home, the amount of money I had on me was just enough to cover the bus fare and not much else. That was all the family could afford. My scholarship covered a limited number of notebooks and other stationery. If I needed any more supplies during the school year, I would have to pay for them out of pocket.

I clearly couldn't do that. At thirteen, I was too young for formal employment—not that it was even an option, given the informal nature of Ghana's economy and the distance from the campus to town. Neither were there any on-campus employment opportunities. I had to be extremely careful managing my resources. I feared that any misstep, however small, could easily send me back to Boadua.

Most of the students in my class used one notebook for every course, which meant ten notebooks each term. I often got by with four. Whenever I took notes in class, I fit two lines of writing in each space of the ruled notebook page. My letters were tiny. To my classmates, that was the weirdest thing they had ever seen. They wondered how I could read my notes. I never explained.

At the end of the first term, I discovered that because I had used my supplies so sparingly, I had money left in my scholarship account. I stuck to the practice, and for the remainder of my years in secondary school, I always had a credit at the end of the term. Although I could not cash out the credit and spend the money on other necessities such as food, I was always happy to be in that position, instead of the other way around. A majority of students brought non-perishable foods—canned fish, evaporated milk, canned beans, crackers—from home to supplement dining-hall meals. What the school provided was not always enough, especially if you stayed up late to study. Those items were well beyond my means, so I never brought anything with me to school. I kept my physical activity to a minimum so as not to drain what little energy I had.

Apart from soccer, the school had track and field sports, field hockey, and table tennis teams. Despite my passion for soccer, I stayed away from it—and every other sport. The academic workload was so arduous that I could not afford to be too hungry to function.

Several weeks into the first term I found out how to get extra food in the dining hall. Some of the students, particularly those from wealthy families who brought a lot of food from home, did not always eat their dining hall meals. Their plates were left untouched. Those lucky enough to have one or two such students nearby could get extra food almost every meal.

Some students seemed to have an aversion to food prepared for the masses. Dining-hall rules prohibited students from moving to other tables during meal sessions. Nevertheless, poor, hungry students often found ways to sneak to other tables where there was extra food. Such students were called "scavengers" and mercilessly teased. The teasers included, ironically, some students who were scavengers themselves. Such food-hunting missions were always carried out surreptitiously. It helped to have a friend at a "well-endowed" table. Hunting missions could then be disguised as brief visits to chat.

Too afraid of becoming an object of ridicule, I initially refrained from looking for extra food in the dining hall. Eventually I decided that my health and well-being were far more important than my pride. I began to take advantage of whatever opportunities I could find. There were some meals almost every student liked; therefore finding an extra plate was nearly impossible. Fried ripe plantains and bean sauce, for example. When it was on the lunch menu, there was no point in going on a scavenging mission.

As was the practice in elementary and middle school, we had comprehensive exams in all subjects at the end of the first term. Fear of failure had driven me to work extremely hard, day and night. After the exam results were released, I was pleasantly surprised to learn that my scores were the highest in most subjects. My perfect score on the English literature exam so impressed Ms. Kontoh that she assembled the entire first-year class to announce it. No one else had ever managed to receive a perfect score in all her years as a teacher.

A couple of days later, after Ms. Kontoh learned about my stellar performances in other subjects, she summoned me after class to ask if anyone in my middle school had done better than me in end-of-term exams. I simply smiled and told her about Francis. She seemed surprised.

"What secondary school did he go to?" she asked.

"He didn't go to secondary school."

"Where is he now, and what is he doing?" Ms. Kontoh asked further.

"In the village, doing nothing. When I was applying to secondary school last year, I tried to encourage him to apply as well. He didn't think his family could afford the fees and didn't apply. I'm not sure what he's going to do now, but I don't think he'll receive any further education."

"What! You're telling me that's it for him?"

"Probably," I replied.

Tears formed in Ms. Kontoh's eyes. I came to see her as someone who entered the teaching profession to nurture children's talents. Hearing that a gem like Francis had been thrown away hit her hard. By then, every teacher in the school knew the story of how I came to be a student there. There were no scholarships Francis could qualify for, but she dearly wished there were.

Seeing how perilously close I had come to suffering the same fate as Francis drove Ms. Kontoh to become extremely protective of me. From the day of that conversation, she spoke with me frequently—every day—always making sure I had what I needed to survive. In many ways, she became a second mother to me. She invited me to eat lunch, and sometimes dinner, at her house on campus. I was particularly grateful for those meals, which meant I didn't have to go on so many scavenging missions.

Because I was a quiet, hardworking student, every teacher loved me. Mr. Korankye, my first-year geography teacher, also spoke to me often both in and out of class to make sure all was well. My music teacher, Mr. Donkor, adored me. He read the newspaper every day, and after he heard my Achimota story and the fact that I discovered the school through reading the newspaper, he began to give me his copies after he finished them. That's how I stayed informed about national and international news, there being no televisions in the dormitories. My classmates marveled at the relationships I was developing with the teachers.

I did not get to see Gladys often. We could leave campus to go to Oda only with permission, and such trips were mostly limited to hospital visits and other emergencies. On average, I saw her once or twice during the school term, either when she visited her friends on campus or I went to town.

* * *

"Have you seen that first-year girl called Catherine?" one upper-class student asked his classmate in the dormitory one evening.

"Yes, I have. She's gorgeous! Everyone has been talking about her. She's the most beautiful girl on campus."

Catherine was in a different first-year class, but I had seen her often in our part of the classroom building. I'd had a huge crush on her since the beginning of our first term on campus. Many other boys had their eyes on her as well.

"Can I speak to you after class today?" Catherine asked me one morning in front of the classroom building. It was a complete surprise because I had never spoken to her.

"Sure," I replied nervously.

"Thank you. Can I meet you in front of your classroom?"

"Yes, that'll be fine." My heart started to beat rapidly as I walked into my next class. *Catherine wants to talk to me? About what?*

"You look distracted today, Patrick. Is something bothering you?" Ms. Kontoh asked a few minutes into her lesson, which happened to be the next class.

"No, Ms. Kontoh, everything is fine," I replied, my voice quavering. *One of the most beautiful girls on campus has asked to speak with me; of course I'm distracted.*

"You don't look like your normal self. Let me know if anything is going on with you," she said before continuing with her lesson.

I rushed out of the classroom immediately after the bell rang at the end of the school day. I couldn't be late for this important meeting.

"Hello, Patrick, thank you for taking the time to speak with me," Catherine said.

"I'm h-happy to," I stammered.

"I have a huge favor to ask. I'm having trouble in math and I was wondering whether you'd be willing to help."

"Absolutely! I'll be delighted."

She seemed surprised. "Really? Thank you so much, Patrick!"

"When would you like to meet?" I asked.

"Whenever it's convenient for you."

"How about this evening at seven o'clock?" I asked.

"That'll be perfect," she replied.

"See you then." Several boys had walked by as we spoke, and I caught their envious looks.

What an honor! Catherine and I were walking together to the dining hall for lunch. We were at different tables, so we parted company as we entered the hall. Although I was quite hungry, I was so excited that I didn't finish my lunch—the first time that had occurred since that disastrous dinner on my first day on campus. *Of all the people on this campus, I'm the one Catherine seeks help from?* I couldn't believe my luck.

Catherine was a tall, slim girl, with flawless skin, dark, shiny hair, and a beautifully shaped face. She had the figure and looks of a supermodel. Apart from her beauty, she also had an elegance that seemed to intimidate even the most self-confident boys on campus. She came from a well-to-do family in Accra and had attended private school. In terms of socio-economic class, we were worlds apart.

It was at the beginning of the second term of first year—a few weeks after Ms. Kontoh had announced my English literature score to the class—that Catherine approached me for help. She had also ascertained that I was a good student she could rely on overall.

After the first tutoring session that evening, we began to meet frequently, a couple of times each week. To increase the time I got to spend with her, I offered to tutor her in other subjects—particularly in science. She readily accepted. Whenever we were together, I kept stealing glances at her beautiful face.

Given the amount of time the two of us spent together, most people assumed we were dating. I had heard rumors that some classmates had begun to date as early as the second year. I would have liked to start dating as well, but I felt that I wasn't qualified to date anyone on that campus. Catherine would obviously be my choice, but she was out of my league. *I'm happy enough to be near her so often; I'm not going to do anything to jeopardize that,* I told myself.

Boys were not allowed to enter the girls' dormitories and vice versa. Catherine and I always met in classrooms where other students were studying. From what I heard, students who had romantic relationships found obscure places on campus where they engaged in "illicit" activities, under cover of darkness.

"Can I talk to you sometime this evening?" I asked Catherine after class one day.

"Yes, normal meeting time?" she asked.

"Sure," I replied.

I liked being around her so much that on days we were not scheduled to meet, I would find sneaky ways to see her. That was the case in this instance. I invited her to talk about a physics problem that we had been discussing the previous evening. It could have waited till our scheduled meeting the following day.

"Was that all you wanted to talk about?" Catherine asked after I finished speaking.

"Yes," I replied, pausing briefly because her question surprised me.

We were standing in front of Red House, only a few yards away from her dormitory. I was baffled by the disappointment on her face.

"What happened?" I asked.

"Nothing," she replied.

We both stood silently as I frantically tried to recall anything I might have said to upset her.

"Are you sure that was all that you wanted to talk about?" she asked again.

"Yes, that's all."

"Goodnight," we both said. She looked sad as she walked away.

I had no idea that Catherine also had a crush on me. In Ghanaian culture in those days, it was taboo for a girl to even hint that she was interested in a boy. That was considered to be slutty behavior, so girls shied away from doing anything of the sort. Girls had to hope that the feeling was mutual, so the boy would take the initiative. I didn't have the courage.

Catherine had told her best friend about her interest in me, warning her not to tell anyone. However, her friend let the secret slip; as a result, there were whispers in some circles. Those whispers didn't filter down to me in time. Convinced that I wasn't worthy of Catherine, I never considered telling my friends how I felt.

At the end of the first five years of secondary school, students had to pass the basic level General Certificate Examination (GCE), a comprehensive and difficult national exam, in order to qualify to study at the advanced level—the final two years of secondary school. Students who failed the basic level GCE could rewrite the exams two more times, although they had to do so privately. Failing at all three attempts meant that a student could not study at the advanced level. In effect, those students had no other avenues to obtain a university education. At the end of the two-year advanced-level studies, students had to pass the even more rigorous advanced level GCE before being accepted to university.

By the third year of secondary school, I was a relatively mature sixteen-year-old and had learned enough about the world to realize that my childhood ambition of studying at Oxford or Cambridge had been completely delusional. In the end, I decided to study electrical engineering at the science and technology university in Ghana. Consequently, I chose the science track in secondary school.

For advanced-level studies, students could choose from any school in the country. Somehow, I once again began to harbor secret hopes of going to Achimota. *If I have the opportunity to study there for these last two years, it would compensate somewhat for the bitter disappointment I suffered in middle school,* I thought.

There was no age limit for Achimota then, and my CMB scholarship would carry over if I were accepted. On the surface, there was no reason not to try. That decision to apply to Achimota was what discouraged me from attempting to date Catherine after I learned of her interest. It was just before making the Achimota decision that I found out—from a classmate who had heard the whispers. I now understood her disappointment the night I spoke to her in front of Red House. By then, we had just over a year left before graduation. It made little sense, in my view, to start a romantic relationship not knowing where we would both be after graduation. I was tempted to reveal my longstanding interest in her but decided against it. We remained close friends.

Applying to Achimota was an enormous risk. Some secondary schools in Ghana did not have advanced-level programs. Students from such schools therefore had no choice but to apply elsewhere if they wanted to study beyond the basic level. That was not the case at Oda. Because I was already a student there and had a good reputation, it would be a safer choice. Any decent performance on the GCE would give me an excellent chance of being admitted for advanced-level studies there. With Achimota, I wasn't so sure. Competition for places in their advanced-level program was said to be even tougher than that for basic-level entry.

If I chose Achimota, did not get in, and had to fall back on my school or my second choice, I would be in danger of not making it to the advanced level. It was an open secret that a student who made a particular school first choice had a far better chance of being admitted there than another who made it their second choice. A risky move, but ultimately worth a try.

The teachers at Oda had done an excellent job preparing us for the GCE, so I felt quite good about my performance at the end of the exam period. The headmaster and my teachers were naturally disappointed when I told them I wanted to attend Achimota for my advanced-level studies, but none of them tried to discourage me. Instead, they all wished me well.

"I'm really sad to see you leave," Ms. Kontoh said on the last day of school.

"It makes me sad as well, and I'm going to miss you. Thank you so much for everything that you've done for me these last five years," I told her.

"It saddens me that we might not have you here for your advanced-level studies, but I know how much you've always wanted to go to Achimota. I'm praying hard for you to get in," she added.

About six weeks after the exams, I received my results. I had done well and was confident that I could get into Achimota. However, I couldn't be sure until I received a formal admission letter. A lot depended on other applicants' results. Another month or so would pass before I knew my fate.

I was elated when I finally received the news that I had been accepted. The school did not conduct admission interviews at that level, so I could begin my preparations right away. Thankfully, there wasn't much to buy because I could take many of the things I'd used at Oda. I eagerly awaited the first day of school.

My father happened to be in Boadua the day I received the acceptance letter.

"I'm so happy for you, Osei," he said, smiling broadly. "You had to wait a few years, but your Achimota dream has finally come true."

"And I'm so happy to hear that your scholarship will carry over," my mother said. "Nothing will stand in your way this time."

"It's been worth the wait," I said.

* * *

I SOON GOT A FEELING for what it's like to be a poor person trying to play on the turf of the wealthy. From the Achimota Junction stop at the northern outskirts of Accra—where I got off the bus that transported me from Boadua—I had to take a taxi to campus.

Typically, four people share a taxi in Ghana. Since most passengers in Ghana carry at least some baggage when they travel, it is sometimes difficult to fit everyone's items into the trunk. Passengers riding in a taxi with a lot of baggage have to pay a fare equivalent to that of four passengers so that some of the baggage can be loaded into the back seats. Alternatively, a passenger in that situation could wait until passengers without baggage come along. For obvious reasons, I chose the latter option.

I got my first hint of how different life would be at Achimota when the cab driver dropped me off at the taxi stop on campus. The stop was at the intersection of the road that connects the east and west sections of the campus and the Accra-Legon road. I was struck by the vastness of the Achimota campus. The Oda campus was relatively small, with the buildings clustered compactly together; Achimota looked more like a small town.

I had been assigned to a dormitory in the western section. With no one at the stop and no directions, I was stranded for several minutes. I was finally able to get directions from a woman who came to catch a taxi to Accra. The building happened to be five hundred yards away from where I was standing.

The campus seemed unusually quiet for a first day of school. I stood near the taxi stop for several more minutes, hoping to find someone to help me carry my luggage. At Oda, I would take a bus from the town's main station to campus. Every first day of school, young boys from the town would be waiting at the campus bus stop, and as students arrived, they would help carry luggage to the dormitories in exchange for tips. Typically, these were boys from very poor homes and any small amount of money was meaningful income.

After waiting for nearly half an hour at the taxi stop, I still saw no signs of life on the Achimota campus. I would have to find a way to carry the luggage myself. In addition to my suitcase and folded student mattress, I had two additional pieces—cardboard boxes containing personal items. I would need to make two trips, at least. I considered the suitcase and mattress to be the most essential, so I picked up those two first. I had no choice but to leave the boxes unattended.

Although I had categorized the two "orphaned" pieces of luggage as non-essential, I knew that I probably could not function in school without their contents. I needed to retake custody of them as quickly as possible before someone carried them away. I tried to walk as fast as I could, but the suitcase was quite heavy, and it slowed me down considerably. I was sweating profusely by the time I reached the dormitory.

A couple of guys stood in front of the building, and they tried to make eye contact. I knew it was rude not to acknowledge them, but I had no time to speak; I had more important business. I hurriedly put down my luggage at the building entrance and ran back toward the taxi stop.

The two boxes were still sitting there untouched when I returned. As I later found out, I should not have worried at all. No one on that campus would have had any use for a poor man's luggage, and the boxes were never at risk. I picked them up, one in each arm, and carried them tenderly like a proud parent carrying twin newborns. *What kind of place have I come to?* I kept asking myself as I walked back toward the dormitory. *Whatever it is, I've become a part of it; I'll have to learn to live with it.*

"Hello," I said to the two gentlemen, who were still standing in front of the dormitory building when I returned.

"Hello, it looks like you're one of our new advanced-level students," the older one said. I was eighteen, and he had guessed correctly.

"Yes, and I'm sorry that I didn't acknowledge you earlier," I apologized.

"That's no problem at all; you had important business to take care of," he said, after I briefly described my luggage ordeal.

"I'm Jim, and I'm the House Eighteen housemaster."

"And I'm Avo. I'm the new house prefect," the younger one said.

"I'm Patrick, and I'm pleased to meet you."

"We're so happy to have you here at Achimota," Jim continued. "Where do you come from?"

"My family lives in a village called Boadua, near Akwatia, but I attended Oda Secondary School," I replied.

Though clearly curious, they said nothing. Boadua and Oda were not familiar names. Students who came from elsewhere to do their advanced studies at Achimota typically attended top-tier secondary schools.

"I'll help you carry your luggage to your room," Avo offered. "This is a typical first day of school at Achimota. Most students arrive late afternoon into early evening. It will be another few hours before the campus really comes to life."

As an advanced-level student, I had a single room. I spent much of the afternoon there unpacking. At five o'clock, I started to hear sounds of students arriving. They were loudly calling out the names of their friends and running in the hallways to hug them. When I emerged from my room, a large crowd of students and their families were assembled in front of the dormitory. I stood there for several minutes without anyone saying a word to me. People were entirely focused on their family conversations. *I'm not sure how I'm going to survive in this place,* I thought. *Did I make a mistake by not going back to Oda?*

I immediately understood why I had not seen anyone at the taxi stop earlier that afternoon. Luxury vehicles had formed a long line to drop off most of the students. They were accompanied by both parents, and in some cases siblings as well. Carrying luggage into the dormitory was generally a family affair.

Very few families owned cars in Ghana at the time. Most cars seen on Ghanaian roads were passenger vehicles with rusted bodies. The sight of all these students arriving in fancy cars made me feel like I was from another planet. Judging by the quality of luggage they carried, my possessions were junk in comparison. *I clearly don't belong here,* I thought.

When the bell rang for dinner, most students were still with their families and in no rush to go to the dining hall. Food was the main reason I had stood in front of the building all that time, so I immediately made my way to the dining hall. It was half-empty. At my assigned table, I was relieved to find that the cutlery was familiar. Also, only two other people sat at the table, and I was able to help myself to a second plate of food without too many eyes looking. As soon as I finished eating, I returned to my room, unpacked the rest of my things, and went to bed.

Opening assembly took place after breakfast the following morning on the east campus. That was the main campus; the administration building, classrooms, main school chapel, and campus police station were all located there. The distance from my dormitory to class was just under a mile. Although a bit tiring at times, particularly when we carried heavy books, it was a nice walk along a tree-lined street. With no on-campus shuttle, everyone had to walk to class. East campus students had only a quarter mile walk from their dormitories to the classroom buildings.

The Achimota campus was large, leafy, and beautiful. It had a hospital, a swimming pool, tennis courts, and a golf course. No other secondary school in Ghana had as many facilities and amenities. The furniture in every building, the bathrooms and the fixtures in them, the student lounges, and everything else at Achimota were far more luxurious than at Oda. Most of the campus buildings were painted white. Unlike at Oda, Achimota dormitories looked more like what you'd see at a college.

At my first class later that morning, I realized I was one of only a handful of new students. The class consisted primarily of students who had attended Achimota for basic-level studies. The school admitted very few students from outside for advanced-level studies. As expected, the new students mostly came from other top-tier secondary schools in Ghana. While not on par with Achimota, those schools were better than Oda, and they generally admitted high-achieving students. When I missed Achimota's cut-off age for basic-level studies, I probably should have chosen one of those schools, but I ultimately decided to stay closer to home.

The Achimota students naturally stuck together initially. As the days went by, I noticed that the students from other schools were beginning to interact easily with everyone else in class. I had difficulty relating to anyone, because socio-economically, we had nothing in common. I had grown up in a village with no amenities. Most of my Achimota classmates lived in mansions in big cities and spent their vacations abroad, in places like London, Paris, and New York. Few, if any, had worked on a farm or done any of the chores I used to do at home. Therefore, conversation was difficult. I heard no mention of scholarships; clearly, no one at Achimota—except me—needed one.

At Oda, there was a good mix of people from different socio-economic backgrounds, so it was relatively easy to socialize with other students. Here, the gap was simply too wide. Although it took a while, I eventually made a few friends and began to interact more easily with the others. Even then, I always felt like an outsider.

Being among this population of rich kids benefited me in one significant respect: I always had enough to eat in the dining hall. Unlike at Oda, I could always find an extra plate of food. Also, I never had to leave my table to look for one. The meals at Achimota were quite a bit better. We had beef and chicken more often, and I was shocked to see so much delicious meat left untouched.

The classrooms, science labs, and other facilities at Achimota were much better equipped than those at Oda. There were fewer courses at the advanced level, but the workload was heavier. The material was a lot more difficult and covered at a much faster pace. What's more, everyone was incredibly smart. Anyone who did not stay alert in class risked falling behind.

Because of the significant amount of material to be covered over a relatively short period of time in preparation for the advanced-level GCE, most students at Achimota attended private classes during the summer between the first and second years. Often, by the time the second year began, they would have covered most of the syllabus topics for each class. They could then devote almost the entire final year to reviewing their notes, studying old test questions, taking practice tests, and honing other test-taking skills.

At the end of the first year, I realized that most of my classmates were applying to summer school. Ideally, I should have applied as well but could not for three reasons. First, I couldn't afford the steep fees. Second, these were private classes held off campus in Accra. I would need to find a place to live in the city and commute to classes each morning. I knew no one in Accra who would accommodate me. Third, it was summer, and my father needed help harvesting the cocoa, corn, and other crops and carrying them to market. At the end of the year, I packed my things and headed back to Boadua.

"The academic work at Achimota is overwhelming, so I need to study throughout the summer in order not to fall behind," I explained to my father when I went back to the farm. "There's a summer school program that most of my classmates are attending and I probably should've as well."

"I agree," my father said. "As for the farm work, we could probably manage without you. The problem is how you would pay the fee."

"I've brought the books with me. I'll try to study on my own," I assured him.

I couldn't do much with the books. The material I needed to study was too complex. It required levels of energy and concentration I could not find, given the work I was doing on the farm and the additional distractions.

As I prepared to return to school at the end of the summer, I had a nagging feeling that the coming academic year was going to be especially challenging. What I experienced upon my return to campus was much worse than I'd anticipated.

A few weeks in, I realized I was in a deep hole, and it was going to require a massive effort to climb out of it. In every class, most of the students knew the material already and could grasp the concepts much more quickly than I. That had not been the case during my first year. I had to spend a considerable amount of time after classes to have the teachers help me catch up.

Each day after dinner, I would return to my room and spend hours reading. I was fortunate to have classmates in my dormitory who were willing to answer my questions, no matter how late it was at night. Obeng was my best friend on campus. He was on the east campus and I often went there to study with him. My dormitory mate, Eric, had also become a good friend, and I studied with him frequently as well.

Obeng, Eric, and I belonged to the small group of students who came to Achimota from other secondary schools. The two of them came from middle-class families and were not as privileged as the Achimota students, which was why it was easier to relate to them. Both were brilliant. Eric was soft-spoken; he kept to himself unless someone needed help, in which case he would drop everything and offer assistance. Obeng was outgoing and more talkative. Through him, Eric and I made more friends on campus than we would have on our own.

Every now and then, I would visit one of my classmates in the dormitory and ask him to explain something to me. Invariably, he was either doing practice tests—in which case I would have to ask someone else—or reading something entirely different from the textbooks I was working with at the time.

I returned to my room after each of those visits totally demoralized. My sleep that entire year was reduced to a series of short naps. I was afraid that if I ever slept normal hours, I would never make up all the ground I had lost. On many nights I felt dead tired but kept going, either from necessity or insomnia.

I was able to get through the year, both physically and mentally. By the time the final examinations came around, I felt prepared. My teachers and some of my classmates had been very supportive, and on a personal level, I had put in the required effort. I had only a short time to revise the materials and do a few practice tests, but I got through enough to give me the necessary confidence.

We took exams in physics, chemistry, math, and general studies. Not surprisingly, my classmates sounded pleased with their performances. I could not be as confident, but I hoped I had done well enough to get the passes I needed to qualify for university. It would take about six weeks for the results to become available, so I said my goodbyes on campus and returned home to help my father on the farm.

In those intervening weeks, I felt anxious all the time. If I passed the exams and got admitted to the university, I would be on my way to becoming an electrical engineer. My older siblings were all in low-paying jobs and could hardly support themselves. As an engineer, I could support myself, help the family, and maybe even get my father to retire from the back-breaking work he had done all his life. I would find out in only a matter of weeks if any of those dreams would ever come true.

After five weeks on the farm, I returned to Boadua. There was no news, but I had a feeling judgment day was near. Two days later, I went to Accra to visit the campus, just to see if I could get any information.

My timing was perfect. The school had received the results that very morning. The few minutes I waited for the woman at the registrar's office to look up my results felt like an eternity. I saw a little smile on her face as she walked back toward me. It was a good sign, but I held my breath.

"Congratulations!" she said, as she handed over the piece of paper with my results. I had passed the exams with strong enough scores to gain admission to the university. It was one of the happiest moments of my life. I couldn't wait to get home and share the great news.

About a month later, I received an offer of admission from the department of electrical engineering at the University of Science and Technology (UST) in Kumasi, Ghana's second city. I was one lucky young man. In a few weeks, I would begin the final leg of what had been a long and often difficult educational journey. The comfortable life I had always dreamed of now seemed within reach.

That, it turned out, couldn't have been further from the truth. Ghana was experiencing a severe drought at the time, so food was scarce and extremely expensive. As a result, the universities could only provide breakfast and lunch. Students had to come up with their own dinner money. Even the two meals the schools provided were never enough. Consequently, although university was still tuition-free, I needed a lot of money for meals and other out-of-pocket expenses. I could not earn that money anywhere because part-time and on-campus jobs for students were still non-existent in Ghana.

I had no idea what that meant until I visited the university campus and talked to some students. Those from poor families were struggling. Some of the engineering students were already thinking about dropping out. Operating on an empty stomach in their demanding academic programs was too great a burden to bear.

This was yet another steep wall to scale.

Me, at Secondary School in Oda

CHAPTER 9

To Moscow with Fear

Two years passed. I was twenty-two, and once again looking for direction. After concluding that it was impossible to study electrical engineering at UST without adequate nutrition, I had abandoned the idea of continuing on at university in Ghana. Because the national economy itself was in bad shape, there were no jobs that I could find with my advanced-level GCE certificate. Instead I spent much of that time helping my father on the farm.

While in secondary school, I had heard of a joint Ghana-Soviet government program that offered scholarships to qualified students to attend university in the Soviet Union. I had not given it much thought, because credentials from Soviet universities were somehow seen as inferior to those obtained from Ghanaian universities.

Whether or not the judgment was valid, for someone who had dreamed of studying at Oxford or Cambridge, getting a degree that few would respect was not an attractive option. But I had reached a dead end.

The deteriorating economic situation in Ghana had made those scholarships difficult to obtain. When I went to the office of the government agency that administered the program in Accra, I learned that the number of applicants was huge. I could see I faced an uphill battle. I spent more than two hours in line for the forms, which I carefully completed and submitted before returning to Boadua.

I was thrilled when I received a letter inviting me for an interview. Candidates would be considered in groups before a panel. That meant operating under the immense pressure of having to compete for air time while coming up with answers.

Two hundred applicants waited at the office when I arrived in Accra on the morning of the interview—all aspiring engineering majors. Hundreds of other engineering applicants had been interviewed in the preceding days.

"Please introduce yourselves to the panel," the leader asked after we were seated.

There were ten of us—all male—seated in a row in front of the panel, which had six members—three males and three females. The interviewers—all Ghanaians—sat behind a rectangular wooden table. The room was fairly large, and I could feel the pressure build as we introduced ourselves.

"Please take turns and tell us why you want to be engineers," one panelist asked at the conclusion of the introductions.

The room fell silent. Although we had only a vague idea of the nature of the interview questions, paralyzing nerves prevented responses to the one question we had been told to expect. Fortunately, I'd had a bit of time to gather my thoughts.

"I loved science in secondary school. As a young, developing country, Ghana desperately needs engineers to help build its energy infrastructure. I would like to study electrical engineering to enable me to contribute to that effort," I offered. The panelists nodded approvingly.

Over the next couple of hours, the panelists asked a series of wide-ranging, often highly technical questions. One panelist asked us to explain how an electrical transformer works. Many of the questions required application of mathematical principles.

The interview was every bit as difficult and stressful as I had expected. However, I felt good about my performance.

* * *

MY FRIEND EMELIA WORKED AS a nurse at the St. Dominic's Hospital in Akwatia. Our friendship led to my first meeting with Patricia.

While I was visiting Emelia at her apartment, her friend Joyce stopped by. Joyce was then a student at the hospital's nursing school. After Emelia introduced us, Joyce mentioned that she'd like to introduce me to Patricia.

Several weeks later, I was walking past the hospital one late afternoon when I saw Joyce and another young lady standing at the taxi stop in front of the main hospital building. The young lady reminded me of Catherine—the slender figure, dark, shiny hair, and beautiful face. Although I didn't have a girlfriend at the time, I hadn't taken Joyce's promise to introduce me to Patricia seriously. I took it that she had said it casually due to the similarities in our names. Joyce and Patricia happened to be classmates at the nursing school.

"It's good to see you, Patrick," Joyce said as I approached them. "This is the guy I was talking to you about a few weeks ago," she said to her friend. I knew right away that it was Patricia.

Wow! Is it possible this beautiful lady isn't dating anyone currently? If she were, why would Joyce promise to introduce her to me? Several questions ran through my mind as I stood there, motionless. I was in a hurry to get answers.

Though I was stunned by her beauty, Patricia seemed unimpressed, judging by her tepid greeting. My heart began to beat rapidly.

"Patricia and I are going to Emelia's place later this evening. Will you be there?" Joyce asked.

"I sure will," I replied. I had no plans to visit Emelia that day, but I smelled an opportunity that I'd be foolish to squander. I tried to act casual about the whole thing, and Patricia's visible irritation at being delayed made me wonder if I should bother.

When I showed up later at Emelia's, she was surprised to see me. She hadn't invited me to the impromptu social gathering she had arranged for that evening, and I implied my presence there was a mere coincidence, saying that I was in the area and decided to stop by for a few minutes to say hello.

I knew Emelia through a mutual friend and had been an occasional visitor for a couple of years. She had no idea that the casual get-together at her apartment that evening was now a high-stakes affair for me. The two of us talked for about an hour before Joyce and Patricia arrived at her apartment.

Patricia looked even more radiant. Over the next few hours, the six of us discussed general matters. I kept looking at Patricia, sometimes making eye contact. Emilia and Joyce had been doing much of the talking and Patricia acted distant initially, though I noticed she gradually warmed to me.

Over the next several weeks, I saw Patricia as often as possible, mostly at Emelia's apartment. My visits became a lot more frequent than they had been prior to my meeting Patricia. The more time I spent around Patricia, the more I fell in love with her. Apart from her outer beauty, she appeared well-mannered and kind, qualities I greatly admired.

Patricia was twenty-one at the time—a year younger than I. She had grown up in Nsawam, a town located about twenty miles from Accra. As it was with Catherine, Patricia's family was well-to-do, so I was once again harboring romantic feelings for someone well outside of my socio-economic class. I wasn't going to repeat the mistake I made in Oda, however. I had to let Patricia know how I felt.

A couple of months after we first met, I asked Patricia out on a date. She didn't say no.

"Are you planning to remain in Akwatia after you complete nursing school?" I asked on that first date. Having no money, I couldn't take her to fancy places. On that date and the next few that followed, we simply sat somewhere and talked.

"Yes, I intend to," she replied. "St. Dominic's is a great hospital and I'd love to stay and work there."

"I'm so glad," I said. "I love being around you."

"I love your company as well," she said, flashing one of her beautiful smiles.

I had been afraid that telling Patricia I loved her would scare her off. One night, when I was about to say goodnight, I pulled her in for a kiss. To my utter relief, she didn't push me away. I was so nervous, my heart felt ready to explode in my chest.

We stood there for a few more seconds, looking intently into each other's eyes, before we said our goodbyes and she went inside her apartment.

Our romantic relationship began after that. My love for Patricia became all-consuming. For a while, I couldn't think of anything else. My parents liked her immediately—and so did my siblings.

Helping my father on his farm began to feel like torture. I couldn't stand being away from Patricia for even a couple of days, but I had no choice but to spend multiple weeks at a time in the jungle.

Whenever I returned from one of those long stays, Patricia would hold me tight and say, "I missed you so much!"

"You have no idea what kind of torture it is for me to be away from you," I would answer.

"It's torture for me, too. You can't do that to me."

"I didn't know you and Patricia were dating," Emilia said when I visited her one day. "You have no idea how many guys in this hospital she's turned down."

I knew that most female Ghanaian nurses dreamed of marrying doctors. According to Emelia, Patricia had rejected the advances of a couple of young doctors at the hospital, among other suitors. I was amazed that she had chosen to date me, a penniless guy from a dusty village who had no idea where his life was headed.

"So, what attracted you to me?" I asked Patricia one day.

She smiled and took a moment to gather her thoughts. "Joyce told me the day she first saw you that you were quite handsome," she finally said. "Honestly, I wasn't that impressed when you walked up to us at the taxi stop that afternoon. What caught my attention was how intelligent you sounded during the conversation we had later that evening in Emelia's apartment. And you seemed to have a gentle nature, which I found admirable. By the way, it took me a while to realize it, but you are indeed handsome."

I pulled her toward me and kissed her. "I love you deeply," I whispered in her ear.

At home by myself the next day, I thought about what Patricia had said. Through reading the newspaper for many years, I had become reasonably well-informed about many issues. That made me come across as intelligent in conversations, much more than I really was. That knowledge had been tremendously helpful numerous times previously—during the Achimota interview, for example. It now appeared to have also helped me win the heart of a beautiful, highly sought-after lady. *That's a pretty good return on investment!* I thought.

* * *

EXACTLY THREE WEEKS AFTER THE interview, I received a letter with the good news. My application had been successful, and I had been awarded one of the scholarships. In addition to paying full tuition, it provided a monthly stipend that covered living expenses. Travel to and from the Soviet Union was also included. The path was finally cleared for me to obtain my university education.

The next few weeks should have been happy, but I began to have second thoughts. The scholarship was for students only, so even if we got married right away, Patricia could not accompany me to the Soviet Union. And I had learned that students typically returned to Ghana only after graduation. It might be six years before I saw Patricia again.

"What? You can't leave me here alone for six years!" she protested, when I finally told her. I knew that she would be upset, but I was taken aback by the look of horror on her face.

"I'm seriously thinking about rejecting the scholarship," I told her. That seemed to take her by surprise.

"Don't be silly," she said, "you can't do that either. This is a great opportunity."

"Let's both take some time to think about what we're going to do about our relationship," I suggested.

"That's a good idea," she said. We hugged each other tightly, tears filling our eyes.

The departure date was six months away—if I decided to leave. Over the next several weeks, we decided that although the separation would be agonizing, we were too deeply in love to simply walk away from our relationship.

"I'm going to do whatever I can to return home to see you before the six years are over," I assured her.

"I really hope so," she replied.

Something else gave me pause. Because the Soviet Union was mostly a closed society, whatever little I knew about it had come from negative things I had overheard people say in secondary school. I decided to use my trips to Accra to learn a bit more about the country where I would be spending the next six years.

"Why on earth would you want to live in the Soviet Union?" a man at the passport office asked incredulously. He had just handed me the application forms.

"I'm going there to study at a university," I explained.

"Why would you want to do that?" he asked again, sneering this time. "Don't you know that Soviet degrees are worthless? Plus, you're going to live in the country with the harshest climate on the planet. Do you know how cold it gets there? Have you heard about the KGB? They'll be spying on you endlessly. The slightest mistake will get you sent to their labor camp in Siberia, where prisoners are worked to death. Not only that, but the Soviets stand in long lines to buy everything; everything is in short supply over there."

This is terrifying! I thought.

I didn't understand much of what he was saying, but I was completely dejected when I left the office that day. During my subsequent trips to Accra, I spoke to various people, hoping to find at least one who had something positive to say that might assuage my fears.

Those fears became progressively worse with each conversation. Everyone seemed to have the same opinion of the Soviet Union, if not worse.

"There'll be spies following your every move, so if you do go, which I don't recommend, you'll have to be extremely careful," one man told me.

During that time, I could not sleep. To travel from my remote African village to an unfamiliar, inhospitable-sounding place like the Soviet Union felt like too much of a leap.

I decided to reject the scholarship. There were still three months left before I would leave, so I had time to look for an alternative that could keep me in Ghana.

Meanwhile, I had become a burden on my poor family, an extra mouth to feed during that period of severe famine. Frequently, because of me, my mother had little or nothing to eat because she gave me her portion. Naturally, I felt guilty and tried to give the food back to her. She wouldn't take it. In her mind, it would only be a few more months before I left Ghana to study in the Soviet Union, so for me, at least, she could see light at the end of the tunnel.

Socio-economic conditions were worsening by the day in Ghana. The relationship between Ghana's new military government and the developed-world governments that traditionally offered financial assistance to prop up the Ghanaian economy had deteriorated to the point where much of that support was no longer forthcoming. That had crippled the economy. I had no choice but to put aside my fears and prepare myself mentally for my transition to a new life in a closed, communist country. I had to bite the bullet.

Patricia and I agreed to put off discussions of marriage for now, given the uncertainties surrounding when I could return for a possible visit.

"I know you'll be busy with your studies, but you have to promise you'll stay in touch as best as you can," she said one night as my departure date drew near.

"It's a shame that you don't have a telephone, but I'll write you a letter every week," I promised. She had by then moved into her own apartment. I spent almost all my time there in those final weeks.

"What have you decided to do about your relationship with Patricia?" my mother asked me one evening.

"It's going to be difficult being separated, but we've decided to stay together," I told her.

"That's so great!" she said, beaming. "Patricia is a lovely person and I think she'll make an excellent wife for you. Since she lives close to us, we'll take good care of her."

"Thank you, Mama," I said.

Classes would be taught entirely in Russian, which I had never even heard spoken. The first time I saw the alphabet—Cyrillic—was when I picked up my visa from the Soviet embassy in Accra. I couldn't even recognize my name. Studying electrical engineering in English was difficult enough; I couldn't imagine how I would do it in Russian.

"It'll be too emotional for me, so I'm not going to accompany you to the airport," Patricia said one week before departure.

"You have to!" I protested.

After several attempts to convince her over the next few days, I reluctantly accepted her decision.

"Do you remember all the promises you've made to me?" Patricia asked when I said the final goodbye to her on the morning of my departure. I had spent the last night with her at her apartment.

"I certainly do, and I'll keep all of them," I replied. We hugged tightly for several minutes as we both began to cry. *Being born into a poor family in a poor country is a real curse,* I thought as we let go of each other and I began my slow walk away from her into the unknown.

My father, a few of my siblings, Francis, and a couple of my friends from the village came to the airport in Accra to see me off that day.

"You've come a really long way," Francis said as we stood inside the airport terminal.

"Thank you, Francis. I really wish we had been together on this educational journey all along," I replied.

He shook his head. "It wasn't meant to be. I wish you the best of luck in the Soviet Union."

"Are you nervous?" my father and my siblings kept asking me.

I had tried to hide the intense feelings of apprehension and sadness that raged inside me, but they could see them written all over my face. The prospect of leaving Patricia, my family, and close friends was painful to contemplate; however, I was at a point of no return. In all my struggles in Ghana over the years, I had taken comfort in the knowledge that my family and friends were there to return to. Now I had no idea how I would find my way home if I got into trouble.

After many emotional goodbyes and more reassurances that I would be fine, I turned around and boarded the plane, beginning my journey into the unknown.

* * *

INCLUDING TWO STOPOVERS ALONG THE way, the flight from Accra to Moscow took sixteen hours. Most of the people on the flight were students like me, with the same expressions of apprehension. No one spoke the entire time; I sat silently, thinking about Patricia and my family and wondering what my first day in the Soviet Union would be like.

Two Soviet gentlemen met us at the Sheremetovo Airport in Moscow. They were Russian-English translators sent to take us through customs. Also greeting us at the airport were a couple of Ghanaian students attending Moscow State University.

The translators accompanied us on a bus from the airport to a hotel in Moscow, where we stayed for the next few days. I was impressed. The city was extremely clean, and unlike in Accra and other parts of Ghana, traffic in Moscow moved in an orderly fashion on wide, paved streets. Most of the buildings were high-rise apartment complexes, freshly painted and well kept.

At the hotel, we met students from several other countries who had just arrived and were waiting to be sent to the cities where they would eventually live and study. We arrived in Moscow the third week of August, and the weather was beautiful. Not speaking Russian or possessing any currency, we could not explore the city. The translators had specific assignments to take us to and from designated places. Showing us the city was not one of them.

Four days later, I was informed that I would be sent to Kyiv, the capital of Ukraine, where I would spend one year in language school. Also going to Kyiv were five other new students from Ghana I had been getting to know. I was happy to learn we would be traveling together.

Our translator met us when we arrived at the station in Kyiv, shortly after six o'clock in the morning, and traveled with us on a bus to the university dormitory. After we checked in, he took us to a cafeteria for breakfast, and then we returned to the dormitory to unpack. After lunch, we went to the university administration building to do paperwork and be officially admitted to the university.

I was surprised to find students from so many other countries in the dormitory at Kyiv State University. It appeared as if every country in the world was represented. This living situation presented a great opportunity to gain exposure to people from other backgrounds and cultures.

I wrote to Patricia and my family a few days after I first arrived in Kyiv. Two months passed before I received replies. Neither Patricia nor my family had telephones at home. Writing letters was the only form of communication. I worried that staying in touch would be difficult.

Four days after arriving in Kyiv, I went to my first class. Each first-year class had twenty students, with class composition based on academic area of concentration. The other five Ghanaians were non-engineering majors and so not among my classmates. In my class, I heard many other languages, including English, French, German, Spanish, Korean, and Vietnamese.

Our first language professor, a middle-aged woman, spoke only Russian. Because she neither spoke nor understood any of the languages of my classmates, she simply went about her business in Russian. It was like being in a United Nations General Assembly meeting without interpreters.

Day-to-day communication was done with hand signals. When we paid a cashier, we had no idea whether we were being given correct change. I realized quickly that I couldn't survive in that mode for long; it was either sink or swim. So, swim it was.

We had classes eight hours a day, six days a week, with only Sundays off. I found Russian to be a very structured language. After we studied the alphabet, learning the language itself seemed to happen in a steady, methodical way. We were required to watch the nightly news on television every evening in the dormitory. The professor told us that the newsreaders were some of the most articulate people in society and listening to them would help improve our own speaking skills.

To my pleasant surprise, after the first few months, I could understand quite a bit and string together a few sentences. I started to venture out and interact with the Soviets. More importantly, I could engage in a bit of conversation with classmates who knew no English.

* * *

DURING MY YEARS IN SECONDARY school, I heard many Ghanaians say that the Soviet government did not offer scholarships to students from developing nations for entirely altruistic reasons. It was said that the Soviets wanted to indoctrinate young men and women from other parts of the world in hopes that when they returned to their home countries, they would help spread communism.

I was constantly on the lookout during those initial months for signs of any overt or covert activities to further that objective. In Kyiv, my roommate was another Ghanaian, Bernard, an international relations major. We shared stories about our backgrounds and prior experiences. Bernard was a fairly small guy, and he loved to talk.

"Did you hear any frightening stories about the Soviet Union in Ghana?" I asked Bernard one afternoon.

"I heard so many that I almost decided against coming here," he replied.
I nodded. "So, what are your impressions thus far?"

"I haven't seen or experienced anything negative, but I'm cautious around the professors at school," he said. We had no Soviet classmates at the time, so the only natives we interacted with were the professors.

"Nothing bad has happened to me either, but I'm constantly nervous," I told Bernard.

"So far so good, and let's hope things stay that way," he said finally.

One morning I heard a knock on the door. My visitor was a young Soviet man, about eighteen or nineteen years old, holding a suitcase. He said something in Russian that I did not understand, but I let him in anyway.

The third bed in our room had been empty since we arrived. The "visitor" set his suitcase down near that bed, offered his hand, and said, "Dmitry Vasilev." I shook his hand and told him my name. For the time being, that communication would have to suffice. He opened his suitcase and started to unpack.

The mere presence of Dmitry in the room injected so much fear inside me that I shook all over. The temperature in the room was perfectly normal, but I began to sweat.

A couple of hours later, Bernard returned. Realizing that Dmitry was the other occupant of the room, he offered his hand and they made their simple introductions. Bernard sat on his bed and looked over at me.

"Why are you sweating so much?" he asked.

"It feels quite warm in here," I said.

I could see Bernard regarding Dimitry suspiciously. *Is he as afraid of Dmitry as I am?* I wondered.

During those first few days before Dmitry arrived, Bernard and I talked a lot whenever we were together in the room. Dmitry's presence changed that. Bernard and I came from the same region in Ghana and so we communicated in that regional dialect. Dmitry could not possibly understand our conversations. Still, we kept silent unless absolutely necessary.

The six of us from Ghana were all housed in the same dormitory and often hung out together at meals and in the lounge. From them, I learned that many of the other foreign students in the dormitory also had Soviet roommates. These Soviets mostly stayed quiet but appeared to be watching their movements.

In those initial weeks in Kyiv, I avoided eye contact with Dmitry. I did everything I could to keep out of the way of this "scary" Soviet.

My body language soon gave Dmitry the impression—rightly—that I wanted him as far away from me as possible. I learned later that his entire life had been spent in a small Ukrainian town. He had never had contact with anyone from outside the Soviet Union, so he didn't know what to expect of his foreign roommates. However, he had been looking forward to welcoming new friends to his country, learning about where they came from, and doing what he could to help them with their language studies.

Verbal communication, understandably, was impossible for the first several months, and my obvious fear prevented Dmitry from interacting with us enough to assuage that fear. Bernard would have been more approachable, had I not drawn him entirely into my corner.

Dmitry, a quiet person anyway, felt completely isolated as a result. He would often sit quietly on his bed and read. When he was not reading, he appeared to be watching whatever move Bernard and I made. That heightened my anxiety, because I assumed he was amassing information to pass on to the Soviet authorities. The atmosphere in the room had become extremely unhealthy, not only for me and Bernard, but also for Dmitry.

"Do you want some fruit?" Dmitry asked us one day, as the three of us sat in our usual silence. That took us completely by surprise.

"No thank you," we both said simultaneously.

"Please take some fruit," Dmitry insisted.

He had just returned to Kyiv from visiting his parents and had brought a bag of fruit. We had studied the language for about three months, so we knew how to construct simple sentences in Russian.

"Go ahead and take one," Bernard told me after he took an apple. As soon as I did, a broad smile appeared on Dmitry's face.

"Thank you for the apple. It's delicious!" Bernard said.

"Thank you, Dmitry," I said as well.

Our use of Russian words brightened his mood even more. From that day onward, Dmitry did his best to draw us closer.

"I know how far away you are from your families. I cannot imagine how that feels," he told us one afternoon. "I've also left home for the first time, and though my parents are far away, it's taken me time to adjust to life in Kyiv. You must be going through something similar."

"You're right about that," Bernard said.

I wondered whether my deep suspicion of Dmitry had been warranted. *If he had evil intentions, why would he make such a kind gesture? Or is it some trick to get us to open up to him so he can gather information about us more easily?* I told myself I should not let down my guard too quickly.

Bernard and I later learned that upon his first visit home from Kyiv, Dmitry had spoken to his parents about us, and they had also taken considerable interest in our well-being. His parents encouraged him to keep trying to get us to relax around him. They were very happy when he reported that we had started warming up to him. From that point on, and for the remainder of that year, whenever he went home, he would bring fruit, baked goods, and other goodies that his parents had packaged specifically for us.

In those following weeks and months, I thought about Dmitry and his parents, and their magnanimity toward us. To them, we were simply human beings far from their homes and families. They'd vowed to do whatever they could to make us feel welcome.

I asked the other foreign students whether their impressions of their roommates had changed as well. To my surprise, the vast majority said yes. As far as they could tell, their Soviet roommates had no mission other than to pursue a higher education.

Dmitry turned out to be one of the most kind-hearted people I have ever met. Although naturally quiet and soft-spoken, he made the atmosphere in our room as lively as he could. As busy as his freshman year was, he always found time to help us with our language assignments and initiate conversations to help us practice.

Dmitry was also wonderfully generous. He often accompanied us to the store to help us find what we needed. Sometimes, when he went grocery shopping alone, he would buy eggs and vegetables to share with us.

During the second half of the year, when communication in Russian became easier, Dmitry asked us frequently about life in Ghana and Africa in general.

"What's the name of the language you always speak?" Dmitry asked us one day.

"It's called *Twi*," I replied.

"Is that what everyone speaks in Ghana?" he asked.

"No, but it's the dominant language, so a majority of Ghanaians know it," I explained.

"What kinds of foods do you eat in Ghana?" he wanted to know.

"Rice and corn, but there are many others, such as cassava and plantain," Bernard told him.

In turn, Dimitry told us a lot about the Soviet Union. He seemed to be non-ideological. Most Soviets in his age group were members of the Komsomol, the youth wing of the Soviet Communist Party, which was the only way to get on a leadership track. Throughout the year, Dmitry never raised the subject of communism versus capitalism. Any views pro or con were kept to himself. I never did ask him outright, curious as I was. I didn't want to open that can of worms.

Toward the end of that year, I began to feel extremely guilty about how I had related to Dmitry those first several months. I was tempted—on several occasions—to explain my initial aloofness, but I decided against it each time. I was reluctant to reveal the negative views of his country I had learned in Ghana, thinking that the conversation would be unpleasant.

I had traveled to the Soviet Union believing I generally could not trust the people there. I wanted as little to do with them as possible. In the end, I was deeply humbled by the kind spirit of a truly good human being. The most powerful lessons I learned during that first year in Kyiv came from living with Dmitry. It forever changed the way I look at the world.

I also came to realize how easy it is for seemingly innocuous prejudicial views to morph into dangerous vehicles that can inflict grave harm on other groups of people. The people in Ghana who shared their views about the Soviet Union with me in truth knew little about that country. They were basing their opinions on hearsay.

What those people in Ghana had said about scarcity and the need to stand in long lines for everything in the Soviet Union also turned out to be inaccurate. The grocery stores were always well stocked with all the basics. The lines were not much different from what I later observed in Western European stores.

Lines for beer and vodka were the exceptions. Because I have never been a drinker, those long lines didn't affect me unless I was entertaining.

* * *

THE CLIMATE IN WEST AFRICA is tropical—hot and humid—with no seasonal variability. I had come from one of the hottest places on earth to live in one of the coldest. After the first month in Kyiv, I bought a thick winter coat, a wool hat, and other gear I needed to do battle with the Ukrainian winter.

One morning in late October, I looked out the window and saw that everything outside was completely white.

"What's that?" I screamed. Bernard and Dmitry rushed to the window.

"It's snow," Dmitry said with a smile.

Our professors had warned us to expect the first snowfall of the season, so I shouldn't have been that surprised. The vast, white blanket was stunning.

"Make sure you put on your coat and hat before you step outside," Dmitry cautioned us.

The temperature was relatively mild, and the air felt fresh and clean. Though I'd lived my entire life in tropical weather, I had always thought that Ghana was too hot and humid. The weather that morning in Kyiv felt pleasant. Many of us foreign students spent several minutes enjoying the powdery snow before going to class. For much of that day, the professor couldn't quite get our attention because everyone kept looking outside the window to admire the snow.

By the next morning, the beautiful weather had disappeared. The temperature had dropped precipitously, and outside, the cold was bone-chilling. I quickly learned that during the winter season even the Soviets made sure that all parts of their bodies were fully protected.

* * *

WHILE WALKING TO CLASS ONE beautiful morning during that first spring in Kyiv, I had a sense of foreboding. I saw small groups of Soviets talking among themselves with an air of concern. I had been in the country for about eight months but still had trouble understanding conversations. The professors did not say anything, and my classmates had no clue what had happened either.

Later that afternoon, we learned there had been an explosion at a nuclear plant in the Ukrainian town of Chernobyl. The explosion had occurred a couple of days earlier, but few people in Kyiv—just eighty miles south of Chernobyl—knew anything. The Soviet government initially did not release any information. Only later, when European countries began to detect high levels of radiation within their borders, was the information made public.

To this day, I don't know if the residents of Kyiv were in danger. I did not see signs of panic, even after the severity of the accident became generally known. Everything seemed normal, as if nothing had happened.

I continued to progress at the language school. The intensity of the full-immersion program helped tremendously. The only time I was not forced to speak Russian was with my friends from Ghana. Even that was discouraged. By the end of the first half of the year, most of us had become functionally literate in the language and were ready to move on to the next phase.

During the second half of the first year, in addition to language classes, we took introductory engineering classes such as math, physics, chemistry, and engineering drawing. Those subjects added another layer of difficulty because we had to learn technical terms in Russian. We also had to adjust to the speaking style of new professors. The Soviets were extremely good in the sciences. Even though taught in a relatively unfamiliar language, the classes were excellent and enjoyable. The professors were extremely dedicated and always made themselves available.

* * *

MY FAVORITE TIME IN KYIV was spring, when the brightly colored flowers such as marigold, mallow, and sunflower in the city's numerous parks and gardens were in full bloom.

The Soviets took great pride in maintaining their public spaces. During the spring, summer, and fall, there were always people sweeping the streets and sidewalks and tending to public gardens. Their massive underground railway system was also a marvel of beauty and efficiency. Many of the underground stations in the major Soviet cities were built to serve as bomb shelters in times of war and could accommodate thousands of people at a time.

I liked Kyiv, and Kyiv Polytechnic Institute had a great electrical engineering program, so I wanted to study there. Unfortunately, at the end of that first year, I was assigned to a university in Kharkiv, the second largest city in Ukraine. I would have to leave my Ghanaian friends in Kyiv and start a new life in a different city.

When I arrived in Kharkiv, I met two other students from Ghana—Jerry and Victor. They were also electrical engineering students, which meant that I would have Ghanaians in my class for the remainder of my time in the Soviet Union. Jerry and Victor had been in language school in Odesa, a port city in the southern part of Ukraine.

The three of us had a rude awakening on the first day of classes. In language school, our classmates were all foreign students, so we spoke the language at the same level. The professors taught at a relatively slow pace in the beginning and made sure no one lagged behind. In the first-year engineering class in Kharkiv, foreign students were a small minority. The large auditorium was filled with over two hundred students, only six of them foreign and all sitting in the front row.

The professor spoke rapidly. Throughout the ninety minutes, the six of us kept glancing around the room to see if our Soviet classmates were having similar problems coping with the speed of the professor's delivery. Nothing seemed to suggest that.

Every foreign student walked out of that first class in a daze, having understood little of what the professor had said. Each of us had hoped that another foreign student had done better in note taking; no one had. The remaining classes were not much different. By the end of the day, we all felt exhausted and dejected.

One of the Soviet students agreed to let me borrow his notes. I could barely read his handwriting. It turned out that for some of the Soviet students, the pace was also too fast.

We realized that learning highly technical, complex material with Soviet classmates in their native language would be far trickier than we had anticipated. Over the next several weeks, I began to harbor serious doubts about my ability to make it in the engineering program, even though I had managed to become fairly fluent in Russian.

Sometime after the first month, Jerry, Victor, and I set up a meeting with a group of the upper-class Ghanaian students. That meeting changed everything. Every foreign student who had ever studied in the Soviet Union had gone through that experience. The idea was that foreign students would not be given any special treatment. The goal was to immerse them fully right away to put them on par with their Soviet counterparts as quickly as possible. The trick had worked in the past, and the professors and school authorities saw no reason why it would not succeed with other foreign students.

Sometime at the beginning of the third month, my comprehension of lectures and my note-taking ability started to improve with each passing day. By the end of that first semester, I could follow almost everything. More importantly, I could ask questions whenever I needed to and was able to answer my professors' questions without much difficulty. The transformation was almost magical.

I was particularly interested in the way university exams were conducted. Most exams had both written and oral parts. At the end of the semester, students were given a list of questions that would appear on the exam. The hundred or so questions covered everything taught in the course. Students received the questions a few days before exams, and they could use any source materials they liked to prepare their answers.

A professor would arrive at the exam room early in the morning and invite in five or six students. On a table would be several three-by-five-inch cards, lying face down. These were called exam tickets. On each of those tickets would be five or six questions, selected at random from the master list.

No two tickets had the same set of questions on them, so picking one was like playing the lottery. A student had one chance to pick a ticket.

Because it wasn't possible to comprehensively prepare and memorize answers to all the questions on the master list, each student could only hope for the best.

That first set of students taking the exam would be given ninety minutes to prepare their written responses. Whoever completed their answers first would approach the professor to begin the oral portion of the exam. If no one volunteered, the professor simply called on someone. That student would hand over the exam ticket to the professor, who would do a quick review of the student's written answers and follow up with questions.

Depending on how well the student had answered the written questions, the oral portion could take anywhere from five to fifteen minutes. After that, the student would receive a grade. Universities in the Soviet Union used a numerical grading scale that ranged from two to five. Two was a failing grade. A three was satisfactory, a four was very good, and a five was excellent. Receiving a two required re-taking the exam a day or two later.

After completing the exam and obtaining a grade, the student would leave the room. Another waiting outside would then take their position.

Depending on the number of students in a class, exams could take all day. A student who was not a morning person could take the exam in the afternoon. I heard numerous debates about the best time to show up. Most students felt the professors were more aggressive in their questioning early on, when they had more energy. I didn't think it mattered one way or the other; mostly I took my exams early.

During the weeklong study period at the end of our first semester in Kharkiv, Jerry, Victor, and I spent many hours, day and night, nervously studying and reviewing for the exams. We had no idea what to expect.

The preparation was probably no more than I was used to doing for other exams; it just felt that way.

I went to bed early on the night before my first exam, which was for an electrical circuits class, and got to school first thing in the morning. Only a few students had arrived, so I joined the first group of five. The professor pointed to the table with the exam tickets. I nervously reached for one. To my great relief, I could answer all the questions in a little more than an hour.

From where I was seated, I could not hear the professor's conversations with the two students who had gone before me for the oral portion, but he seemed to be smiling each time I looked up. I signaled to him that I was ready to show him my written answers. His smile became even broader.

I was the first foreign student he was examining that day, and he was probably trying to get me to relax. He took my exam ticket and answer sheet. After reviewing them for about five minutes, he asked me several questions. Most related to the answers I had provided already. However, a few were general. At the end, he congratulated me on a job well done and gave me a five grade for the course.

I became a big fan of the Soviet method of conducting exams. A student's course grade was not determined solely based on written answers to a few randomly selected questions. Invariably, a professor asked several general questions to ensure that the student had a comprehensive knowledge of the material covered. If a student could not fully answer one of the questions, the oral portion provided another opportunity to demonstrate sufficient knowledge to earn a passing grade.

Conducting exams in that manner made cheating unlikely. No two students had the same set of questions and so could not collaborate. It allowed for maximum flexibility as well. A student with an emergency could reschedule without the professor having to worry about answers already becoming public information. The system had benefits for everyone.

* * *

DURING THE FIRST WINTER BREAK in Kharkiv, I traveled to what was then Western Germany with Jerry and Victor. On the way, we stopped for a few hours in the Polish capital, Warsaw. Traveling students mostly used that time to do some shopping in the city. The prices in Warsaw were lower than in Western Europe.

There were no readily available official channels at the train station or elsewhere in Warsaw for students to exchange foreign currency into zlotys, the Polish currency. Students relied on ordinary Polish citizens at the train station who exchanged zlotys for foreign currency at black market rates.

Those people were not easy to identify. They simply walked around in the station and made gestures signaling foreigners that they had zlotys to exchange. As with most transactions of that nature in the Soviet Union and its satellite countries in those days, they were illegal but generally accepted as a necessary evil.

During a stopover on one trip to Germany, I was standing in the middle of a crowded main train station in Warsaw when a young Polish guy made eye contact with me. I moved in closer, discreetly took out a hundred-dollar bill from my wallet and handed it to him.

"Stop! Where are you going?" I ran like a madman after him. For a minute, he had pretended to reach into his pocket to retrieve the zlotys before suddenly taking off.

"What's going on, Patrick?" Victor yelled as he ran after us.

"The guy took my money and is running away with it," I replied, panting heavily.

"Hey! Stop!" Both Victor and Jerry were shouting at the guy. They had just completed their own transactions a few feet away, in another corner of the station.

"I can't see him anymore," I heard Victor shout. He had given the guy a good chase before he disappeared into the crowd.

"How much money did you give him?" Jerry asked.

"A hundred dollars," I replied.

"We have to find the guy!" Jerry insisted. That was quite a lot of money.

"He's probably outside the station already." I stopped running, dejected. "I'm going to report the matter to those policemen over there," I told Jerry and Victor. I took a few steps and then, realizing the futility of it all, said, "Let's just go and wait for the train to Germany."

The attempted transaction was not legal in the first place. Telling the police would just get me in trouble.

"Are you sure you don't want to report the incident?" Jerry asked.

"Yes," I replied.

My previous currency trades in Warsaw had been completed without a hitch, but on this occasion, it was a complete disaster.

* * *

THE UNIVERSITY WE WERE STUDYING at in Kharkiv was primarily known for its architecture program. Its relatively new electrical engineering program did not have a particularly good reputation. At the end of our first year in Kharkiv, Jerry, Victor, and I petitioned the Soviet authorities, through the Ghana embassy in Moscow, to transfer us to a place with a stronger program.

Our persistence paid off, and our petition was ultimately granted. We were transferred to a university in Donetsk, a major city in Ukraine's Donbas region. Donetsk is smaller than both Kyiv and Kharkiv, but it was an enjoyable place to live. We completed the remaining four years of the program there.

* * *

THE SOVIET UNION HAD BEEN in existence for sixty-three years when I arrived in the country in August 1985. President Mikhail Gorbachev was only six months into his tenure as general secretary of the Politburo, the highest governing body of the Soviet Communist Party. As a result, I got to see Soviet society pretty much as it had been throughout its history before the reforms initiated by President Gorbachev kicked into gear. Those reforms led to the union's disintegration six years later.

Prior to becoming a part of the union, each of the fifteen Soviet republics had at some point in its history been a separate country with its own language and culture. The older Soviet citizens from the other republics occasionally communicated in their native languages. The younger generation spoke Russian, the official language.

With the Cold War still at its height, ordinary Soviets were not allowed to travel outside the country. As a result, the vast majority rarely met any foreigners. On numerous occasions when I went to the underground stations to take a train, even in some major cities, I was the only Black person. I always received curious glances from the groups of Soviets gathered on the platforms. For many, it was the first time they had seen a Black person. At other times, a bus full of people would pass by and someone on it would point a finger at me, laughing or gesturing. I was always highly amused.

I remember one incident in particular. I had gone to a farmers' market in Donetsk with Victor to buy produce. In addition to local farmers, others from nearby small towns sold produce there as well. Shortly after we arrived at the market, a middle-aged Soviet man walked up to us. From his demeanor, we could tell that he was drunk.

"Why are you so black?" he asked.

Before either of us could say a word, he swiped one of his fingers on my arm. He seemed confused when he looked at it and found no black stain.

Victor and I both broke into hysterical laughter. The man had clearly never seen anyone who looked like us. Our vigorous laughter must have scared him because he retreated quickly. Victor and I later wished we could have engaged him in conversation to find out whether he was asking an innocent question out of curiosity, or whether he was so drunk that he didn't have a clue what he was asking. The curious looks and such isolated incidents were as far as things went. There were never any outward expressions of hostility toward me throughout my time in the country.

In the first few months after I arrived in the Soviet Union, I was still unsure what motivated the Soviet government to bring foreign students into the country to study. It seemed logical that it was an attempt to win our hearts and minds. Apparently, quite a few Africans returned to their home countries to assume top-level government positions, then tilted their countries' domestic and foreign policies in favor of the Soviet Union. I never observed any concerted efforts by my professors to convince any of us to change our political views during the entire time I lived in the country.

Most of my Soviet classmates and professors were members of the Communist Party. In many of our conversations over the years, they always adhered to the official party line. That, to me, was normal, given that they knew hardly anything other than their own socio-economic system. Most were curious about Africa, its people, and its culture.

What I found most surprising was the degree to which ordinary Soviets were isolated from the rest of the world. Along with being forbidden to travel outside their country's borders, they had no access to foreign television programs that would have introduced them to what life was like elsewhere. It was somewhat the same for me growing up in Boadua with no televisions. In the Soviet Union, almost every home had a television, but they received only Soviet programming. Most people were in the dark as to how the rest of the world operated.

The Soviet Union was a massive country, with a geographic territory that spanned eleven time zones. As people were getting ready for work early in the morning somewhere on the western tip of the country, it would already be early evening on the eastern tip. Within that expansive territory, the Soviets were allowed to travel freely, so even if they could not see the rest of the world, they had a lot to explore.

As foreign students, our travels across that giant landscape were not restricted either. However, we were required to obtain visas from the local Soviet government authorities—in the cities and towns where we lived and studied—to travel anywhere. For us the trip from Kyiv to Moscow, for instance, required a visa. Very few Soviets owned cars then, and foreign students generally did not drive, so long-distance travel anywhere within the Soviet Union was either by train or airplane. The flight from Moscow to Kyiv took less than ninety minutes.

I later realized that the visa requirement made sense, in that it allowed university officials and other authorities to track students' whereabouts. Because train travel was relatively inexpensive, whenever I had the time, I took a train ride somewhere. It was one of my favorite things to do in the Soviet Union.

Traveling long distances by train gave me the chance to see some of the most beautiful landscapes of the Soviet Union—lakes, picturesque mountains, and charming small villages. In addition to spending time in cities such as Kyiv, Moscow, St. Petersburg, Odesa, and Minsk, I visited small towns and villages in Ukraine, Russia, and some of the other republics.

No place was more beautiful than St. Petersburg, with its Parisian architecture. The Hermitage Museum was my favorite destination there. Unlike other famous museums in the West, the Hermitage was hardly ever crowded.

I never felt in danger anywhere in the Soviet Union. In the small towns and villages, most of which had no major universities and therefore no foreign students living in them, the number of curious looks from the locals was always far greater than in places such as Kyiv and Moscow. No one asked what I was doing there. Most people were quite friendly and ready to answer questions and provide whatever help I needed.

For many decades, leaders of the Soviet Communist Party had told their country's citizens that the communist system was far superior to capitalism and that the Soviet Union was much more powerful, militarily and economically, than the U.S. and its Western allies. Based on numerous conversations with ordinary people in various parts of the Soviet Union, I got the sense that although a majority believed what their leaders told them about the East-West power balance, significant numbers of Soviets dismissed it as propaganda.

Ordinary Soviets appeared to be split along ethnic lines on that issue. Russians I spoke to were far likelier to have total belief in the communist system and its superiority, while a majority of the skeptics were from other republics.

My conversations with non-Russian Soviets led me to believe that many felt they were living under colonial rule. Russia, which includes Moscow and St. Petersburg (Leningrad in those days), was by far the largest and most dominant of the fifteen republics that constituted the Soviet Union. Because many of the republics had at one time been invaded by Russia prior to joining the union, their citizens saw themselves as involuntary members, thus explaining some of the ethnic tensions within the Soviet Union.

I saw myself as a neutral observer in those debates and listened to every viewpoint with equal interest. Asked about my own views, I simply said I did not know enough to judge. That was true initially—until I made my first visit to Western Europe.

Prior to its disintegration, the Soviet Union largely traded with other Eastern Bloc countries, which were communist states in Eastern Europe. Most stores offered only Soviet-made goods. The lack of variety meant shopping trips were always quick. A shopper walked in, selected whatever item was on the shelf, paid for it, and returned home. That was the case with both basic consumer products and big-ticket items, such as refrigerators. On the roads, one saw only two makes of cars, Lada and Volga, both Soviet-produced.

To enter West Berlin from the Soviet Union-to-Western Europe train route, passengers had to pass through a customs border in East Berlin, the capital of the former East Germany. Setting foot in West Berlin for the first time, I was immediately struck by the stark contrast between the city and all the other places I had seen along the way from Moscow. Whereas most of the buildings in Moscow and East Berlin—and to some extent Warsaw—looked rather dull, gleaming buildings graced every corner of West Berlin. There were beautiful markings and brightly colored stoplights on the busy streets, which teemed with people and all kinds of luxury vehicles.

West Berlin's perfumed stores were stunning, with nicely arranged aisles and shelves filled with many varieties of beautifully packaged products. I began to question whether the Communist Party leaders in Moscow really believed what they were telling their own people about their "superior" system. Unlike ordinary Soviets, party leaders traveled to the West frequently. Although I knew that quality of life could not be measured solely in terms of material things, I doubted that any reasonable person could look at those two portraits and claim life in the East was better.

* * *

IN THOSE DAYS, THERE WASN'T much for a foreign student to do in the Soviet Union during school vacations. Most of us traveled to countries in Western Europe. During summer break, students normally worked for two or three months in places like London and Paris to earn supplemental income. Winter breaks were too short for that purpose, but they were long enough for shopping trips to Western Europe.

The Soviets were generally unfamiliar with goods manufactured elsewhere, but those who were knew that most domestically produced goods were inferior in quality. As a result, some ordinary Soviets were always looking for ways to buy foreign-made goods.

Foreign students who traveled to Western Europe typically bought clothes, shoes, and basic supplies such as soap and toothpaste. Some also bought electronic goods, such as televisions and VCRs. Many Soviets relied on foreign students to buy them goods from the West. The Soviets' wish list began with jeans and electronic goods. Those were the items most students brought back to sell.

Some foreign students even traveled during the school term to buy goods that they sold upon their return for profit. Although I bought and sold a few electronic and other items during those years, I mainly stuck to my day job as a student.

The summer of my first year, I made my first trip to England. Once again, I took the train from Moscow and traveled through Poland and Eastern Germany before entering Western Europe. Because I was going to spend three months in London that summer, I didn't need to do any shopping in West Berlin, so I continued on to the Netherlands, where I would take a ferry across the North Sea to Harwich, England. From Harwich, I would catch a train to London.

A family friend from Ghana lived in Amsterdam at the time so I visited him before going to England. When I ascended the escalator into the main terminal at the Utrecht train station, there were long lines at all the many ticket counters. Utrecht lies in the central part of the Netherlands and is a major hub, so its train station is always busy. Seeing those long lines made me nervous. I had only a few hours to make it to Amsterdam and back, and I couldn't miss that last train going from Utrecht to The Hook of Holland, from where the ferry to Harwich would depart later that evening; my ticket was confirmed for that day only.

It was already too late to change my mind about going to Amsterdam; the train that brought me to the Utrecht station had left. During those couple of minutes contemplating what to do, several more people had joined the line I had chosen. My indecision had made an already unpleasant situation worse. I reluctantly stood in that line.

I was shocked when, less than twenty minutes later, I had my purchased ticket in hand. The woman at the counter was issuing tickets at an astonishing speed. That high level of efficiency contrasted starkly with what I had generally experienced in the Soviet Union.

To purchase train tickets to anywhere in Western Europe from the Soviet Union, we had to visit an office in Moscow. Because there were multiple legs on those journeys, the tickets were in the form of booklets. There was a separate page—ticket—for each leg of the journey. On any given day, about five or six people sat behind a counter and issued tickets. It took each issuer a couple of hours to complete one ticket. Each booklet contained at most five or six pages. The job wasn't extraordinarily difficult. It's just that the workers were in no real hurry.

Buying a ticket in that office was always frustrating. There were never many people there—few traveled to the West—but it always took hours. Sometimes I would wait an entire day at the office without getting my ticket and would have to return the following day and spend another several hours in line.

That lackadaisical approach to work was all too common in many parts of the Soviet economy. Because all enterprises were owned by the state, there were no competitive markets and, consequently, little attention was given to productivity, product quality, or customer service. Workers received the same remuneration regardless of their productivity level, and no one ever got fired for making poor-quality products or providing inadequate customer service.

In truth, the vast majority of ordinary Soviets I interacted with were highly patriotic people who took pride in their work. They knew they were in competition with the West for both military and economic supremacy, and they operated with the national interest in mind. The problem was that the yardstick they used to measure themselves was defective.

The workers at the Utrecht train station were well aware that their jobs depended on their productivity. Also, if they consistently left their customers unsatisfied, they could get into trouble with their bosses. Those two factors served as powerful motivators.

After that experience in Utrecht, I got into the habit of observing people at work. In the West, the competitive spirit and its accompanying positive motivations seemed ever-present. That dynamism was what made places like West Berlin, Utrecht, Amsterdam, and London look and feel the way they did. Lacking that energy, the Soviet Union was gradually crumbling beneath the surface.

During my first summer in London, I found a job in a warehouse that supplied bagged potatoes to various grocery stores in the city. On weekends and other days off from work, I explored London by bus and subway. I usually bought a day pass (ticket) that was good for both buses and trains. On most days, I did not return home until well past midnight because I wanted to make maximum use of my ticket. By the end of that summer, I knew almost every corner of London.

Compared to both Kyiv and Moscow, London was a lot more vibrant, with so much to do and see. Additionally, I had complete freedom of movement. In spite of the relatively better quality of life there, I never considered abandoning my studies in the Soviet Union to live there permanently, as a few students did. With the little money I had saved from my summer job, I bought myself some clothing, shoes, and a few other basic items and returned to Kyiv.

* * *

IN THE ENTIRE TIME I was in the Soviet Union, on only one occasion was I questioned about an item I was carrying into the country from Western Europe. I had brought a small New Testament Bible with me from Ghana, and I took it on my first trip to England. Upon my return at the end of the summer, the Soviet customs officer who checked my luggage at the border checkpoint between Poland and the Soviet Union found the Bible and asked what it was. When I told him, he took it and disappeared into an office. I didn't know whether he showed it to someone or did anything with it, but after several minutes, he brought it back to me and asked no further questions.

Officially, the Soviets were atheists. We had received no formal instructions about practicing our religions. The ordinary Soviets I spoke with never discussed religion, so I did not know whether it was completely forbidden. In my subsequent trips to Western Europe, I continued to carry my Bible and was never questioned about it again.

Because most foreign students interacted with their Soviet classmates and non-student friends on a daily basis, many Soviets had opportunities to learn about the Western world through us. They saw the consumer items we brought back from Western Europe and recognized their superior quality. That is why many ordinary Soviets got into the habit of asking foreign students to buy them various items from the West.

We brought back Western movies and tape recordings of foreign music. Our Soviet friends got to watch some of those movies with us on our imported television sets and listen to the music we played on imported stereo systems. In essence, we gave those Soviets the exposure their government had denied them through restrictions on travel, foreign television programming, and certain types of literature.

Over time, I came to realize that most of the Soviets who were skeptical about communism also happened to be those who interacted with foreign students. I often wondered whether the authorities ever considered our unrestricted travel to and from Western Europe and other parts of the Western world to have been a strategic mistake.

As it turned out, the gradual collapse of the broader Soviet economy under its own weight, due to misallocation of its rich natural resources toward strengthening the military, was known to the country's leadership. However, most of the leaders had chosen to ignore the problem. It took the emergence of President Gorbachev as leader for the badly needed reforms to be introduced.

President Gorbachev began his reforms by trying to get ordinary Soviets to change their way of thinking. He made frequent and lengthy televised speeches to the nation. In those speeches, he would explain why it was necessary to introduce openness or *glasnost* into the country's administrative sphere. Gorbachev aimed to keep the Soviet Union intact while empowering the people to have a greater say in their lives. *Perestroika* is the Russian word for "restructuring." He was seeking to introduce into the Soviet system the type of competitive spirit I observed during my travels in Western Europe.

As part of the reforms, Gorbachev opened the Soviet Union's borders so that ordinary Soviets could travel abroad freely. During my first four years in the country, there were rarely any lines at the Western embassies and consulates. That changed after the Soviet borders were opened. Suddenly, thousands of Soviets stood in lines every day to apply for travel visas.

I saw some of the longest lines at the U.S. embassies and consulates in Moscow and St. Petersburg. That, to me, was fascinating. The Soviet leaders had spent decades telling their citizens that America was their greatest enemy, but as soon as the borders were opened, that was where the Soviets were most eager to travel. It was a clear illustration of the disconnect that often exists, in country after country, between official policy and the attitudes of ordinary citizens toward adversarial countries. In my thousands of conversations with ordinary Soviets, I detected little anti-Americanism.

I had become used to seeing President Gorbachev on television almost every day, either giving a speech or attending a public event. Therefore it felt strange when, for several days in the summer of 1991, he did not appear on television. Rumors began to circulate that he had been taken ill while on vacation and was resting at his vacation home in Crimea. Soon after, news about the failed palace coup by hardliners determined to hang onto absolute power began to filter out.

Gorbachev, who had been placed under house arrest in Crimea, refused to resign as President. Other reformers in the Soviet leadership quickly called for mass protests against the coup. That effort was spearheaded by Boris Yeltsin, president of the Russian Republic. Thousands of ordinary Soviets poured into the streets in response. President Gorbachev was released and flown back to Moscow. The events of those few tumultuous days had so weakened his authority that they led to his resignation in December of 1991. Yeltsin replaced him as president, and within days, the Soviet Union disintegrated.

It was a rare privilege to bear witness to one of the most significant historical events of the twentieth century—*perestroika*. And, because of my back-and-forth travels between the Soviet Union and Western Europe, I was one of the few who had the opportunity to observe life as it really was on both sides of the Iron Curtain during that historic period.

I spent parts of the next four months in Ukraine watching events unfold in the aftermath of the Soviet Union's collapse. It was a chaotic period, with ordinary people in the newly independent republics (states) wondering how life would change in the coming months and years. I was extremely fortunate, in the sense that I had graduated earlier in June of that year. The government of the Soviet Union had granted me the scholarship. Now that the Soviet Union was no longer in existence, I wondered how my status as a foreign student would have changed had I been a continuing student.

As the Soviets were emigrating in droves, I was preparing to return to Ghana. I planned to marry Patricia, help build Ghana's energy infrastructure (as I had promised in my scholarship interview), and repay my father the huge debt I owed him.

Unknown to me, something terrible had happened at home in Ghana. It would change everything.

Jerry (left), Victor (middle) and their friend walking on a Moscow street

Me and my Ghanaian roommate Bernard (in Kyiv, 1985)

*My elementary school classmate Francis (in striped shirt), my sister
Charlotte, and me hanging out with another friend in Boadua during
one of my visits home from the Soviet Union*

Me (in the middle) and some of my classmates in Donetsk

*Me, preparing to DJ at a party in Donetsk (I was a DJ for
African student parties in Donetsk)*

147

Me, in Moscow   *My wife Patricia*

*Me (in the middle), Jerry, and a Ghanaian female student
in a dorm room in Donetsk*

CHAPTER 10

A Tragic Loss

MY FOURTH YEAR IN THE Soviet Union, I was finally able to visit Ghana and see Patricia and my family again. By the time I decided to go, it was too late to send a letter, so I traveled there unannounced in June of 1989. My sister Charlotte, who had just started working as a nurse in Accra, was so excited to see me that she decided to accompany me to Boadua.

"What happened to this place?" I asked Charlotte after we stepped out of the taxi that had brought us to the bus stop in Boadua.

"What do you mean?" she asked.

"It looks as if a hurricane swept through and leveled everything."

Charlotte scanned the area, searching for anything unusual. "Nothing happened," she assured me.

In the four years I had been away, I had become so accustomed to looking at skyscrapers that the sea of brown thatched roofs in Boadua appeared to be level with the ground. My entire frame of reference had shifted.

"Didn't you see me, Papa?" Charlotte asked in surprise as my father bolted past her.

"Out of my way!" he commanded as he rushed toward me.

We had just walked into the house from the bus stop, and the unexpected sight of me made my father so excited that he ignored everything else in his eagerness to hug me.

My mother rushed out of the kitchen. "Let go so I can hug him too!" she yelled at my father. She wrapped her arms tightly around me. Within minutes, a large crowd had gathered at the house to witness the scene.

My mother hurriedly fetched me a cup of water, since we never had drinking glasses at home. Nothing had changed in the four years I had been away: the water was as brown as what I had fetched from the river as a child. What had changed was that I no longer had the same level of immunity, and drinking that water would be a huge risk. I hesitated, but not wanting to spoil the joy of the occasion, I gulped down the water.

No one in the large crowd at the house had ever met someone who had traveled in an airplane before, so questions began flying at me from all directions.

"How does it feel to be so high up in the air?" one woman asked.

"Do you see God up there?" another woman inquired. In the village, we were taught that God resided high in the heavens.

"No, you can't see God from an airplane," I replied politely.

My parents and siblings were having a tough time getting in any of their questions because of the crowd. Because I would be spending a few days in Boadua, I knew there would be plenty of time to talk with my family, so I patiently answered as many of our neighbors' questions as I could. Unsurprisingly, none of the questions concerned my university education in the Soviet Union. No one in the crowd really knew what the Soviet Union was or what, exactly, I was doing there.

"I'm sorry, I have to go," I said after an hour. As much as I enjoyed their company, I was in a hurry to see Patricia. Being also a nurse, Charlotte had become close friends with Patricia, so she accompanied me to the hospital to see her.

"Who are you?" Patricia asked when she saw me, pretending not to recognize me. Before I could say anything, she jumped into my arms, holding me tight for several minutes. Charlotte stood by quietly. "Why didn't you tell me you were coming back to Ghana?" Patricia asked, after loosening her grip.

"I decided a couple of weeks ago, and there wasn't enough time for a letter," I replied.

"I'm so happy to see you again, Patrick!" she shouted from pure joy. This was the reunion we had both dreamt of for four years. "How long is your visit?"

"Four weeks," I replied.

"That's so short! You're not going to leave my sight for the next month," she declared.

"I'm here for you," I promised her.

Other than three short visits to Accra, I spent most of the time in

Akwatia with Patricia. We made daily visits to Boadua to see my parents and siblings.

"It's so nice to see you two together again," my mother said to us one evening.

"I feel like I'm the luckiest woman in the world right now," Patricia said, smiling.

"It won't be long before he's back permanently so you can get married and start a family," she told Patricia.

"Thank you for all you've done for me while Patrick has been away," she said to my mother.

"It's been a great pleasure. We're looking forward to having you as a daughter-in-law."

Patricia and I went to Nsawam to see her parents. She had wanted to introduce me to them before I had left for the Soviet Union originally, but scheduling difficulties had prevented it. However, I had written to them, so they knew something about me.

I'm not sure I would fit in comfortably with this family, I thought as I looked around the spacious and beautifully furnished living room in her parents' two-story mansion in Nsawam. Patricia had just formally introduced me, and we were engaged in conversation, but I was distracted by the opulence of the place. I feared that if her parents learned more about my family's socio-economic status, they might not approve of me as a potential son-in-law.

Just as those worries started creeping into my mind, I suddenly remembered what Patricia had told me: that education was a top priority of her father's. *Will he view me positively due to my being a university student?* I asked myself. The longer we talked that evening, the more I was convinced that her parents liked me. It was a huge relief.

We spent the night with them in Nsawam before continuing to Accra the next day to see Ellen, Patricia's older sister who lived there with her family. She was the only member of Patricia's family I had met previously. I had gone to see her at her office in Accra a week before I left for the Soviet Union.

"We've lost a lot of precious time in our relationship," Patricia said one night as we lay in bed.

"It's been a huge sacrifice," I said, "but we both had to make it. The education I've received will lead to a much better future for us."

"I can't wait to start a family with you," she said.

"I'm looking forward to that as well!" I replied.

* * *

OUR FAMILY HOUSE IN BOADUA had already started falling apart by the time I completed secondary school. Large cracks ran through each wall, and the entire building had become structurally unsound. Whenever it rained, the roof leaked, and metal buckets were placed on the floor in every room to collect the water.

There being no other free space in the house, Ernestina stored her baskets full of fish, vegetables, and other wares in my parents' bedroom. The baskets were never more than a couple of yards from their bed because the room was so small. My parents not only slept in a room that reeked of fish but also shared their space with mice, ants, and other creatures, attracted by the contents of those baskets.

When I was midway through the program in the Soviet Union, Daniel, Felicia, and Christina moved to Accra. Although they were still struggling to find their footing and could not afford to live in fancy places, their new circumstances offered my father a fresh perspective when he visited. In Accra, the houses had living rooms adjoining the bedrooms, with chairs for relaxation. Also, most people there slept on foam rather than straw-filled mattresses.

Inspired by Accra, my father decided to rebuild the family house. No one, my parents included, had ever enjoyed much privacy at home. A highly disciplined person, my father liked to have things arranged neatly— an impossibility due to the number of occupants. The new building plan provided for a master bedroom with a dedicated sitting area.

"The master bedroom will be off limits to everybody," he told us one afternoon during my June 1989 visit, as he inspected the freshly poured foundation. He joked, "I'll keep it locked and the keys will be in my pocket at all times."

He was in his late seventies when construction began. For over two decades, he had worked the same grueling hours on the farm. Fortunately, many of us had left home by then, and with the financial burden somewhat eased, he could spend more time in Boadua to oversee the project. Unfortunately, he did not have the funds to keep the construction moving as fast as he wanted.

"As you all know, I don't have many more years to live," my father said.

He had arranged this meeting with my siblings prior to my unannounced visit, and since I was home, I was able to participate. He was asking for financial help to speed up the construction.

"There's nothing I want more than to finish this building and get a nice place to live for the remainder of my life," he continued.

My siblings had low-paying jobs, and there wasn't much they could do. With the little money my father could make from his cocoa harvest each year, it would take another several years to complete the building. Although he was still in excellent health, he had a sense that time was running out.

I'm going to do whatever I can, as quickly as possible after graduation, to help my father realize his dreams, I vowed upon my return to the Soviet Union. He had sacrificed so much to help each of his children get a better life. Without him, I could not have ultimately found myself in the Soviet Union, where I had lived well. Giving him a decent place to live during his twilight years would be the best way I could reward him for his sacrifices. I could not wait to return to Ghana and help make that happen.

Typically, about a year before graduation, foreign students in the Soviet Union started to buy household items such as refrigerators, freezers, ovens, dinnerware, and cutlery. Those items were relatively inexpensive, so students could afford to ship them home when it was time to leave. I began that process immediately after I returned from that visit. Within a few months, I owned a few items I planned to give my father for his future bedroom.

* * *

PATRICIA AND I GOT ENGAGED in August 1990 when I visited Ghana a second time. I would graduate in less than a year, so it was time to start planning our future. Over the next six months, I returned to Ghana two more times to look for employment. The first of those visits occurred in March 1991.

"I'm so proud of you, Osei," my father told me during that visit.

"Thank you, Papa," I replied. "I've been able to accomplish so much because of the incredible sacrifices you made for us. I look forward to returning permanently, so I can help the family financially and make it possible for you to retire. I know how much you're looking forward to that master bedroom."

He beamed at me. "That'll make me so happy. I can't wait!"

"Tell Mintah I'll come to Accra to visit him Wednesday of next week," my father told me prior to my return to the Soviet Union. "I know you'll be leaving that Thursday, so it'll also give me a chance to say goodbye to you."

Daniel's middle name is Mintah, which is what my parents called him at home. Whenever I visited Ghana and I was in Accra, I stayed with him and his family at their apartment.

Charlotte was pursuing additional nursing studies at a hospital in Kumasi, Ghana's second largest city. I had scheduled a day trip to visit her on the Wednesday my father was due to arrive at Daniel's place in Accra. My plan was to return from Kumasi that evening, spend the night with Daniel and my father, and then leave Accra the next day to travel to Moscow.

"Where's Papa?" I asked Daniel when I returned from Kumasi.

"He hasn't arrived, and it's quite late so I don't think he made the trip," Daniel replied. There being no telephones in the village, we couldn't determine the reason for his absence.

I was extremely disappointed, but I'd be back to Ghana in less than six weeks and could see my father then.

Patricia had written six months earlier to inform me that she was pregnant. We were both ecstatic, because starting a family had already been delayed quite a bit by my being away for those six years. Her due date was the second week of May, which meant that my next visit would allow me to be present for the birth of our first child as well as follow up on a couple of job opportunities.

* * *

"ARE YOU LOOKING FOR MR. ASARE?" one of the three young girls playing nearby asked me. She must have been about nine years old, and her parents were Daniel's next-door neighbors. It was five o'clock in the afternoon. I had just arrived at Daniel's apartment for the May visit. No one was in the apartment, and the doors were locked. This was highly unusual because his wife and children were normally home by that hour.

"Yes," I told the young girl.

"His father died, and they left for his funeral," she explained.

A vast emptiness opened up all around me. I stood still, staring blankly, a knot forming in the pit of my stomach. "What did you say?" I asked in a panic.

"Mr. Asare and his family went to his father's funeral," she repeated.

She must have this completely wrong! I said to myself. I was in no mood to continue this conversation, so I picked up my luggage and began to walk away, unsure where I was headed.

"Mr. Asare left the keys to his apartment with my dad—I can get them for you," the girl offered.

"Thank you," I said as I stopped to wait for the keys.

By then my entire body was shaking and my knees were buckling. The simple task of unlocking a door suddenly seemed extremely complicated. My hands trembled so terribly that I couldn't get the key into the keyhole.

"Do you want me to open the door for you?" the young girl offered.

"No, thank you. I can do it," I replied.

After I finally succeeded in unlocking the door, I threw my luggage into the narrow hallway, handed the keys back to the girl, and ran back to the nearby taxi stop to take a taxi to the bus station, from where I would travel to the village.

I made sure not to make eye contact with anyone as I left Daniel's apartment. I wanted to avoid having the little girl's message confirmed.

When I'd left Ghana only a few weeks earlier to return to the Soviet Union, my father had been in excellent health. *That girl just can't be right*, I kept telling myself.

Daniel didn't have a phone in his apartment, so I couldn't reach out to anyone from there. Felicia and Christina also lived in Accra; logically, I could have sought out either of them. Finding them home would confirm my suspicion that the young girl was simply mistaken. That option never crossed my mind, however. I wanted to go straight to the source. *If indeed Daniel and his family went to a funeral, could it be some distant relative who passed away?* I wondered.

I hadn't slept for more than twenty-four hours and had been looking forward to getting some rest at Daniel's place. Now I was wide awake. I sat quietly in the bus during the three-hour journey, feeling a vague sense of unreality.

I arrived in Boadua around nine thirty p.m. Someone had seen me after I stepped off the bus and alerted my family. When I got to within a few yards of the house, I heard wailing. It turned out to be Felicia. She ran over and gave me a big hug, still crying uncontrollably and calling out our father's name. The entire family was assembled when I entered the house, and their somber expressions appeared to confirm what I had refused to believe for the past three hours: my dad had indeed passed away. My mother and my siblings all wore traditional black funeral attire.

I was in such a state of shock that I could not feel my existence for the next several minutes. *Am I just having a terrible dream, or is this real?* I wondered. The entire place became eerily quiet.

"Bring Osei a cup of water," Ernestina finally asked one of our nieces.

"No, thank you, I don't want anything. What's going on?" I finally asked.

Throats were cleared all around, followed by several seconds of total silence. No one had the courage to break the news to me. Although we all loved our father dearly, I had a special relationship with him.

"Can anyone tell me what has happened?" I pleaded.

Emmanuel finally pulled up his chair a little closer. "Patrick, I'm sorry to tell you that Papa has passed away."

"What!" My scream startled everyone. "What happened?" I screamed again.

"Do you recall that Papa had promised to visit Daniel the day before you were scheduled to leave for Moscow?" Emmanuel asked. He paused, waiting for an answer, but I simply stared at him silently. "He made the trip to Accra, as promised. Unfortunately, as he was crossing the street from the taxi stop near Daniel's apartment, he was hit by a bus and died on the spot." As Emmanuel spoke, I sat stoically, staring blankly at the floor of the verandah where my father had held so many of his "court" sessions over the years. I had kept clinging to the hope that I was stuck in a bad dream. I would wake up soon, and everything would be all right.

This is indeed real! I burst into tears. My heart was being ripped from my chest. The taxi stop where my father had attempted the crossing was a mere twenty yards from Daniel's apartment. After surviving all those years surrounded by poisonous snakes and other dangers in the jungle, he'd been killed crossing the street.

* * *

THERE HAS NEVER BEEN A good system of identification in Ghana. Hardly any place in the country—even today—has a street address, and few homes had telephones back then. For most Ghanaians, there is no such thing as a form of identification, such as a driver's license (few people own cars) or a social security number—documents and identifiers that most people in developed countries carry wherever they go.

The Cocoa Marketing Board issued identification cards to farmers who sold their cocoa to the agency. Apart from the holder's name, little else was on the card. My father had his card on him that day, which meant the police at least had a name to work with. The bad news was that, with neither a telephone number nor a street address, they could not inform the family. They took my father's body to the mortuary at the main hospital in Accra.

The best the police could do was to ask the radio station in Accra to make an announcement, in hopes that someone who was related to or knew the victim would hear it. No one did. Multiple announcements had been made on the radio over a three-week period, but the body remained unclaimed.

"Papa said he would be in Accra for only a few days, so why hasn't he returned?" my mother asked Ernestina one evening, more than a week after he left on that trip.

"Maybe we should send someone to Accra to investigate," Ernestina suggested.

One of my nephews was dispatched to Accra.

A massive search effort began after the family realized my father was not in Accra and had never made it to Daniel's.

"Where on earth could he be?" my mother asked in a panic. It was already late when my nephew returned from Accra, so early the following morning, my mother traveled to my father's ancestral hometown, one hundred fifty miles away, where he occasionally went to visit distant relatives. No one there had seen him either.

Word spread quickly—both in Boadua and Accra—that my father had been missing for over three weeks. Soon thereafter, one of Daniel's friends in Accra came over to his apartment to inform him that he had heard—over the radio—about a fatal accident involving a victim with the same last name as his. Asare is a common surname in Ghana. Knowing that my father did not live in Accra, Daniel's friend hadn't made the connection.

"Thank you for this information. I'll go to the police station, just in case," Daniel said to him.

"Our father has been missing for three weeks, and we've just learned that a victim in an accident that occurred recently had the same last name as his," Daniel told the officer at the desk that evening. He had gone to the police station with Ebenezer, who happened to be in Accra.

"What are your names?" the officer asked them.

"I'm Daniel Asare Mintah, and my brother's name is Ebenezer Asare Adu," Daniel replied.

"Wait here, I'll be right back," the officer told them. He went into an adjoining room and brought out a small suitcase.

Daniel and Ebenezer broke down in tears as soon as they saw the suitcase. It was the luggage my father had been carrying that fateful day. For confirmation, the officer opened an envelope that had been taped to the suitcase and took out my father's cocoa farmer's identification card. He handed the card and suitcase over to Daniel, and he and Ebenezer drove straight to the mortuary, where they identified my father's body.

"I'm so sorry for your loss, gentlemen," the attendant told them after the identification process. "I know it's a difficult situation for you, but things could have been worse."

"How?" Ebenezer asked, as he and Daniel exchanged glances.

"Sometimes," the attendant explained, "we have so many unclaimed bodies that the mortuary fills up, forcing us to bury corpses in mass graves. Your father's would have been buried a couple of days ago, together with several others, had the grave-digging equipment not broken down. At least your family can give him a proper burial now."

The attendant told them it was not uncommon for the bodies of accident victims to remain unclaimed for weeks—even months. That is why mortuary operators sometimes had to handle the unpleasant task of sending bodies for mass burial. Daniel and Ebenezer were left to wonder what might have occurred had it not been for that farmer's card. It's quite possible that the family might never have confirmed his death. We would never know whether he routinely carried the card on his travels … or if he just happened to be carrying it that day.

My father's accident had taken place late in the afternoon on the day I returned from visiting Charlotte in Kumasi. I had taken a taxi from the bus station to the same stop where he had attempted to cross the street. His body had been removed from the scene just over an hour before my taxi arrived at that stop. If my timing had been different, I would have been the first family member to see his body.

There was no indication that anything out of the ordinary had occurred at that taxi stop. I went to sleep that night and took the flight to Moscow the next day without knowing that my father had died just hours earlier, and only a few yards away.

Making matters worse for me, my father had been buried two days before my arrival. After the family learned of his death, Daniel had gone to the airport in Accra and hand-delivered a letter to someone traveling to Moscow. He explained that my father had passed away and implored the man to mail the letter immediately upon arrival in Moscow. The letter did not reach me in time.

Actually, my trip to Ghana had been scheduled for the week before, and I had a confirmed ticket for the flight from Moscow to Accra. Because there were large numbers of students traveling back and forth in those days, Aeroflot (the Soviet airline) flights from Moscow to Accra were always overbooked. Most people camped out overnight at Sheremetovo Airport to be first in line for the five-a.m. flight to Accra. Although I had spent the night at the airport, holding my confirmed ticket, and was at the head of the line when check-in was announced, I did not get on the flight. Someone had paid a bribe to obtain my seat—a common occurrence in those days. Had that not happened, I would have been in Ghana in time for my father's funeral.

* * *

"I'm so sorry, Patrick," Patricia said, hugging me tightly. Although it was quite late, someone had gone to notify her of my arrival, and she had rushed to the house to see me. "I know how close you were to your father. I had become close to him as well, so this situation is extremely difficult for us both."

I was inconsolable. I did not sleep a single minute the entire night. All I wanted was for daylight to break as quickly as possible, so I could visit my father's grave.

Ernestina, Richard, Daniel, Felicia, and Emmanuel accompanied me to the cemetery around five o'clock in the morning. I stood silently by the grave, overcome by emotion. For several minutes, no one spoke.

"I'm going to carry on your legacy as best I can," I promised my father as I looked down at his grave. I wasn't exactly sure what I meant. His shoes were much too big for me to fill, but I knew in my heart that I must keep his memory alive for as long as I lived. I would find a way—whatever it was—to do that.

My daughter Jennifer was born exactly a week after I learned about my father's death. As I held her in my arms in the hospital, I could see some resemblance to my father—the grandfather she did not get to meet. That made me happy. Having a child who would always remind me of my adored father was an extraordinary gift. My parents already had several grandchildren, but my father had told me he was particularly looking forward to Jennifer's birth, given what Patricia and I had endured.

"Jennifer looks a lot like your father!" my mother-in-law said when she saw her for the first time. She had traveled from Nsawam to spend time with Patricia and Jennifer.

"I thought so myself," I said. I was a proud father; only, that happiness was dimmed by my dark frame of mind.

My mother was in terrible shape—both mentally and physically—in those weeks. One of the good things about Ghanaian culture is that in hard times a few family members stay for as long as necessary to offer emotional and other support. More than two weeks after the funeral, there were, apart from three of my older sisters, other people in the house to keep her company. I spent as much time there as I could. Often I would sit on my father's chair, in his favorite corner of the verandah.

"Do you have to go back to the Soviet Union?" my mother asked me one afternoon as I sat in that corner, in a deeply pensive mood.

"I have no choice," I replied.

"When do you plan to leave?"

"In a week."

"Are you sure you can go back so soon? I worry how you'll manage all by yourself in this state of mind."

Those were the very questions running through my mind. "I'm going to try," I told her.

Thankfully, because graduation was six weeks away, I had completed all my coursework. All that remained was to make one final revision of my thesis, get a few copies bound, and present the work in front of a panel. Under the circumstances, the task would be extremely difficult, but I was determined to get through it and graduate.

I'm lying to myself, I thought. I had no desire to do anything. Almost everything seemed meaningless. I had, with dogged determination, overcome one obstacle after another for so many years. Now I was mere weeks away from attaining my university degree. I'd looked forward so much to celebrating that achievement with my father. It felt as if all that hard work and sacrifice had been for nothing.

It had not been easy to stay in touch with Patricia and my family during those six years. Patricia and I sent pictures of ourselves in every letter we wrote to each other. My father and I communicated through letters as much as we could. In just a few more weeks, I would have been permanently reunited with him, sharing his final years. It wasn't meant to be.

Throughout the eleven-hour flight back to Moscow, I sat quietly, wondering how I would cope in Donetsk without the emotional support of my family. *Even if I do manage to keep from falling apart, will I have the energy to complete my thesis and defend it?* I wondered.

I found myself in uncharted territory. I had always dealt with any obstacle that came my way by drawing on some lesson learned from the coach—my father. Now I could not readily find anything in his playbook to help me face the challenge presented by his passing. The great coach was gone forever; I would need to develop my own playbook. I had become a father myself and would be doing my own coaching in the years ahead.

As expected, those next few weeks in Donetsk were extremely difficult. I was constantly distracted by thoughts of my father. Victor and Jerry provided what support they could. About one month later, I completed my thesis and submitted it to my adviser. I successfully presented it in front of the full faculty committee the following week.

My mission in the Soviet Union was accomplished. Universities there did not have formal graduation ceremonies. Following completion and defense of a thesis, a student would simply go to the registrar's office a few days later to pick up their diploma. My completion of formal graduation forms brought my Soviet Union education to a close. I felt a deep sense of pride the day I received my electrical engineering diploma and my Russian language teaching certificate.

After I stepped out of the registrar's office, I burst into tears, saddened by the thought that I wouldn't be able to show those two precious documents to my father. He wouldn't be able to read them, but I could imagine the joy on his face from simply holding them in his hands.

What now? I asked myself as I stared at the diploma lying on the table in my dormitory room. During my last visit I had not followed up on the job leads in Ghana. I had to figure out my next move. My classmates were busy shipping their belongings to their home countries, in preparation for their return.

In my state of indecision, I left my belongings in storage and flew back to Ghana. I spent the next several weeks with Patricia and Jennifer in Akwatia, visiting often with my mother, who was only a couple of miles away. The passage of time did not bring clarity regarding my future.

"I think I need to go somewhere else for a while," I told Patricia one evening.

"What do you mean?" she asked.

"I can't stop thinking about my father. Whenever I visit my mother and see the unfinished home he was working on, the intensity of feeling is too great to bear. I need a change of scene."

"And where exactly do you plan to go to?"

"I don't know," I told her. "Somewhere unfamiliar would help me heal."

"Do you plan to take us with you?"

"Since I don't know where I'd be going and haven't made any arrangements, it may not be possible to take you and Jennifer."

"What! You mean after living apart for six years, I have to subject myself to another indeterminate period of uncertainty? Patrick, I fully understand what you're going through, but we have a new baby and we're planning to get married soon. You cannot do what you're suggesting."

"I know, let me give it some thought."

Several weeks passed and nothing changed. If anything, I grew more depressed. *It doesn't make sense to leave my new baby and soon-to-be wife and go to an unknown place, but I can't help believing it is the only remedy,* I kept thinking.

As the subject of my going away kept coming up, Patricia ran out of patience.

"You must be out of your mind! If you do go away, you can forget about me! I've been through a lot already and I'm certainly not going to put up with this any further," she exploded in anger one evening.

I tried to make her understand. "You know how much I love you, Patricia. I'm just having a hard time coping with my father's death. The only way I'm going to get better is by going away for a while."

"Then forget about marrying me," she insisted. "I won't talk about this anymore. Go ahead and make your own decision."

Patricia's ultimatum finally drove home the depths of her anger. We didn't say much to each other in the ensuing days. I fully understood her position and was extremely sad to put her in that situation. I was, however, too depressed for rational thinking. The nature of my father's death had been bad enough, but I seemed to be even more bothered by not being able to pay my last respects. I was mired in sadness and anger.

"I'm going away for a while," I told my mother one afternoon.

"Back to the Soviet Union?" she asked.

"No. I've graduated and can't live in that country anymore. I'm constantly reminded of Papa while I'm here, so I'm going to go somewhere for a while and heal."

"Will you take Patricia and Jennifer with you?"

"No, I'm not sure where I'm going."

"Are you crazy? You can't do that! She's already suffered enough by waiting six years for you. You're not going to make her suffer further. You have to rethink this!"

Ultimately, I failed to convince Patricia and my mother, but I knew in my heart that I needed to go away. *Wherever I end up, for however long, I will find a way to fulfill my parental duties,* I said to myself.

It is unfathomable to me now that I actually followed through on my decision. Leaving Patricia and Jennifer at that time was extremely inconsiderate. It is something that, in hindsight, I judge myself particularly harshly for. I also know that many would side with Patricia and my mother. They would be fully justified.

My decision to leave was driven mainly by depression. I did not believe that in my present state of mind I was any good to anyone. Moreover, I didn't think I'd be gone for long. I had the example of my father, who did what was necessary to support his family, even when that meant being away from us for extended periods.

I never intended to abandon Patricia and Jennifer. Wherever I ended up, I would find a way to earn some income and send as much money as I could to Patricia for their welfare. I also knew that Jennifer would be well cared for by Patricia's extended family.

During my time in the Soviet Union, I had always wanted to visit America. I'd obtained a U.S. visa and had planned to visit before the end of my final year. The visa was still valid. America seemed like the perfect place: far away and unfamiliar. I flew back to Moscow to prepare for the healing journey.

*My father and my sister Charlotte in the yard
in front of our house in Boadua*

My father in front of our house in Boadua

CHAPTER 11

The Rude Awakening

My journey to America began with a short evening flight from Moscow to Prague, the capital of the Czech Republic. I stayed in a hotel overnight and then took another flight bound for New York the next morning.

Prague is one of the most beautiful cities in Europe. As the bus from the hotel to the airport traveled through the city center that gorgeous spring morning, several American tourists kept admiring the beautiful architecture and neat gardens. I looked at the surroundings dispassionately, deeply absorbed in my own thoughts. From the tourists' conversations, I concluded they were happy people. In all likelihood, they had good lives to return to. I, on the other hand, was like a bird cut loose from its flock, randomly searching for a safe branch to perch on. I had absolutely no idea what I would do in America.

I was traveling alone to a strange country where I knew no one. I left Moscow with less than eight hundred dollars in my pocket, not enough to sustain me for even one week in New York if I had to pay for a hotel and meals. I took some comfort in having purchased a return ticket. If I ran out of money, I could catch a flight back to Moscow, and from there, find a way back to Ghana.

At the last minute, I remembered that one of my Ghanaian college mates in Donetsk, Joe, had an older brother, Ernest, who was a medical student in America. Joe and Ernest had both been ahead of me in secondary school in Ghana. I called Joe, who was visiting Ernest at that time, to see if he could get Ernest to host me at his apartment for a brief period. Ernest had agreed, so I knew I had a temporary place to stay. From there I would figure out my next move.

It also dawned on me that this visit would allow me to explore pursuing a graduate engineering degree in America. I hadn't intended to pursue this longstanding dream immediately after graduation from the Soviet Union. Considering my lack of money and specific preparation, whatever I did toward fulfilling this goal would only be an exploratory exercise.

From JFK Airport in New York City, I traveled by bus to the Port Authority Bus Terminal (PABT) on Eighth Avenue. From there I would take another bus to Buffalo. Ernest was studying at the State University of New York (SUNY) in Buffalo at the time. It was around nine p.m. when I arrived at the PABT, only one block away from the city's famous Times Square.

How busy the city seemed! Even that time of the night felt like rush hour, with everyone moving briskly about. Standing outside the terminal, I was shocked to see how much taller the buildings were than in Europe. The bright lights of Times Square were dazzling. My luggage prevented me from venturing too far outside the terminal. I simply stood there, mesmerized, and watched people go by for about an hour before catching my bus to Buffalo. It left shortly after one a.m. and arrived in Buffalo around nine a.m.

"It's great to see you! How was the journey?" Joe asked when my taxi arrived at Ernest's apartment that morning.

"It was good but quite tiring," I replied.

"Welcome to Buffalo," Ernest said.

"Thank you. And thank you for agreeing to host me."

It was a huge inconvenience for Ernest to be hosting Joe and me at the same time, so I intended to leave his apartment as soon as I could. The two-bedroom apartment was located in the northern part of the city, about a fifteen-minute walk from the SUNY south campus. The living room was small, and opposite the kitchen was an even smaller den where Ernest did his studies. Joe occupied one of the bedrooms, and he was kind enough to share his bed with me.

I had spent very little of the money I had left, so I decided to hang on for as long as I could before making my next move. Since I didn't really have anywhere to go in Buffalo, I spent much of my time in the apartment, either watching television or doing some casual reading.

Ernest was two years my senior, so I hadn't known him well in secondary school. He seemed quieter in Buffalo, which was understandable given that he was a busy third-year medical student. He would leave home early in the morning and return late in the evening. After dinner, he spent several hours by himself studying in the den. We didn't talk much.

Watching the hustle and bustle in the area around the PABT that first night, I wondered whether the whole of America was like that. In New York City, everyone seemed to be in a hurry. Life in Buffalo, in contrast, appeared to be a lot calmer. Joe took me to various parts of the city during the first week. The buildings weren't as high as in New York City, and people in Buffalo made more eye contact. Complete strangers would smile and say hello as they passed you on the streets. *Americans seem quite friendly,* I would think.

The more I watched television, the more fascinated I became with the American way of life. I had spent most of my life in places—Africa and Eastern Europe—where average citizens had little say in national governance. Even in Western Europe, where I lived during summer vacations, I did not witness the same level of citizen engagement as in America. The lively debates I watched on television were both entertaining and educational.

In Buffalo, I saw some places that were not as glitzy as the America I had pictured. Parts of the city met my expectations, with nice houses, impeccably manicured lawns, and tree-lined, smoothly paved streets. In stark contrast, other parts were visibly run down, with many dilapidated houses. Lawns and public spaces were clearly not well kept, and some streets had potholes, which I had not expected to find in America. The population in those parts of the city was predominantly Black. During the day, when most people would be at work, there were always people sitting in front of houses or walking about. Their lives seemed anything but comfortable.

In the nicer part of the city, the population appeared to be predominantly White. I got my first sense of the divide between the lives of Blacks and Whites in America. Later on, I would realize these conditions were not just dictated by race. There were "haves" and "have-nots."

Ernest's apartment, while not in the richer part of the city, was in a diverse, pleasant middle-class neighborhood. About a month after my arrival in Buffalo, he told me I was welcome to stay with him and Joe in the apartment while I contemplated what to do in America. It was a gracious offer, given his circumstances, and I was extremely grateful. That bought me the extra time I so badly needed.

Soon after that conversation with Ernest, I wrote to Patricia to let her know I would be in America for a few months at least. The change of scenery had helped to lift me out of my deep depression. Although I deeply missed her and my daughter, I knew in my heart the trip had been necessary.

As the days and weeks went by, I increasingly fell in love with life in America. I kept hearing people say that it was a land of opportunity where anyone could develop their innate talents. In those early days, I didn't know enough about American society to judge the accuracy of that portrayal, but I liked what I saw. I had grown up in a society that denied large numbers of people the opportunities they needed to live happy, prosperous lives. American society seemed to have space for everyone—from scientists to writers, athletes to artists, and everything in between. I greatly admired the energy of the place, and I wanted to experience it for more than just a few months.

Education had cleared the path that took me from my remote village in Ghana to Buffalo. If I had any hope of staying in America for a meaningful length of time, education might be my ticket once again. I knew my Soviet degree would not be recognized by American employers, and so finding professional work would not be possible immediately. My best bet would be to find a way to be educated in America.

"I'd dearly love to go to school in this country," I said to Ernest one weekend.

"It won't be easy," he said matter-of-factly. "If you manage to get accepted into a graduate engineering program, you could apply for a research or teaching assistantship position, which would pay your tuition as well as provide a monthly stipend. However, the schools that can provide that type of funding are extremely difficult to get into."

Ernest's pessimism didn't worry me. I was prepared to do whatever it took to make myself a competitive applicant. The real problem was that I couldn't afford the application process. I saw no visible path forward.

The burning desire to remain in America would not go away, so I woke up one morning and decided to begin the process of applying for admission into a graduate program. Because Ernest and Joe had generously shared most of their meals, I had spent little of my money. I went into a nearby bookstore that morning and bought a book to prepare me for the Graduate Record Exam (GRE), required for admission by most graduate engineering programs.

I studied intensely, day and night, for the exam. Ernest was so impressed with my determination that he promised to do anything he could to help. I ended up living in his apartment for a few more months.

Ernest always bought the Sunday edition of the *Buffalo News*, the local newspaper. One Sunday afternoon, while reading the paper, I saw an advertisement for a job opening at a local elementary school: a Russian language teaching position. *Could this be my lucky break?* I wondered. I couldn't wait to find out.

In addition to my engineering studies in Ukraine, I had become certified as a Russian language teacher. That program was offered to foreign students who were interested in teaching Russian in their home countries upon completion of their studies. It was open to all of us, regardless of our majors. Having no intention of becoming a teacher, I initially thought pursuing the certificate would be a waste of my time. For some reason, I changed my mind and applied for the program.

When I arrived in Buffalo in April 1992, relatively few Soviets lived outside the Soviet Union, so I doubted there would be many Russian-speaking people who could speak English fluently and were also certified teachers. I stood a good chance of getting the job.

Nervousness and excitement kept me awake that entire night. I woke up early the next morning and arrived at the Board of Education office long before anyone who worked there.

When I explained the purpose of my visit, the receptionist directed me to a woman standing behind a counter. I asked for an application form for the Russian language teaching position. She looked at me for several seconds without speaking, clearly wondering if I was a prankster.

"Do you know what the qualifications are for the position?" she finally asked.

"Yes," I replied simply.

My answer seemed to annoy her.

"Listen, I'm not in the mood for joking on this Monday morning, and I hope you will excuse me," she said.

"Madam, I'm not joking. I think I'm qualified for the position."

I realized I would alienate her completely if I continued the conversation in that fashion, so I promptly handed over my Russian language teaching certificate and my passport, which I had wisely carried to prove I was the owner of that certificate. She was stunned when she opened both documents and realized I was telling the truth. She immediately called her colleagues over to review my documents.

"How on earth did you manage to go from Ghana to the Soviet Union to earn a teaching certificate there?" one woman asked incredulously.

"I received a Soviet government scholarship to study engineering and happened to obtain the teaching certificate in addition to my engineering degree," I replied.

"Did you know any Russian before you went there?" another woman asked.

"No, I had to learn it from scratch," I replied. Every jaw in the room dropped.

"What was the place like? Did you like it there? Were the people friendly?" one man asked. As I answered his rapid-fire questions, many more came at me from all directions.

"I'm so sorry for my rudeness," the woman I had spoken with at the beginning said.

"I wasn't offended at all," I assured her.

I was hired on the spot, and one week later, I started work as a teacher at the school. As I had rightly guessed, the pool of qualified candidates had been small.

I could not believe my luck. When I reluctantly decided to complete the teacher certification program in Ukraine, I had no idea that it would open a crucial door for me.

Because of my engineering background, I was asked to teach math in addition to Russian. I initially worked as a substitute teacher. Each day, after my Russian language classes, I would go to another school to take the place of an absent math teacher. When a regular teacher went on medical leave, I was offered a long-term teaching position in math. That teacher told me she had asked the principal to hire me because she thought the school needed a Black male teacher to serve as a role model.

I started teaching in October. By then I had lived in Ernest's apartment for six months. With the money I earned, I could now afford to live on my own and rented an apartment two blocks away. I couldn't thank Earnest enough. Without his crucial support in the beginning, I certainly would not have found my footing in America.

Communicating with Patricia and my family had become easier than in the Soviet Union. Letters took about ten days to travel between Ghana and Buffalo. Although Patricia still didn't have a phone in her apartment, I could call her from Ernest's apartment whenever she visited Ellen in Accra. In the Soviet Union, the student dormitories didn't have telephones, so if I wanted to call Ghana, I had to book a time to call from a post office telephone booth. It was a complicated process, so I rarely called home.

I came to America on a temporary visitor's visa. To stay longer, I had to submit an application to the Immigration and Naturalization Service

(INS). "Obtaining a permit is a multi-year process," Ernest told me when I consulted him about it.

I could remain in the country while my application was being considered by the INS, but travel outside the country would be highly restricted.

For an indeterminate period, I couldn't return to Ghana to visit Patricia and Jennifer. If I left America, my INS application would be nullified, and I would not be able to re-enter. And, until I had the permit that would allow me to stay in America long-term, I could not bring them over to join me.

Should I just give up and return to Ghana? I asked myself repeatedly during those difficult weeks. I ultimately decided to hang on. Whenever I spoke to Patricia on the phone, I could sense the anger in her voice. The relationship felt shakier than ever.

At the elementary school, I taught Russian to students in grades one to four. Each class had about twenty-five students. They were adorable children who appeared eager to learn the language and always gave me their full attention. At that early stage, most of the lessons covered the alphabet— completely different from the English alphabet—and basic vocabulary. I also taught them how to construct simple sentences.

There were three other Russian language teachers at the school. One of them was a Russian woman who had recently immigrated to America with her family. She had been a teacher in the Soviet Union and also knew English, so she was able to communicate easily with the students. The second teacher was a Polish gentleman who had also recently immigrated to America. In addition to his native Polish, he spoke English and Russian— both learned in Polish schools.

The third teacher was a woman born in England to Ukrainian parents. Her parents had been taken from Ukraine to Germany during the Second World War. After the war, they both moved to England, where they met and married. Soon after my colleague was born, her family immigrated to America. She spoke Ukrainian with her parents at home and had majored in both Russian and French in college. She taught French in addition to Russian.

Although I lived in Ukraine for six years, I never mastered Ukrainian. During that time, the vast majority of Ukrainians spoke Russian, the official language of the Soviet Union. Some older folks spoke their native language at home, but most of the younger people I was exposed to spoke only Russian. Ukrainian is similar to Russian, so when Ukrainians speak, I can understand quite a bit.

Together, the four of us formed a great team and constantly exchanged ideas about teaching methods. I also got to know the families of those three colleagues, which allowed me to become part of the network of Russian-speaking people in Buffalo. I was invited to so many social activities that, after a while, I felt like a member of that extended family.

Although my father was much on my mind, I was feeling a little healthier psychologically. The novelty of America and the intellectual discussions I regularly listened to on television had served as welcome distractions.

Then, everything changed.

I returned from school one afternoon to find a letter from Daniel. I had exchanged a couple of letters with him since I arrived, so I was quite up to date with family matters in Ghana. The letter, I assumed, was just a follow-up on some mundane issues.

"I regret to inform you that Mama has passed away," read the first line. *What!* I screamed. I must have passed out, because my mind blanked for the next several seconds. When I regained consciousness, I read that first line again. *Could I be having a bad dream?* I wondered.

My mother had never recovered from the shock of my father's tragic death two years earlier. She had been in and out of hospitals a few times, including time spent in a psychiatric hospital in Accra. I knew about her medical issues, but I had no idea they would lead to her passing so quickly.

After reading the rest of the letter, I sat on my bed and cried. *What do I do now?* I asked myself after drying my eyes. The funeral date was only two weeks away. I had to figure out quickly how I was going to make it to Ghana to be present for the burial.

Oh my God! I yelled seconds later when it dawned on me that my pending INS application precluded me from overseas travel. As I understood it, the circumstances might allow me to obtain special permission to travel to Ghana and back, but that would require submitting a different application. The two-week timeframe was too short for me to go through that process. Even then, I couldn't be sure permission would be granted.

Maybe I'll just leave and forget about returning to America, I said to myself. After considering that option for a few hours, I decided against it. The intensity of my sadness following my father's death had driven my decision to leave Ghana. The psychological trauma had led to my mother's untimely death. *How would things have turned out in my case? Would it have helped my recovery?* I wondered. I barely slept that night. In the end, I made the extremely difficult decision to stay.

"I won't be able to travel to Mama's funeral," I informed Daniel during our telephone conversation the next day.

"It saddens me to hear that, but I was afraid that would happen, given the timeframe," he replied. "We'll handle matters here. Take good care of yourself, and let's stay in touch."

"I'm so sorry, Patrick," Patricia said when we spoke two days later. I just kept sobbing without speaking. "Are you coming back to attend the funeral?"

"No," I said simply.

"What?" she asked in disbelief. "Why are you doing this to yourself? How could you be absent from both your parents' funerals?"

I had asked myself that very question over and over again in the preceding days.

"I'm unable to for logistical reasons," I explained. She stayed silent for almost two minutes.

"It's your decision so I'll leave it up to you," she finally said.

On the day of my mother's funeral, Ernest invited me to his apartment. He had assembled a few of his friends to keep me company. They did their best to console me and get me through that incredibly difficult day. I kept imagining the events taking place thousands of miles away at the family house in Boadua, as my mother was readied to be laid to rest.

Over the next several weeks, Ernest, his friends, and my colleagues at work collectively provided an incredible level of emotional support. There were days when I felt so numb I almost couldn't get out of bed to go to work. But my soccer days had taught me that winning important matches sometimes required playing through pain. Though my pain threshold in this case had been set extremely high, I had no choice but to play through it.

* * *

IN THOSE EARLY WEEKS FOLLOWING the start of my teaching career, I was fascinated by the stark contrast between the advanced world classrooms in Buffalo and the makeshift classrooms in the Ghanaian village where I had begun my own educational journey. The classrooms in Buffalo were well equipped, with proper furniture and plenty of resources. This was a school with a well-stocked library, a cafeteria, a nice playground, and professional teachers who were some of the friendliest people I had ever met. The school environment in Buffalo was pleasant to work in, and I looked forward to going to work every morning.

Everything changed quickly, however, shortly after I began teaching math in other schools in the city. Unlike Russian, I taught math not only in the lower grades but also to middle and high school students. My lower-grade math students, for the most part, were as cooperative as those I had in my Russian language classes. The upper grades were a different story.

When I walked into the classroom where I was going to substitute-teach math for the first time, I was completely shocked by what I witnessed. It was a ninth-grade class. I was used to seeing chairs and desks arranged in perfect order in my Russian language classrooms, but in this math class, disorder reigned. Desks were facing in all directions, with the students talking among themselves and completely ignoring my presence, although the bell had rung for the lesson period to begin. My repeated pleas to get the class to settle down fell on deaf ears.

Shell-shocked, I just stood in front of the class for several minutes, desperately trying to get the students to cooperate. By then, the noise level was so high that it had to be disturbing other classes nearby. I closed the door and continued pleading for silence for a few more minutes. The more I pleaded, the louder the students talked.

I began to feel nervous, certain that my inability to control the classroom would reflect poorly on me. The principal and other teachers might judge me as unqualified, which could jeopardize my entire teaching career. Those fears led me to barricade myself in the classroom with the students and wait until the period was over before opening the door. That way, no one would know what had transpired. I would sign out at the office when the period ended and live to fight another day.

Do these students have any idea what impact their actions could have on me? I wondered as I observed them. A lot of things had needed to fall into place for me to be standing where I was at that moment. This one hour of chaos could ruin everything. If the principal found out and sent a report to the Board of Education office, I could easily be let go as a teacher.

Then I would be back to square one. I wouldn't have the money to pay my rent and cover other basic expenses. There was no guarantee I would find another job quickly, and I couldn't even imagine having to return to Ernest and ask him to take me in again. At that moment, I was mostly thinking of myself. The damage the students were inflicting on themselves and their future well-being had not even registered.

About halfway through the period, the situation escalated to the point where I had to do something. By then, I had more than loud noise to deal with. Pushing and shoving in one corner of the room had led to desks being rammed into the walls. I ran to that corner and tried to get those students to calm down, without much success. This was clearly a storm I couldn't simply ride out.

Rather reluctantly, I opened the classroom door and rushed to the office. If only the principal would not be there .... I wanted this issue to be below the radar, if at all possible. One of the staff members saw the expression on my face as soon as I walked in and realized that something was terribly wrong.

"What's the matter?" she asked, a worried look on her face.

"There's pushing and shoving in the classroom, and I can't get the students to calm down," I told her in a hushed tone, avoiding a detailed explanation.

"Let's go. I'll see what I can do," she said. She walked with me back to the classroom. What happened next shocked me even more.

After several pleas by the woman for the students to put their chairs in order and quiet down, they seemed to feel even more empowered to continue their disruptive behavior. I had assumed they misbehaved because I was a substitute teacher—that they wouldn't treat their regular teachers and other school authorities the same way. I was wrong.

"Wait here, I'm going to look for the principal," the woman said as she stepped out of the room. I almost blurted out my fears about getting the principal involved, but quickly realized I had run out of options and deferred to her judgment. Within minutes, she and the principal entered the room.

Upon seeing the principal, most of the students returned to their seats. Even then, a handful seemed unfazed by her presence, and she had to raise her voice a few times before they obeyed her commands. She warned the students sternly that if they continued to make it impossible for me to do my work, they would be put in detention, and that she would suspend any students who instigated more fighting. Those warnings were taken to heart, but much of the class time had already been wasted. After the principal left, only ten minutes remained for me to do my job.

Given the time constraints, all I could accomplish was to collect the students' assignments. The teacher had left instructions to record the names of those who didn't have anything to submit. To my surprise, fewer than ten out of the twenty-four students took out their work. I glanced at the papers as they were handed to me; most didn't have much written on them.

The students who brought nothing gave a variety of excuses. A few didn't bother.

Soon after, the bell rang to signal the end of the period. The students rushed out of the room unceremoniously, pushing and shoving to get through the door first. During that mad rush, chairs and desks were knocked over, spilling books and papers everywhere. In less than a minute, an eerie silence prevailed. It seemed as if a hurricane-force wind had blown through the room.

No other class was scheduled the next period, giving me time to restore order. With trembling hands, I began to pick up the papers and furniture from the floor. It was my only class of the day, so after I put everything back in its place, I went to the office to sign out.

"How was your day?" the office staff asked in unison. They all knew it was my first time at the school.

"Just look at his face and you'll get the answer," the woman who had tried to help me earlier told them before I could utter a word. I tried but failed to force a smile.

"I'm sorry you had a bad day in class. Don't worry, we look forward to seeing you again soon," one woman said.

Although I knew she meant well, her words felt like a curse. After the experience I had endured, coming back anytime soon seemed like the worst thing anyone could wish for me.

"Thank you, I also hope to see you soon," I lied.

Still in a daze, I headed to my car in the school parking lot. Given my state of mind, it was a big mistake to drive off right away. The school zone had many stop signs, and I almost got into an accident at the first intersection.

I failed to see the stop sign and was driving past it when, from the corner of my eye, I saw another driver coming through that intersection at a fairly high speed. He did not have a stop sign. I instinctively stepped on the gas pedal and sped through to avoid being hit. The other driver was forced to slam on his brakes to avoid hitting my vehicle. From my rearview mirror, I could see him swearing at me—justifiably. No police were nearby so I didn't get into legal trouble. More importantly, I was lucky to escape what could have been a serious accident.

I drove under the speed limit the rest of the way to my apartment. I had not eaten lunch before class. It being the first time at that school, I had delayed lunch to give myself extra time to travel, just in case I got lost.

Hungry as I had been before that math class, I now had no appetite. I went home and lay on my bed.

A million thoughts ran through my mind. I worried what the principal would think of me, and what she might say to the people at the Board of Education office. From the way the students had responded to her and to the woman from the office, I knew I had not been entirely at fault. However, I was being paid to do the job, so it was up to me to find a way. My fear was that I would be equally helpless in future similar situations. My job, and by extension my entire future in America, was on the line.

Dinnertime came and went, and I still had no appetite, so I ate nothing for the remainder of that day. Normally, I took a stroll around the neighborhood in the evenings before starting my readings and preparation for school the next day. With no desire to do any of those things, I paced restlessly for a few minutes then went to lie down again. The next day, I was exhausted. Sleep had been impossible.

As soon as I walked into the elementary school that morning, my colleagues sensed my despair. Fearing their reactions, I had planned to keep my problems to myself. Would they see me as an incompetent teacher and start to relate to me differently? As the minutes ticked by, they grew increasingly concerned by my silence. They knew I had just come to America alone and was still adjusting to life here. They'd done everything possible to help smooth that transition.

Upon their insistence, I related my story in all its gory detail. To my surprise, they began to chuckle. They told me not to be too hard on myself because no reasonable person would hold me responsible. At that time, they all taught only at the elementary school; they did not have to deal with the disciplinary problems that seemed concentrated in the higher-level grades. However, they knew what teachers in other schools had to deal with every day.

"Some of the students have serious behavioral problems, and that's the primary cause of the chaos in classrooms," one of my colleagues explained. "We're lucky at the elementary school only because the students haven't started acting out yet."

I knew from my middle and secondary school days in Ghana that teenagers tend to act irresponsibly, which is part of the growing up process. What I had witnessed went far beyond. Whatever the cause, this was a new environment to adjust to.

My colleagues had set my mind at ease somewhat, and I was able to at least function during the school day. With no math to teach, I knew I could go straight home afterward and get some rest.

I seriously considered telling the Board of Education that I no longer wanted to teach math. Despite my colleagues' assurances, I doubted my ability to manage another unruly classroom situation. Perhaps native teachers had specialized training to deal with such classroom environments. If so, it might be better to make way for someone who could do the job properly.

"Don't do that. Trust us, you'll be fine," my colleagues assured me when I told them my plans the following morning.

"All teachers who work in the district schools, regardless of their training, face the same challenges," one of them said. "Over time, you'll learn how to manage it."

"Thank you. I sincerely appreciate your advice and support," I said.

I continued to enjoy my work at the elementary school, but I was extremely nervous whenever I was assigned to teach math. As a substitute math teacher, I was sent to a different school almost every day. My experience that first day turned out to be more or less the norm.

In nearly every math classroom where I taught, whether in a middle or high school, I spent more than half the lesson period trying to get the students to keep quiet and stay in their seats. Consequently, I almost never got to complete my class plan. My biggest worry was that the students would not have another opportunity to learn that material. Many would finish every school year with significant knowledge gaps.

Most of the district's schools had racially diverse student populations. Over time, I observed noticeable differences in how the Black, Hispanic, and White students approached learning. A vast majority of the Black students showed no interest. They congregated in the corners, where they talked and laughed, oblivious to the current lesson.

At the time, I had no idea what a significant role race plays in America's education system and in broader society. That lack of awareness caused me to do the unthinkable. One day, I had written a set of problems on the chalkboard for the students to solve. I found it quite strange that most of the White and Hispanic students were hard at work, while almost all the Black students were doing other things unrelated to the assignment. A few of them had arranged their desks in a circle in one corner of the room. They were talking loudly and disturbing the class, ignoring my repeated pleas for quiet.

"Why are the Black students the only ones not working and disturbing the class?" I blurted out.

Every head in the room shot up. From their expressions, the students couldn't quite believe their ears. For several minutes they simply sat there, frozen in their seats. I didn't realize that I had made a racially charged statement that could easily have gotten me into deep trouble. The students eventually returned to whatever they had been doing. No one said a word.

It was only after I told one of my colleagues about the incident that I came to understand the students' reaction. "The only reason you got away with it is because you're Black," she said. I had spoken without malice, purely out of frustration. After that conversation with my colleague, I never repeated that mistake.

Over time, I became somewhat accustomed to the classroom dynamics in the middle and high schools and was better prepared psychologically to deal with most of what I encountered. Still, there is one particular incident I will never forget.

Close to the end of my lesson period, two students from another classroom barged into the room where I was teaching. One of them carried a big cup of water. They had been arguing, and the one holding the cup chased the other through the hallway and into my classroom. Before I could intervene, he threw the cup at him, splashing water everywhere. My presence made no difference. They ran out seconds later, having spilled water on several of my students and their books. I have since heard horror stories from other inner-city schools that make this incident seem minor, but at the time I was shocked.

My mother, photo taken in Boadua

*Ernest (wearing jean jacket), another friend from
secondary school, and me; Ernest was my host in Buffalo*

CHAPTER 12

"Acting White"

DURING MY TIME AS A teacher, one student stood out, a Black boy named Antoine. He was always quiet and studious. Whenever I taught his eighth-grade class, he would sit by himself amidst the chaos and try to do the assignment. I was impressed by his attitude. Academically, Antoine wasn't the best student, but he was my favorite because he was making a serious effort despite all the distractions.

Jamal, another Black boy in that class, was the exact opposite of Antoine. He never did his homework and never paid attention in class. School, for him, was just another place to hang out with friends and party. He was always either singing or using his desk and others nearby as a set of drums, playing various beats that the others seemed to enjoy dancing to.

Jamal also happened to be the most popular boy in the class. Everything seemed to revolve around him. To have any control of my classroom, I had to bring Jamal under control, and that was impossible. He had no fear, and he also seemed to know that he had enormous influence over his classmates. Whenever I attempted to discipline him, he would employ various tactics to get the students on his side, nullifying any authority I had as a teacher. Over time, I realized that Jamal always got the upper hand. Weary of these fruitless skirmishes, I learned to ignore him as much as I could.

What bothered me most was that Jamal never left Antoine alone. It was obvious how deeply he resented him. Whatever Antoine tried to do, Jamal did his best to disrupt. Students had assigned seats, but I always moved Antoine to another corner to keep him as far away from Jamal as possible. That did not help. Antoine, for some reason, was Jamal's prime target.

One day, as the students were filing out of the classroom at the end of the period, I asked Jamal to wait so I could speak with him, alone, for a few minutes. They had study hall next, which meant I wouldn't be keeping him from a class. That wouldn't have mattered to him anyway. His mission did not appear to be acquiring knowledge, at least at school.

I told Jamal I would walk him to study hall after we spoke. He was reluctant to stay behind at first. Partying in study hall was even greater fun for many of the students, and he didn't want to miss a single minute. In the end he agreed, but he told me it better be quick.

When we were alone, Jamal complained that Antoine was "acting White."

At first, I didn't understand. I asked him to explain.

Jamal was visibly angry. I was wasting his time, and he wasn't going to let me keep him from his more important business any longer. He started to walk toward the door, signaling the end of the conversation. I didn't want to squander this opportunity, so I stood in the doorway to block his path. Jamal wasn't a particularly big boy, and I knew that I could restrain him, if necessary. I succeeded in keeping him from leaving.

"Explain to me what 'acting White' means," I pleaded.

"You don't understand?" he asked incredulously.

"I don't," I replied.

"WHAT PLANET DID YOU COME FROM?" Jamal shouted at the top of his voice.

"Africa," I replied, before realizing I shouldn't have implied that Africa was its own planet.

"Oh, that's why you talk funny all the time," he said, smirking.

Although I had done my best to speak formal English in class, I couldn't hide my accent. I had never told the class I wasn't born in America, and Jamal admitted that he and many of his classmates had always wondered why I talked the way I did. His mood brightened a bit.

"What language do you folks speak in Africa?" he inquired.

"We speak a number of different local languages, but English is the official language in Ghana, where I grew up."

"What is an official language?" he asked.

"Because people from different tribal groups in Ghana speak different languages, we had to find a common language that everybody could understand, one we could use for national-level communication," I explained. He still looked puzzled.

"Are there any White people in Ghana?" he asked.

"No," I replied.

"Then why do you use their language?" he asked further.

Jamal was much more intelligent than I had realized. His eyes shone with curiosity as he questioned me. I hadn't expected it, given his behavior in class. He seemed genuinely interested in learning more about Ghana. I gave him a quick history lesson on colonialism, explaining that because Ghana used to be a British colony, English was adopted as the official language after the country gained its independence.

"Why didn't you use one of your local languages as the official one and make everybody else learn it?" he asked.

"I wasn't even born when the decision was made to adopt English as the national language, so I can't explain their reasoning," I joked. I ventured a guess: "Maybe they wished to avoid offending people in the other tribes whose languages would have ended up not being the official one."

"Why would they be offended?" was his next question.

"People from the other tribes whose languages were not chosen would have felt discriminated against. Choosing something neutral was a way to avoid trouble."

"I guess that makes sense," he said with a nod.

The conversation, which I expected would last five minutes at most, wound up lasting more than half an hour. Because I didn't have to teach that period, I could afford to carry on. He seemed to be enjoying the conversation so much that he completely forgot about the party in study hall. It was only after the announcement came for students to go to their next period classes that we both realized we had talked the entire study hall period. He thanked me for teaching him about Ghana, and I told him I was happy to do so.

Because of the impression Jamal made on me that day, I invited him for a second chat the following week during another study hall period.

"Do your parents speak with you at home about your grades?" I began. I had learned from his regular math teacher that his grades were generally poor, which didn't surprise me.

"My parents don't talk to me about school," he replied.

"Do they work a lot?" I inquired, assuming that was the reason.

"My mom doesn't work," he replied.

"What about your dad?" I asked.

"I live with my mom. I've never met my dad."

"How old is your mom?"

"Twenty-nine."

Jamal was fourteen, meaning that his mother gave birth to him when she was fifteen. She subsequently dropped out of school.

"Do you like school?" I asked Jamal.

"It's a complete waste of time," he replied. His response left me speechless.

I initiated short conversations with Jamal as frequently as I could. I tried hard to convince him that education was his only ticket to success in adulthood, regardless of what he decided to do with his later life. My sermons did not bring about any miracles. However, I was delighted to notice improvements in his behavior. He became a little less disruptive in class, and more importantly, he bothered Antoine a lot less than before.

* * *

"ACTING WHITE," AS I LATER came to understand it, is a pejorative term used mostly within Black communities in America. It refers to Black people who conform to socio-cultural attitudes typically associated with White people. They are seen as betraying their culture.

In schools, the term is used by some Black students to refer to others who make a serious effort to excel academically. A Black boy or girl doing something as normal as reading a book risks being seen as "acting White" by Black peers. The "offender" could become a social outcast within Black circles. It is only natural that Black children would try to avoid that label. Even adults do whatever they can to "fit in," both professionally and socially.

I had always found it strange that whenever Antoine was reading a book or doing math problems, he would frequently glance at Jamal, as if checking to see if he was watching him. Antoine always looked fidgety, and I wasn't sure why. I never bothered to ask. As long as he was getting his work done, I had no reason to question his behavior.

One day, I chatted with Antoine during a study hall period, just as I had with Jamal. I wanted to compliment him on his hard work, to encourage him to keep it up. When we started talking, his polite manner impressed me the most. He listened intently and, unlike Jamal, asked hardly any questions. He simply kept nodding, clearly absorbing everything I was telling him. We also ended up spending the entire study hall period together.

"Who do you live with?" I asked Antoine during that conversation.

"My mom and grandmother," he replied.

"Where's your dad?" I asked.

"He visits occasionally, but I've never lived with him."

"Does your mom work?"

"Yes, she works long hours so I'm often home with my grandma."

"Do they ever speak with you about school?" I inquired out of curiosity, recalling what Jamal had told me.

"Yes, all the time. My mom and my grandma both say that education is very important, so I have to work hard in school always. We don't have much at home, but they're always doing their best to get me what I need to succeed in school. So I know I have to work hard."

That brought a smile to my face. Antoine was also born out of wedlock, but in his case his mother had her high school diploma.

"Why do you always cast your eyes around the classroom?" I asked Antoine midway through the conversation.

"I've heard many stories of Black children bullied by other Black children in school for acting White, so I try to avoid being seen as a serious student. I'm afraid I'll get bullied."

I was stunned. Learning was considered a criminal activity in some segments of his community. Although I did my best to suppress my anger, Antoine could tell that I was unhappy. He looked as if he was about to ask whether he had said something wrong.

"Don't ever let anything like that discourage you from learning," I blurted out. "If you are ever threatened at school for studying, tell the authorities, and let your mother and grandmother know right away."

"I will, Mr. Asare." He thanked me as he walked out to his next class.

To ensure that Antoine would never again have to hide his studying activities, I repeated the message to him every day he came to my class. He later confided in me that Jamal was the person he feared most in the entire school. Jamal often teased him, but thankfully he hadn't done anything else. He was afraid that the teasing would turn into something worse. That was why he tried to avoid letting Jamal see him study. He was quite relieved when I told him I had spoken with Jamal about his general behavior, and that he should stop worrying so much.

I couldn't stop thinking about how Antoine's efforts to better himself were being seriously undermined by external factors beyond his control. I had learned that most of the other teachers at the school also spent inordinate amounts of time trying to maintain order in their classrooms, drastically reducing the amount of time they could devote to teaching. By then I also understood that this was a pervasive problem in America's urban K-12 public education system. Across the country, there were many Antoines whose lives were being ruined by Jamals. That began to haunt me.

I grew up in an environment not vastly different from that of my Buffalo students. In some ways, Ghana was worse. The poverty was much greater, and the schools I attended as a child were rudimentary in comparison. In spite of that, I was able to travel all the way to the Soviet Union for a college education and then to America to teach. I doubt I could have made the same journey if I had been born in urban America. I could have been forever trapped in poverty.

As I continued to think about Antoine, I began to appreciate the irony. How lucky I had been to be born and raised in the poorer of the two countries! In Ghana we had tribalism and crushing poverty, but there were counteracting social and cultural influences that made it possible for the schools there to function reasonably well, allowing me to obtain the basic education that provided my ticket out of the village.

Children from America's poorer urban areas contend with such high levels of violence that even getting to school safely is not guaranteed. The threats of violence do not stop when they enter school buildings. It is becoming increasingly common to find guards—sometimes armed— patrolling hallways. I never had to worry about my physical safety when I went to school in Ghana, meaning that I had one less mental burden to carry with me to school.

The tragedy is that children like Antoine and Jamal often have to navigate their difficult terrains without parental guidance. Neither boy had his father adequately present in his life. There are indeed many external factors contributing to the poor educational outcomes for Black children, but the absentee-father problem is widely viewed as one of the most important. It negatively impacts the lives of urban Black boys in a massive way.

It was not Jamal's fault that he did not know the importance of education. Every child needs guidance. Without a high school diploma or any clue as to how to serve as a role model, his mother could not help him. She herself had been failed by someone—or something—else. Like too many others, Jamal and his family were trapped in a vicious cycle of poverty. Through Jamal, that curse could spread to Antoine.

Apart from being fortunate to grow up in an environment that was more conducive to learning, I was also blessed with a powerful role model in my childhood. I had always had enormous respect for my father and was grateful for all the things he did throughout his life to fulfill his responsibilities toward his children. Examining how my experience differed from Antoine's and Jamal's led me to retrace the magical journey that started in my Ghanaian village, and to reflect on the many lessons I'd learned along the way.

* * *

ALL ALONG, I HAD BEEN working on pursuing a graduate degree in engineering in hopes of ultimately finding employment in the industry. Each day after school, and on weekends, I spent hours studying for the GRE and researching schools. I selected a few that offered programs in the area of energy sources and systems, my field of study during my undergraduate studies in Ukraine.

My GRE results made me confident of getting into some program, but Purdue University was the school I most wanted to attend. It was a long shot. Located in West Lafayette, Indiana, Purdue is widely known to be one of the best engineering schools in the world. It also has one of the best electrical engineering programs, even among the top schools in America. The School of Electrical Engineering sent me a glossy brochure in addition to the application forms.

I was in middle school in Boadua when I first learned about the moon landing of Neil Armstrong, the first person to set foot on that celestial body. For many years after that, I considered him to be the most famous person on earth, so when I discovered he had not only graduated from Perdue but had also majored in electrical engineering, I couldn't contain my excitement. If accepted into Purdue, I would be in the same department where he obtained his degree. I would walk in the same halls and sit in the same classrooms where he had studied.

The moon had a special significance in our village. With no electricity, moonlit nights were much anticipated. They were celebratory occasions when entire families would gather around wood fires in the open air and tell stories late into the night. We would look up in the sky at the full moon and wonder what was up there.

My special regard for Neil Armstrong intensified my desire to gain admission to Purdue University. Each day, as soon as I returned from teaching, I would pore over the brochure. Some days I was so tired that I just wanted to sleep, but as soon as I started looking at the professors' pictures in the brochure—reading about them and their various areas of research—I would get a burst of energy that fueled my study session well into the night.

I started to get nervous when, several weeks after I received acceptance letters from some of the other schools I applied to, I still hadn't heard from

Purdue. I didn't have to respond right away to any of the schools, so I could afford to hold out awhile. After waiting in vain for a few more weeks, I began to prepare myself for what felt like inevitable disappointment.

Just when that resignation set in, I came back from school one afternoon to find a surprise packet in my mailbox. There were a few letters, but this one was in a large brown envelope. I gasped when I saw it was from Purdue University. I tore it open and found that I'd been accepted.

I could not believe I had managed to gain admission to such a prestigious school, given my circumstances only a year earlier. I was in a hurry to get into one of those classrooms where I would feel the presence of Neil Armstrong. I called Ernest right away to relay the good news. He was proud of me, and I thanked him for helping me achieve that dream.

The admission package contained information about financial aid options. I was advised to contact professors in my area of interest in case they were looking for research or teaching assistants. I would have to go through an evaluation process to determine whether I was qualified for the position. My dream of attending Purdue was still a long way from becoming a reality.

I had already identified a couple of professors in the electrical engineering department I planned to speak with if I were accepted. One of them was Gerald Heydt, an expert in the electric power industry. I traveled to the campus to meet with him, my first trip outside the state of New York since I came to America. I liked what I saw when I arrived in West Lafayette. The bucolic campus, with its red brick buildings, was simply gorgeous.

After an extensive interview and a thorough review of my academic records, Professor Heydt agreed to consider me for a research assistantship. He then referred me to a professor he had collaborated with in the mechanical engineering department for another interview. Professor Heydt told me afterward that they were looking for a graduate student to help research a specific project: a number of electric utility companies in the Midwest had provided funding for the department to research the impact a mass deployment of electric-vehicle battery chargers would have on the electricity grid. He thought I'd be a good candidate.

A couple of weeks after the interview with Professor Heydt, he called to offer me the position. I felt like the luckiest man ever born. In a relatively brief period of time, I had gone from a state of near hopelessness to one of endless possibilities. A graduate degree from Purdue would certainly be a huge step in the direction of a great professional career. I was extremely happy.

My colleagues had mixed feelings when I broke the news. They had known I was waiting to hear from Purdue and so were happy for me. However, they were sad that I would be leaving Buffalo. The four of us at the elementary school had become close friends. I had come to love teaching and liked to be with the students, particularly those at the elementary school. Although I would be a fair distance away, I promised my colleagues I would keep in touch and visit as often as I could.

About a week after I received the formal appointment letter from Professor Heydt's office, I wrote a letter to the Board of Education to inform them of my decision to resign from my position at the end of the school year. I left Buffalo in the summer of 1994 to begin my new life in West Lafayette.

* * *

MY INS APPLICATION WAS APPROVED two weeks before I was scheduled to start the program at Purdue. With my permanent residency (green card) granted, I could now travel overseas. I was eager to visit Ghana to see Patricia and Jennifer before school started, but it was too late. I needed to start gathering research material even before classes began.

It wasn't until the spring of 1995 that I was finally able to fly to Ghana. My relationship with Patricia had become strained by more than two years of absence. Even so, we had been in constant communication, and I had regularly sent money to help take care of Jennifer.

"Hello, Jennifer, I'm so glad to see you!" I said as I hugged my daughter.

She had grown into a tall, beautiful four-year-old. She simply looked at me and smiled. Being only five months old when I left Ghana to come to America, she didn't quite know who I was now, even though Patricia had told her I'd be visiting. I held her for over five minutes before I sat her down and gave Patricia a hug as well.

"I'm so sorry to have put you through this ordeal," I told her.

She said nothing but began to cry. I started to cry as well.

Although a green card allowed me to stay permanently in America, I couldn't easily sponsor any family member to join me. U.S. citizenship was required for such sponsorship, and it would be another couple of years before I would qualify. For the time being, I would have to rely on annual visits to Ghana.

As a student in the Soviet Union, I had obtained a U.S. visitor's visa fairly easily. It would be extremely difficult for Patricia and Jennifer to obtain visitors' visas from the U.S. Embassy in Ghana. For ordinary people in developing nations, it has always been difficult to obtain visas to travel to most places in the developed world. That is why hundreds of thousands of people attempt illegal entries into the U.S. and Western European countries each year.

On the morning after my arrival in Ghana, Emmanuel and Ernestina, who had moved into the family house, accompanied me to my mother's grave. My siblings had managed to complete the new building my father had been working on before his death. Sadly, because my mother had been ill and was living for much of that time with Felicia in Accra receiving medical treatment, she didn't get to enjoy the new house in Boadua much before she passed away. It was fitting that Ernestina, who had sacrificed so much for the family over the years, now lived there.

As soon as I saw my mother's grave, I started to cry. I remembered the many times she gave me her meals and went to bed hungry. Sadly, I didn't get to repay my enormous debt to her. "Thank you for being such a wonderful mother," I said, looking down at her grave. Ernestina led us in prayer. "May your beautiful soul rest in eternal peace," I said before we left the cemetery.

Before returning to Indiana, I spent three weeks with Patricia and Jennifer in Akwatia. I graduated from Purdue six months later and began working as an engineer at a Caterpillar, Inc. engine-manufacturing facility in Lafayette, only a few miles away from the Purdue campus.

In 1997, I became a U.S. citizen. Patricia and I finally wed in the summer of 1999 in Nsawam.

"Thank you so much for your patience," I told her after the ceremony. "I love you dearly."

"We were meant to be husband and wife," she replied. "I love you, too."

It was the happiest day of my life.

I submitted the immigrant visa applications for Patricia and Jennifer to the INS as soon as I returned to the U.S. after the wedding. Though approval would take several months, we could finally look forward to living together as a family. Just as relief set in, we were dealt another severe blow.

The INS required mother and child applications to be filed separately. Although I had mailed them on the same date, a month had passed following receipt of Patricia's approval letter, and nothing had arrived for Jennifer. It wasn't until I called the INS office to follow up that I realized

Jennifer's application had been lost. After an unsuccessful search, the INS asked me to resubmit Jennifer's application.

Patricia's visa had been issued for travel to America. Immigrant visas have short expiration dates, so we were forced to make the difficult decision to let Patricia come to America and leave Jennifer behind while her application was processed. We couldn't risk Patricia's visa expiring.

Since I had assumed they would both join me, I hadn't planned to travel to Ghana that summer. I reversed that decision. I hadn't seen Jennifer for a year, and another year might pass before she could come to America. I flew to Ghana in the summer of 2000 and spent three weeks with her and Patricia.

We arranged for Jennifer to stay with Ellen in Accra, enrolled at the same school her children attended. After Jennifer's application had been approved, Ellen would take her to the U.S. embassy in Accra to obtain her visa.

The day Patricia and I left Ghana was difficult for us both. Jennifer was nine years old, and we had explained the situation to her. She took the news surprisingly well. Patricia and I both had tears in our eyes as we hugged her at the airport. I had expected her to cry, but she did not.

"I love you, Jennifer. I'm going to bring you to America as soon as possible," I assured her.

"I love you too, Daddy," she said.

Throughout the flight, Patricia and I sat quietly. What should have been a happy occasion had been spoiled. Immediately after arriving at our home in West Lafayette, we called to speak with Jennifer and Ellen. She sounded sad, but Ellen assured us she was fine.

Because of my firsthand experiences with the U.S. immigration system, I have followed the long-running immigration debates with considerable interest. I know the pain of leaving loved ones behind. Whenever I see pictures of struggling immigrants, I wonder about their personal stories and what drove them to leave their homelands.

CHAPTER 13

In the Deep End

IN THE POWER SYSTEMS DIVISION at Caterpillar, we designed and manufactured engine-generator systems that we sold through the company's global dealership network to customers all over the world. Some of the systems were used for emergency power generation during periods of grid-electricity loss. Hospitals and critical-care facilities, and various industries with sensitive operations that could not withstand even momentary loss of power, constituted the target market. We designed other systems for baseload (continuous) power generation on ships and in remote locations—those inaccessible to the main electricity grid—around the world.

In my six years at Caterpillar, I rose through the ranks to become a senior electrical engineer. The work was particularly gratifying. Not only was I doing something I had spent many years training for, but I was interacting with people across the globe. After those six glorious years, I decided to return to school to obtain my MBA.

* * *

PLEASE DON'T! SHE'S GOING TO think I'm too old! As the thought flashed through my mind, I was mentally scrambling to come up with an excuse to spare me from going, but the Tuck admissions officer was already a couple of steps ahead, so I was forced to follow him. He had just finished interviewing me as part of my application to the MBA program at the Tuck School of Business at Dartmouth College, and he wanted to introduce me to the director.

"Mary, this is Patrick Asare. He has quite an interesting background," he told the director. "I think he'd be a wonderful addition to the class."

"I'm so pleased to meet you, Patrick," she said, shaking my hand. "Oh yes, I remember reading Patrick's application. He has a fantastic life story."

Maybe she didn't notice my date of birth? As we talked, I was searching for facial clues to get a sense of her impression of me. Despite her smiles, I was uneasy.

The Wall Street Journal had just ranked Tuck the number one business school in the world. It is the oldest program in America and has been consistently rated among the best. The school's top ranking in 2001—the year I applied—didn't surprise anyone. For me, it meant the already long odds of my getting admitted had become a whole lot longer.

I was thirty-nine years old—thirteen years older than the average applicant. From what I had learned while researching MBA programs, the top schools preferred applicants in their mid to late twenties. The vast majority of applicants had near-perfect grade point averages (GPAs) and admission test scores, as well as interesting work experiences. My GPA and test score, while decent, did not quite match the typical student profiles I saw on the top schools' websites. My one advantage was the length of my work experience. I had eight years, versus the average four or five for the typical applicant. The top programs emphasized a decent level of work experience, but even then, I wasn't sure whether in my case that was good or bad; it probably revealed my age more clearly.

This is one of the most beautiful places on earth, I thought as I drove through Maine, New Hampshire, and Vermont. I had been on a road trip from Indiana to Canada in the summer of 1998 and was returning from Quebec to upstate New York en route to Indiana. The greenery, mountains, and lakes in those three states made the area a paradise. *I'd love to live in this part of America someday,* I thought.

I knew that Dartmouth College was in New Hampshire and that it had a business school. However, at first I didn't know much about Tuck. Because I was interested mainly in the top schools, Tuck appeared on my list of choices.

Of the top full-time MBA programs in America, Tuck's is the only one without a PhD program. Unlike its competitor schools, where some MBA classes are taught by PhD students, Tuck's world-renowned faculty is fully dedicated to teaching MBA students. Tuck also has the smallest student population of the bunch. Thus Tuck students have unparalleled access to its top-notch professors. Its reputation and beautiful surroundings drew me more and more to the school as I narrowed down my choices.

"Thank you, it was very nice to meet you," I said after my interview with the director of admissions had wrapped up. *What a pleasant woman,* I thought.

* * *

"JENNIFER RECEIVED HER IMMIGRANT VISA from the embassy today," Ellen said as soon as I picked up the phone.

"That's great! Thank you so much for your hard work on this, Ellen," I told her.

The nightmare would soon be over. It had been a tough year for both Patricia and me, and while Jennifer seemed to have handled the separation well, I knew she would be relieved at the prospect of joining us in America.

Patricia had passed her certification exam and would be qualified to work as a registered nurse as soon as the New York State Board of Nursing finished processing her paperwork. Although we lived in Indiana at the time, she had chosen to apply for a New York nurse's license; the licensing process there was streamlined, relative to other states. The Board of Nursing would endorse the New York license in any state we moved to in the future.

It had been four months since my Tuck interview. The schools would be making their decisions within days so I was constantly on edge. I had learned that in some business schools, admissions office personnel called some admitted students to notify them in advance of their formal letters. I certainly wasn't expecting such a call.

"Can I speak to Patrick, please?" the woman on the phone asked.

"Speaking," I replied nervously.

"Hello, Patrick, this is Mary Smith from Tuck. I have great news for you! I'm so glad to tell you that you've been offered admission to Tuck," she said.

"Oh my God, I'm speechless. Thank you so much. I'm so happy!" I screamed with joy.

After I calmed down a bit, she said, "Patrick, we'd be extremely happy to have you as a member of our incoming class. I know you are considering other schools, but I sincerely hope that you'll decide to come to Tuck."

What! She thinks I'm going to select some other school over Tuck? I paused, then said, "Tuck has been my dream school all along. I'll definitely enroll."

"I'm so glad to hear that, Patrick. I look forward to seeing you again in the fall," she replied.

"Thank you again, Ms. Jaeger. I can't wait."

The acceptance call came late in the evening, so Patricia and I celebrated the next day. She submitted paperwork to the New Hampshire Board of Nursing right away to apply for that state's license. Simultaneously, she applied for employment at the Dartmouth-Hitchcock Medical Center (DHMC), only a couple of miles from the Dartmouth College campus. I informed my superiors at Caterpillar that I intended to resign later that summer to pursue my MBA.

* * *

"IT'S GREAT TO SEE YOU!" I said excitedly as I hugged Jennifer at the JFK airport that afternoon. Now ten years old, she had just arrived—unaccompanied—from Ghana to begin her new life in America.

"I'm so glad to see you both!" she replied as Patricia hugged her.

Patricia and I had packed up and left West Lafayette at dawn that day and had been driving for about twelve hours when we picked up Jennifer from the airport. From there, we drove on to White River Junction in Vermont, where we had rented an apartment. We had traveled nearly eighteen hours by the time we arrived around eleven p.m.

White River Junction lies on the border between Vermont and New Hampshire. Our apartment was a ten-minute drive from campus. Patricia had been offered a nursing position at DHMC a few days before we left Indiana, and her drive to work was about ten minutes as well. We registered Jennifer at the White River Junction Elementary School the day after we arrived. For the first time, we were together as a family. Everything was in place for us to begin our new lives.

"We're so happy to have Jennifer here," the elementary school principal told me when we registered.

"Thank you," I said. Jennifer would be the only Black child in her class. In every respect, it was going to be a major adjustment for her.

"We'll make every effort to ensure the transition is as easy as possible," the principal added, after I told her more about Jennifer's background and that she had just immigrated to the country.

After the first day of school, I asked Jennifer, "How were your classes and your teachers?"

"Everything went well. The teachers and the students are all nice," she replied. "They asked me so many questions about Ghana and Africa ….
Sometimes I didn't understand and couldn't answer them all," she added with some concern.

"I'm really glad to hear that classes went well. Don't worry at all about the language problem," I assured her. "You'll pick it up quickly."

Although classes in Ghana were taught in English, what she heard in Vermont that day sounded different to her. She missed her friends initially, but within weeks she made new ones and settled into her new environment nicely.

I too was acclimating to a new school. My class at Tuck was full of students with undergraduate degrees from Ivy League universities, as well as top schools such as MIT, Stanford, and Duke. The overseas students had similarly studied at the elite universities in their home countries. *This is going to be a tough environment to operate in*, I thought.

I believed I had prepared myself mentally for the challenge ahead. The actual experience was even harder than anticipated.

Because I had never taken courses in accounting, capital markets, and managerial economics, much of the material was new to me. The professors assigned voluminous amounts of reading. Additionally, there were numerous assignments and projects to work on.

Holy cow! How am I going to get through this program? I asked myself one afternoon, as I stared at the stack of papers I was supposed to read for my study group meeting later that evening. Everything seemed to be moving at such a blistering speed that I couldn't keep up.

There were students from all parts of the world in my class. Some of them had worked on Wall Street and in top-tier consulting and accounting firms for a few years after their undergraduate studies. As a result, they were familiar with most of the concepts being taught. Still, quite a few other students in the class were as unfamiliar with the concepts as I was, due to their undergraduate majors and work experiences. As far as I could tell, they were coping relatively well. I was studying with some of the most brilliant people on earth.

The pace was such that everyone in the class, regardless of level of brilliance, academic background, or nature of work experience, had to work like crazy, day and night, just to keep up. I decided I would need to work twice as hard as everyone else. Although prepared to do just that, I could not find enough hours in the day.

* * *

"I'M PREGNANT," PATRICIA TOLD ME one evening after I returned from class.

"That's great news!" I said enthusiastically. "When did you find out?"

"I suspected about a week ago, but I wanted to be certain before telling you."

Both of us had wished for another child. We immediately began to prepare for the little one's arrival. Jennifer was overjoyed that she would soon have a sibling.

We had one car at the time. Given my hectic schedule at school, we had been planning to buy a second one so that Patricia could drive herself to work. Now we gave up on that idea as too expensive. Jennifer took the school bus to school, so we didn't have to worry about transportation for her.

On most days, Jennifer stayed in the apartment by herself after school, because I was either in class or study group meetings and Patricia was working. It wasn't ideal, but we couldn't afford after-school child care. I had no income, meaning that Patricia was the breadwinner. At least the condominium complex we lived in had a locked main entrance door.

Patricia worked twelve-hour shifts at the hospital, three days a week. I drove her to work at seven in the morning before going to school. I would pick her up around seven thirty p.m. Often, I had to leave study group sessions and rejoin them after I dropped her off at the apartment. She occasionally called for a taxi, but because we were on a tight budget, we tried to avoid that expense.

The back-and-forth driving was a significant burden. It was always a mad scramble to get Patricia to work and then go to my first class. As much as I hated being late, I often couldn't avoid it.

I probably wouldn't have survived the first quarter at Tuck without the incredible help I received from my study group. Teamwork is a key focus of the Tuck MBA program. In the first year, each student is assigned to a study group of four members who work together throughout the year. Groups are structured so that each has members with a variety of skill sets—different academic, professional, and personal backgrounds.

Most class assignments are discussed within groups, although each student must submit their own written answers. Participation in study group discussions requires extensive preparation—long readings, problem solving, and other preliminary work. Given the large number of assignments and projects during the first year, each group meets for several hours daily, often late into the night.

Tracy, James, and Rao were the other members of my first-year study group. Tracy obtained her bachelor's degree from the University of Pennsylvania, James obtained his from Harvard, and Rao had completed his undergraduate studies at the University of International Business and Economics in China.

"How do you folks do it?" I often asked my study group mates during our meetings.

"I skim a lot of the readings," was the usual answer.

How could anyone have such command of the material from simply skimming it? I wondered. Judging by the way they spoke during discussions, they appeared to have read everything. I couldn't understand how they could find the time to get through all that material.

My group mates were all in their mid-twenties. Rao was married but had no children. His wife didn't work so he had none of the driving duties I had. Tracy and James were both unmarried.

Although I did as much of the assigned readings as I could and completed my homework for each study group meeting, I often felt woefully unprepared.

James popped in and out of study group meetings because he traveled a lot to visit his girlfriend in New York City. Having worked in consulting for a few years, he seemed to know everything we covered already. Although they surely had better things to do, Tracy and Rao stayed as long as necessary to help me complete my assignments. I had many questions, and in those late hours, nowhere else to turn. I was amazed by their patience and truly grateful.

Often, I returned to my apartment and continued reading until the early hours of the morning. Most nights I got by on only two or three hours of sleep. It was a grueling schedule, and I felt as if I were swimming against a tsunami. The first term was broken into two five-week modules. By the time the second module ended just before Christmas break, I was exhausted. I had survived what is generally considered to be the most difficult part of the program at Tuck. What I did not appreciate at the time was that I was accumulating a massive amount of knowledge.

In the second term, the pace did slow somewhat. Along with a few required core courses, we could take electives. For the first time since I started the program, I felt in control of events. I could finish reading most of the material, complete assignments, and participate in study group meetings much better. I was enjoying the program the way I had hoped.

* * *

"Where's Mom?" I asked Jennifer one afternoon when I called home from study group.

"She went to the hospital."

"Why? What's wrong?" I asked nervously.

"She wasn't feeling well so she decided to go to the doctor."

"How did she get there?"

"She called a taxi."

The fact that she hadn't gone in an ambulance was a good sign, and I was slightly relieved.

I always had the car, and because Patricia's due date was getting closer, I had gotten into the habit of calling often to check on her. Neither of us had mobile phones because they were not as ubiquitous then, meaning that we couldn't exchange text messages. I had to call from a wall-mounted phone located in the classroom building.

"I have to rush to the hospital," I told my study group mates as I frantically picked up my papers and laptop.

This study group was for a managerial accounting class—one of the first-year classes for which we could form our study groups independently.

"What's wrong?" they asked in unison.

"I just learned that my wife is in the hospital, but I'm not sure what's wrong."

"Don't worry about this meeting. We'll take care of the assignment. Our best wishes to her," they all offered.

I rushed to the parking lot and drove straight to the hospital. Patricia was lying on a bed in an observation room when I arrived.

"What happened?" I asked.

"I began to have contractions and was feeling dizzy. The doctors already ran some tests. They said there is nothing overly concerning, but they want me to stay for further observation."

One doctor came by a few minutes later. "We're going to monitor you for a little while, but it's looking like we may have to deliver your baby through cesarean section," he said after performing a quick examination. "The fact that your first child was delivered through cesarean section increases the likelihood that your next child will also have to be delivered via that method. The nurses will check on you periodically. I'll be back in another hour or so and then we'll decide."

It was getting to be quite late at night, and Jennifer had been by herself in the apartment for much of the day. Because it was a Sunday, she had been at home since morning, when Patricia left for the hospital.

"How are you doing, Jennifer?" I asked when I called from the hospital.

"Everything is okay. I'm doing my homework."

"I'm glad to hear that. It seems as if I'm going to be here for a little while. Stay inside the apartment and keep the door securely locked."

"Okay, I'll do that."

The contractions became more frequent as the night wore on. Shortly after ten p.m., the doctor and two of his colleagues entered the room.

"We're going to need to perform a cesarean section," he said after another examination. One of the nurses brought me a gown to wear so I could accompany them into the operating room.

"He's a handsome boy!" one of the nurses said as she handed our newborn baby to me.

"Thank you. I'm a proud father!" I replied enthusiastically as I cradled him in my arms. Rather reluctantly, I handed him back to the nurse so she could attend to him.

"Do you have a name for your son?" a nurse asked. "We need to create a record of his birth."

Patricia and I exchanged glances. During those last few months of her pregnancy, she had suggested several times that we choose a name. Because I had been so busy with schoolwork, I never found the time.

"Patrick Osei Asare Jr.," I said after a moment of hesitation. I looked at Patricia to see if she approved.

"That works for me," Patricia said. "Oh, I'd like to add 'Sam.' It's a name I've always liked."

Our son's name was thus officially recorded as Patrick Sam Osei Asare Jr.

Patricia's three-month maternity leave provided a much-needed respite. Not having to do the daily back-and-forth driving allowed me to better focus on my schoolwork. I wasn't constantly distracted in study group meetings by having to leave to pick her up or call to check on her at home. Still, there was the stress of a newborn baby to contend with. I would sometimes cut short my sleep to take care of Patrick Jr. when he woke up at night.

The DHMC had a day care center, and we had been on a waitlist there for several months before Patrick was born. No space had opened up by the time Patricia had to return to work. We found a small day care center that a couple operated in their house, about a mile away from where we lived.

I can't do this, I thought as I sat in the car in the empty parking lot with Patrick in his car seat. I had just dropped Patricia off at work and was taking Patrick to day care for the first time. The thought of leaving him with complete strangers for the entire day was extremely difficult to bear. I sat quietly for the next several minutes, contemplating what to do. Then it struck me that my first class of the day was about to start. As I resumed driving to the day care, tears filled my eyes.

Several other parents were dropping off their children when I arrived. *Are any of these parents feeling the same way I am?* I wondered as I watched them come and go. It looked as if many of them were used to the practice, because they quickly exchanged greetings with the owners, said goodbye to their children, and left. In contrast, after handing over Patrick to the woman, I lingered, watching intently and trying to get a sense of how he was feeling. He seemed quieter than usual, which made me anxious.

"Don't worry, Patrick, your son will be in good hands," the husband and co-owner told me.

"Thank you. This is an entirely new experience for me and I'm finding it difficult to handle," I replied.

"I perfectly understand, but I can assure you your son will be fine. Did you ever take your daughter to day care when she was a baby?"

"No," I replied. "She grew up in Ghana. Over there, extended family members are always available to assist with child care, so there are no day care centers in the country."

"That's really interesting," he said.

I felt a pang of sadness. My family and I were alone in a distant land with no close relatives, causing us to grapple with the emotional anguish of placing our baby in the hands of people we didn't know.

"I have to go!" I blurted out, interrupting the man's next sentence. My class had just started. I had completely lost track of time.

"No worries. I'd love to hear more about Ghana next time you're here," he said.

I gave Patrick a quick kiss on the cheek and hurriedly drove to campus, arriving fifteen minutes late to class.

Time seemed to move a lot slower that day. I couldn't wait for classes and afternoon study group meetings to be over so I could pick up Patrick from day care, which closed at five p.m. He was quiet and seemingly tired when I arrived, but as soon as I strapped him into his car seat, his mood brightened, and he started to smile. It was clear that he was happy to be back in familiar surroundings.

* * *

TUCK WAS EVERYTHING I EXPECTED—AND more. Because of the school's small size, none of the classes were oversubscribed, as was common at other schools. We had easy access to our professors. Any student could walk into any professor's office at any time. I had countless one-on-one interactions with professors during those two years.

The school administration and faculty placed as much emphasis on campus social life as they did on academic preparation. Every Thursday evening, administrators, faculty, and students gathered for *Tuck 'Tails*, a happy-hour event in the school's magnificent Stell Hall, where students, professors, and school administrators mingled and enjoyed drinks and refreshments.

There were student parties almost every weekend. Those were typically held in students' off-campus apartments, and people went freely from one party to the next, hanging out with friends until the early morning hours on Saturdays and Sundays. Tuck students competed with students from other MBA programs in hockey, soccer, and golf tournaments on campus.

The world-renowned Killington, Sugarbush, and Stowe ski resorts were all about an hour's drive from campus. In my class, both avid skiers and novices wanted to take advantage of their proximity to the resorts. During the winter months, many students spent the bulk of their free time on the slopes.

Parental and driving duties left little time for extracurricular activities, meaning that I missed out on much of the fun. Having to drop off Patricia and Patrick before going to class in the mornings meant waking up earlier than ever. After picking up Patrick from day care late in the afternoon, I typically stayed with him and Jennifer in the apartment for about an hour before going to pick up Patricia. Jennifer was extremely helpful during that time. She took care of Patrick while I prepared for study group meetings.

After handing Patrick over to Patricia, I would rush back to campus for my meetings, or to work in the library till late at night, only for the drill to begin all over again a few hours later. That juggling of home duties and school work began to feel like the arduous routine I had endured as a young boy in Boadua.

On one particular day, it all became too much. In almost every class, there were several case studies we had to prepare for during the quarter. In managerial accounting, during each class session, the professor called on one student from a study group to present the group's analysis of that day's case. Typically, that student was interrupted repeatedly to answer a series of wide-ranging questions. The ability to answer those rapid-fire questions required careful reading of the often-lengthy cases.

Most students dreaded case presentation. At first it appeared as though the professor called on students randomly. We soon realized, however, that his selection was based on a student's background. Because we were analyzing business cases, he'd typically call on someone with expertise in the type of business that day's case was about.

I have a strong feeling I'll be called on to present this case, I thought as I read through it before going into my study group meeting later that evening. The case concerned an electrical engineering-related business. I was one of a handful of electrical engineers in the class, and the only one in my group.

"You're definitely going to be the presenter tomorrow," one of my study group members remarked as soon as I walked into the meeting.

The others agreed.

"That's what I suspect too," I replied. "I'll have to make sure I know this case inside and out."

It had been an exhausting day, and now a long night lay ahead of me. I would need to read the case thoroughly more than once to prepare. By the time I returned to the apartment, it was well past midnight.

"Are you going to get some rest tonight?" Patricia asked. Everyone was already asleep, but she woke up when she heard me open the door.

"I'm extremely tired, but I don't think so," I replied. "I still have homework to complete and a case to prepare for tomorrow."

"Good luck," she said and went back to bed.

I hurriedly completed my homework assignments and read the case one more time. I also spent extra time going over the spreadsheet and other analysis the group had prepared.

"You really need to get a bit of rest," Patricia said as she walked by on her way toward the kitchen.

"Oh my God, it's past four o'clock!" I said in a panic, looking at the clock on the living room wall. Patricia woke up around that time each morning to prepare for the day. "Please wake me up in an hour," I said as I dashed toward the bedroom.

As I drove from day care to campus that morning, I mentally outlined my presentation and answers to some of the possible questions. Although I had a few minutes to eat breakfast in the cafeteria before going to class, I decided to use the time for one last review of the spreadsheet. *I'm well prepared for this case and should be able to present it well,* I thought as I walked into the classroom.

"Patrick, please come and present today's case on behalf of your group," the professor said as soon as I sat down. My study group members looked at me as if to say, "We told you so." This was a fairly large class, so it was held in one of two large auditoriums. I descended nervously to where the professor stood at the center.

After projecting the spreadsheet onto the large electronic board, I tried to recall my introductory remarks, which I had rehearsed multiple times throughout the night and that morning. I stood still for more than a minute but just couldn't remember what I had planned to say. My attempt to look at the spreadsheet on the board to help kick my mind into gear made matters worse. When I managed to speak, my words were utterly incoherent: my mind was frozen. *Relax! You've prepared exhaustively*, I told myself. *You need to calm down and get on with this.* Nothing worked. Silence filled the auditorium, and all eyes were on me.

"Get back to your seat, Patrick," the professor finally said, after what felt like an eternity. I had made another couple of attempts to jumpstart the presentation but had remained incoherent, and the professor finally concluded I couldn't do it. He called another student from a different study group to present the case.

Utterly humiliated, I walked slowly back to my seat, unable to lift my feet easily because they felt so heavy. I sat quietly through the entire class incapable of mentally processing anything anyone said. *How on earth did that happen?* I wondered.

I had been working frantically, almost nonstop for over twenty-four hours, and had made the disastrous mistake of not giving myself at least a few minutes to decompress before going into class that morning. Standing in front of that large class in that amphitheater-like space was quite intimidating. That, combined with my less-than-ideal mental state, contributed to my inability to get my brain to function.

"Don't be too hard on yourself, Patrick," Anna said to me. Anna was one of the Harvard graduates in the class, and one of the nicest people I've ever met. I had remained in my seat as people were filing out of the auditorium. Seeing my misery, she had decided to try and lift my mood.

"Thank you, Anna," I replied in a low voice.

She spoke to me for several more minutes, and her kind gesture helped restore my sanity. *At least in this instance I didn't receive cane lashes,* I consoled myself as I finally packed up my stuff and left the auditorium. The experience had reminded me of my elementary and middle school days in Boadua.

My study group mates had hurried out to go to their next classes, so I didn't get the chance to speak to any of them after the class. I apologized later that afternoon. My disastrous non-performance likely gave the professor—and the rest of the class—the impression that my group had not spent enough time preparing, which couldn't have been further from the truth. They all graciously told me not to worry too much about it.

"Good afternoon, Professor Sansing," I said to the professor when I went to his office the next day.

"Hello, Patrick, how are you?"

"I'm well, thank you. I want to apologize for what happened in class yesterday. My group and I did prepare thoroughly for the case, but I had been working round-the-clock, nonstop, at home and at school, and was completely exhausted when I came to class. I had a brain freeze, and that is why I was unable to present the case."

"Don't worry too much about it, Patrick. I realize you're combining school and caring for a new baby," he reassured me.

"Thank you so much, Professor Sansing."

A disastrous performance impacted the grade not only of the presenter but also of group members. I could deal with the unpleasant consequences of a bad grade, but I worried about the negative impact on the rest of the group. The reactions of my group members and the professor helped assuage those worries somewhat.

One thing that never ceased to amaze me at Tuck was the down-to-earth nature of the students. These were high-achieving individuals, mostly from wealthy families, and I had expected them to act aloof. Instead, Tuck was a place where it seemed that no one, regardless of socio-economic background, race, or national origin, felt isolated. As I later learned, the Tuck admissions office makes a sincere effort to identify and admit students who would fit in with the school's renowned collegial culture.

Despite the enormous stress, I was enjoying every minute of my time at Tuck—both academically and socially. There were so many good classes on offer that at the beginning of each quarter I felt like a kid in a candy store. Typically, students took four or five classes per quarter so that by the final quarter, they had three classes to take in order to graduate. That allowed extra time for job hunting. In my class, several students had a Monday-Tuesday schedule in that quarter, leaving the rest of the week open for interviewing, golfing, and skiing.

How will I fit all these classes into my schedule? I asked myself when I looked at the course list at the beginning of final quarter. Although I only needed to take three, I was interested in many others. Fortunately for me, I had already accepted a job offer. *I'm not going to have another chance anywhere else to take such interesting classes from this type of faculty; I have to maximize the opportunity,* I thought.

I registered for the required finance, strategy, and negotiations classes. Of the five others that caught my eye, I could possibly handle four—two accounting, one strategy, and one corporate restructuring. The fifth, a marketing class, conflicted with a required class. Taking five classes in any quarter at Tuck was an extremely heavy load; the seven I was considering, on top of my family responsibilities, would be unthinkable. However, I couldn't pass up the opportunity.

As I agonized over it, a workable solution occurred to me: auditing. I could simply attend the classes without having to do the homework assignments and take the exams. *Would that be acceptable to the professors?* I wondered.

It was such a relief when I visited their offices and each agreed to let me sit in on their classes. I attended every class session for all four classes, which meant I had to be in school every day of the week. My classmates thought I was crazy, and there were times when I was inclined to agree. It was painful to see them having so much fun while I sat in classrooms all the time.

"How is the final quarter going for you?" the dean asked, as he stopped to talk to me at a cookout in the main yard of the Tuck campus.

"It's quite busy, but I'm having a great time."

"How many classes are you taking?" he inquired.

"Seven," I said.

"How many?" he asked again, an incredulous look on his face.

"I'm taking seven," I repeated.

He appeared to be astonished. "I didn't know it was possible to take so many classes in one quarter!"

"There were so many interesting classes on offer. This is my last quarter here, so I decided to take as many as I could fit on my schedule."

"That's quite a feat. You're really getting your money's worth."

Wanting to keep him impressed, I didn't clarify that I was auditing four of them.

I made many lifelong friends at Tuck. When Tracy found out that my family and I would be moving to eastern Pennsylvania after graduation, she was extremely happy. Her parents lived in Newtown, Pennsylvania, about a two-hour drive from Wyomissing, the location of the company that had hired me. She visited her parents often, and we looked forward to continuing to socialize after graduation. She had accepted a job in San Francisco.

Tracy returned to Pennsylvania for the Christmas holidays that year. Because we were new to the state, she felt we would be lonely and invited us for Christmas dinner with her family in Newtown. The following year, Tracy visited us in Wyomissing with her boyfriend, Jeff. At her wedding to Jeff a year later in Napa Valley, California, Tracy wanted Patrick Jr., whom she had known since the day he was born, to serve as a ring bearer. We gladly flew out to California to attend their beautiful wedding. Beverly and Ted, Tracy's gracious parents, hosted us in their home in Newtown on a few other occasions after that first Christmas, until they moved to California to be closer to their grandchildren.

Most of my classmates, and many of the Tuck alumni I have encountered over the years, have said they would have preferred to live near Hanover and be close to Tuck after graduation. The New Hampshire-Vermont-Maine area is simply gorgeous, particularly its summer greenery and brightly colored fall foliage. That is a large part of the attraction, but it is the Tuck experience itself that most students find difficult to let go of.

Patrick Jr. and Patricia in the foyer of the Dartmouth-Hitchcock Medical Center in Lebanon, NH, where he was born

CHAPTER 14

Race in America

WHEN JONATHAN, MY GOOD FRIEND in Vermont, told me discouraging things about Berks County, Pennsylvania, it started to look as if I was destined to hear negative opinions about every place I was about to move to. I was two months away from graduation at Tuck and had received a job offer from UGI Energy Services, a diversified energy services company based in Wyomissing, Pennsylvania.

Throughout my time at Tuck, my goal had been to work in finance in the energy industry post-graduation, preferably on the East Coast. The job as a financial analyst at UGI was a perfect fit. I was quite excited when I broke the news to Jonathan, a White man and Vermont native. He wasn't a student at Tuck, but I'd met him during the first year through friends on campus, and over time, we had become close. We had many enjoyable conversations during those two years I lived in Vermont.

"I'm happy for you," Jonathan said. "It sounds like the perfect job. I am, however, concerned that the company is located in Berks County," he added, after a brief pause.

"What's the problem with Berks County?" I asked.

"It's Pennsylvania Dutch country. The people are known to be unfriendly toward foreigners, and I'm afraid that you and your family won't feel welcome."

"What is Pennsylvania Dutch?" I asked. I had never heard that term before.

"They are descendants of German immigrants, and they constitute the majority population in that part of Pennsylvania."

"Have you lived in that area before?" I asked.

"No, but I've heard many stories."

"Thank you," I told him. "I sincerely appreciate your concern, but we'll make the move. If we find the place too hostile, I'll apply for a job somewhere else." I could tell all his information was based on hearsay, but he was such a good friend that I knew he meant well.

Although not convinced by Jonathan's words of warning, I began to worry. Jennifer was twelve years old and about to enter seventh grade. If there was any truth to what he said, then she might find it difficult to make friends at school. Patrick was just over a year old, so I didn't worry as much about him, though it could become an issue in a few years.

While teaching in Buffalo, I had become aware of how critical relationships among students at school were, especially in middle and high schools. If Jennifer was lonely at school because she couldn't make friends easily, her academic performance and psychological well-being might suffer. That was an issue I could not take lightly.

I decided against telling my family what I had been told about Wyomissing. I didn't want to alarm them to the point where they tried to discourage me from taking the job.

I knew it was selfish to withhold the information. However, the decision to move to Wyomissing was one I was better suited to make on behalf of the family. This was a movie I had seen before. The fear I'd confronted before going to the Soviet Union was much greater, yet I had been pleasantly surprised by my reception there. The reality might be no different in Wyomissing. It made no sense to throw away such a good opportunity on such flimsy evidence.

Moreover, I had visited Germany during each of the six years I spent in the Soviet Union. I recalled nothing unusual occurring in any of the German cities I visited. Most of the average Germans I met in stores, nightclubs, and other places could speak English, and I had many conversations there over the years. Those interactions had been mostly pleasant. I could not imagine that descendants of German immigrants in America would be hostile enough that a foreigner like me could not stand to live with them, as Jonathan seemed to suggest.

In addition to the Soviet experience, I had an even more recent one as a reference. A few days after I broke the news about my acceptance to Purdue to my colleagues in Buffalo, one of them—an African American woman who happened to be a good friend—told me privately that she didn't think Indiana would be a good place for me to move. The state was not racially diverse, and as a Black person I would find life there very difficult.

Although relatively new to America, I had heard enough about the ugliness of racism in some parts of the country to make me worry. Like Jonathan with regard to Berks County, and the Ghanaians who almost persuaded me to throw away the Soviet scholarship opportunity, my colleague had never lived in the Midwest. Nevertheless, because she was a native-born Black and surely knew more about race relations than anyone I had met in America until then, I thought it unwise to completely dismiss her advice. Another school I was considering was on the East Coast; she thought it would be a better fit for me.

As I agonized over that issue for a few days, I thought about life in the Soviet Union. It was unquestionably one of the least racially diverse places on earth when I lived there, but I had been able to cope very well. Indiana could not possibly be worse. And, the master's program would take only two years, so I wouldn't have to live there too long if things didn't turn out well.

A couple of weeks after our conversation about Indiana, my colleague asked me what I had decided. I told her I appreciated her advice and had given the matter considerable thought; however, I had decided to go to Purdue. It was where I really wanted to study so I would make whatever sacrifices necessary to get a degree from there. She didn't seem totally convinced, but she wished me well.

Apart from Chicago and a handful of other cities and large towns in the Midwest, what my colleague said about the Midwest not being racially diverse was correct. Although the population was indeed predominantly White, her fear—that a Black man would find life difficult there—turned out to be unfounded.

Over the entire seven-year period I studied and worked in Indiana, I experienced only one noteworthy incident clearly triggered by racial animosity. I had gone to pick up clothes from a dry cleaner in Lafayette one Saturday morning. I had only recently started taking my clothes there. When the attendant at the counter—a White woman—gave me the shirts, I noticed that one of them still had a stain, one that I had specifically pointed out when I dropped off the shirts. I politely asked the woman to have the shirt returned for the stain to be removed.

At most dry cleaners, this would not be a problem. However, the woman refused to have the shirt sent back. Before I could say another word, a White guy rushed out to the counter from the back of the room. He was the woman's husband, and he was visibly angry. Having made my point politely, I could not understand why he was so upset. He began yelling at me, using racial epithets. That didn't satisfy him, so he charged toward me as if intending to punch me. His wife, realizing that her husband could be in trouble with the law if he made physical contact with me, rushed to restrain him. Unbeknownst to me, another woman at the back of the room had already called the police.

Within minutes, an officer arrived at the scene. He asked me to step outside so that he could speak with the couple. Several minutes later, he came out to interview me. Based on what I told him, and what he had learned from the couple and the other woman inside, he had concluded that I had done nothing wrong. There had been no physical assault, so he could not charge the man. He advised me to walk away and simply take my business elsewhere. I had already come to that conclusion on my own.

I'll never know what prompted the man to behave in such a manner. Based on the racial epithets he used, he clearly harbored ill feelings toward people of color. The ugly incident left a bad taste in my mouth for several days afterward. However, it was an isolated one. In those seven years, I had tens of thousands of interactions with White people all over the Midwest with no problems of a similar nature. I could not use that one unpleasant incident to indict the White population in that entire region.

On the whole, I loved life in the Midwest. Most places were not densely populated. Having grown up in a small village, that suited me perfectly. I found the overwhelming majority of people, regardless of their race, to be polite, humble, and generous. I attended countless social and other events in various settings and always felt welcome. After seven wonderful years in the Midwest, it was difficult to say goodbye when it came time to leave for the MBA program in New Hampshire.

Given those two previous experiences, I was confident that things would turn out well in Wyomissing. I actually became curious, rather than fearful, as the time approached for us to leave Vermont. I was eager to find out whether the pattern would repeat in Wyomissing.

It wasn't long before I had my answer.

* * *

WYOMISSING IS A SMALL TOWN just outside of Reading, Pennsylvania. Patricia got a job at the Reading Hospital and Medical Center and started work soon after our relocation. I began my job at UGI the same week. The hospital had a good day care center for Patrick. A few weeks later, Jennifer started seventh grade at the Junior-Senior High School, only a few yards away from the apartment complex where we lived.

In those first few weeks, I got the impression that Wyomissing was a good place for a family like ours to live and work. Both Patricia and I had short commutes, and on the surface, the town appeared safe. That impression did not change by the end of our first year, so we bought a house less than a mile from the high school.

I thought about my father constantly the day we moved in. The standard four-bedroom, two-bathroom house in a nice neighborhood would have pleased him no end. Growing up, I could never have imagined living in such a grand place. I was quite happy, but also sad as I thought about my father and his unfulfilled dreams.

The population of Wyomissing is predominantly White. Of the town's approximately ten thousand residents, almost ninety percent are White. We are presently the only Black family in our neighborhood. Within the first couple of days after we moved in, two couples—neighbors from next-door and across the street—came over to welcome us. They brought house-warming presents, gave us their contact information, and asked us to reach out if we needed any help.

Another family across the street had a swimming pool. Their daughter, who was two years older than Jennifer, was also a student at the high school. The parents invited Jennifer to swim in their pool soon after we moved to the neighborhood. Afterwards, they told her that she was welcome to come over and swim whenever she wanted.

In the little over ten years since I'd immigrated to America, I had always lived in rental apartments. This was my first house, and the first time anyone had given me a house-warming present. Even more unexpected were those parents who knew almost nothing about us but felt comfortable enough to invite Jennifer into their home. I was so pleasantly surprised by the kind gestures of those three neighbors that I decided to use them as a teaching moment for my family.

I had not told Patricia and Jennifer about my debilitating fears prior to leaving for the Soviet Union, and how close I had come to giving up that opportunity. Nor had I told them about my colleague's attempt to discourage me from going to Indiana. Throughout our first year in Wyomissing, I had also never shared Jonathan's warning about the people in that city. I realized that Jennifer, being at that formative age, would particularly benefit from those lessons I had learned in both the Soviet Union and the U.S. Midwest about not making important personal decisions based on the expressed views of others.

Our collective experiences in Wyomissing during that first year had been positive. My family enjoyed life in this town. Patricia and I both liked our work and our colleagues. Jennifer had made a good number of friends at school in a relatively brief period. Whenever we dropped off Patrick at day care, the teachers and other parents we met were friendly. There simply wasn't much for us to complain about.

"There's something I have to tell you," I said to Patricia and Jennifer one Sunday morning.

"What is it?" Patricia asked, concerned.

"It's nothing bad," I assured them. "When we were about to leave Vermont to come here, a friend of mine strongly discouraged me from bringing my family to Berks County because he thought the people were hostile toward foreigners." Then I recounted my conversation with Jonathan.

"Why did he say that?" Patricia asked. "The people here are quite friendly."

"The man has never lived here, but he had heard negative things about the people in this area from other sources," I explained.

"I like it here, so it's a good thing you didn't listen," Jennifer interjected.

I continued, "I chose not to tell you in Vermont, because I was afraid you'd be so worried that you'd want us to look for somewhere else to move to."

"That was a good decision," Patricia said. "We certainly would have been worried."

I went on to tell them about the warnings I'd received about the Soviet Union and the Midwest. Even though they had never been to the Soviet Union, they had, over time, listened to my many stories about the place, and about the Midwest. They knew my experiences had been overwhelmingly positive.

"That's so terrible that people make up things about other people like that," Jennifer said after I finished speaking.

"It absolutely is," I said. "Let these stories serve as lessons for you. Don't believe everything people tell you."

"I'll keep that in mind," she said, giving me the reaction I was looking for.

We have lived in this neighborhood in Wyomissing for eighteen years now. Apart from three families that have moved away during that time, with three new families moving in, all the people we first met still live here, and we have gotten to know them quite well. Many families have invited us to their homes for Christmas, birthdays, graduation parties, and other social events over the years. In turn, our invitations have always been readily accepted, and we have welcomed many of the neighbors into our home for similar social events.

Thus far, I have never heard anyone in any social gathering discuss ancestry, so I am not quite sure who has German, Irish, Greek, or some other lineage. Sometimes last names offer clues, but what I have found is that, generally, people in the neighborhood don't pay much attention to who is what. People here look out for each other and are always ready to offer help when needed.

Our experiences in the broader Wyomissing community and beyond in Berks County have similarly been positive. The population in Berks County as a whole is a little more racially diverse than that of Wyomissing. We have gotten to know some Black, Hispanic, and other non-White families quite well and, thus far, we have not heard any complaints that would indicate the presence of significant levels of racial disharmony in the county.

What has pleased me the most since we moved to Wyomissing is the relationship Patrick developed with his friends. Because he was only a year old when we sent him to the Reading Hospital Day Care, where almost all the children happened to be White, and he went to elementary, middle, and high schools with many of those children, almost all his friends in Wyomissing are White. As I watched him interact with them—playing, going for bicycle rides and to the movies, arranging play dates and sleepovers with them, year after year, I have been struck by how colorblind he and his friends are. For them, the difference in skin color is a non-issue. That, in turn, has made it easy for them to relate to one another in ways that adults of different races seem to find difficult.

* * *

FROM MY OBSERVATIONS OF PATRICK's relationships with his friends, and taking into account the nature of my family's relationships with our neighbors, I have lately begun to think differently about the issue of race relations in America. Racism is alive and well in some parts of the country. However, there are also many hopeful signs that some of the progress American society has made to address the issue will endure. It is important to recognize those positive signs. Equally important, in my view, is the way conversations about race are framed.

Too much of the talk about racism in America tends to be on a strictly Black-and-White basis. I have heard many White people lament that they are too often painted with a broad brush and labeled as racist by Blacks, even though they are not. Like most people of color in America, I have experienced subtle forms of racism such as being carefully watched and followed in stores, or sometimes being ignored by salespeople in upscale stores who don't think I qualify to shop there. I know how awful it is to be judged solely on the color of one's skin. For that reason, I am particularly careful when I talk about White racism in any setting nowadays.

Following the recent spate of shooting deaths of Black men by White policemen, I have heard many Black parents say that they fear for the safety of their sons and feel compelled to talk to them about how to navigate what they consider a racist society. In particular, such parents want to talk to their children about how to conduct themselves in encounters with the police.

Considering the shooting cases in question, these reactions are understandable. Having that conversation is an unpleasant prospect, however, for any parent. But it was a subject I had to broach when Patrick turned sixteen and started learning to drive.

I thought long and hard about how to frame the conversation about his responsibilities as a driver. My dilemma was whether to focus on the routine obligations all motorists have—regardless of their race, gender, or age—to respond appropriately to the police when stopped, or to go beyond and talk about the racial factor. I was deeply torn. In the end, I broadened the conversation to include the subject of insidious racism, given the sheltered life Patrick had lived until then.

I certainly would not have needed to contemplate such a conversation if my family and I lived in Ghana. Although we have our own tribal tensions there, the racial factor underlying these ugly incidents between the police and Black men—in particular—in America is not an issue in Ghana due to the country's racial homogeneity.

Unlike in the corporate world, where it is a business imperative for people of all races to coexist amicably, my White neighbors in Wyomissing have no obligation to be welcoming. They don't have to invite me and my family to Christmas parties and other social gatherings, but they do; they didn't have to bring us vegetables from their gardens, but they did; they didn't have to welcome my son and daughter into their homes, but they did; and nothing compels them to be so kind to us in numerous other ways, but they have been.

I am cognizant of the fact that my level of education and my profession greatly influence my neighbors' perceptions of me and my family. If I were less educated and didn't have the professional job I have, I probably wouldn't be living in this neighborhood to begin with. The Wyomissing police I pass on my way to work and other places operate quite differently from those in urban areas, given the suburban-urban environmental differences.

My family and I are thus far removed from some of the urban-area environmental conditions that generate the ugly race-related incidents we read and hear about almost daily. That recognition causes me to exercise caution in the way I think and speak about race relations in America. It does not, however, diminish in any way the positive impression our neighbors have made on me—and my family. They are, in our view, genuinely good people who have gone out of their way to make us feel welcome.

As illogical as it may sound, I now believe that sometimes it pays not to have other options. I was extremely fortunate that when I had to make the difficult decision to leave Ghana for the Soviet Union, it was my only option. Given how I felt then, I most certainly would have chosen any available alternative, no matter how bad. I would not trade the totality of the fantastic experiences I had in the Soviet Union during that historic period for anything—perhaps not even a university degree from Oxford or Cambridge.

Unlike leaving Ghana for the Soviet Union, going to Indiana from Buffalo was not my only option. I had been accepted to a few other schools on the East Coast and could have easily chosen one of them instead. Any other choice, however, would have been inferior to Purdue. Without my experience in the Soviet Union, and the valuable lessons I learned from living with Dmitry, I might have lacked the courage to move to Indiana. That would have meant denying myself a great opportunity to study at a world-renowned university with exactly the type of electrical engineering program I was looking for.

If I had made the wrong decisions in those two instances, I would have borne the negative consequences alone. That was not the case with the job offer in Wyomissing. My decision had the potential to affect the rest of my family negatively.

Based on our cumulative experiences over the past eighteen years, I can say with confidence that Wyomissing is among the very best places to live in the entire country. It has one of the top-rated school systems in the state of Pennsylvania, and indeed in the country. The safe environment, the good school system, and the welcoming nature of our neighbors gave Jennifer and Patrick the opportunity to grow up in the best circumstances any parents could want for their children.

Most of my Tuck classmates are shocked when they find out that I
still work for the company I joined immediately after graduation. At our
ten-year reunion on campus in 2013, I found out that quite a few of them
had changed jobs three or four times already. I'm not sure what they will
think when we meet at the twenty-year reunion next year and they find out
I am still at UGI. The fact is, I like working there, and I absolutely love
Wyomissing. I see no justifiable reason to go elsewhere.

Given how I grew up in Ghana, I probably should have been wiser.
Even though Ghanaians are generally a tolerant people, I had, during most
of my childhood years, heard many negative and blanket statements made
by various people about entire tribal groups. There are many tribes in
Ghana—the dominant one being Akan, to which I belong. Each tribe has
its own dialect and cultural norms. The dialects are so different that often
a person from one tribe cannot communicate with someone from another,
unless they both know a common language, such as English.

Ghana is a predominantly Christian nation, but it also has a sizable
Muslim population, as well as small minorities of people who practice other
religions. Although the various tribal and religious groups in Ghana have
coexisted peacefully in the decades since independence, there have always
been stereotypes that tend to highlight some perceived undesirable traits
associated with people from certain tribes.

My best friends in elementary and middle schools happened to be
children from some of the minority tribal and religious groups that were
often maligned. I played with them frequently and knew their families well.
To me, they were not any different from the other families and children in
the village. They were humble, hardworking, honest, and generous—more
so, in my view, than many I knew from the majority tribe. That exposure
should have been enough to make me understand, even at an early age, that
I should not take anything said about other people at face value and make
critical decisions on that basis.

My parents were open-minded people with no evident tribal or other
biases. They rarely said anything bad about other people at home. It seemed
as if everyone in the village, regardless of tribal or religious background,
was my father's friend. My mother, who was a devout Christian, similarly
got along well with everyone. Clearly, that positive home environment had
not been enough to properly influence my thinking while I was making the
decision whether to go to the Soviet Union.

It took living with Dmitry in close quarters for an entire year for
me to become properly educated in the art of judgment formation about

other people and places. I am extremely blessed to have been given that opportunity. It taught me that problems such as racism, tribalism, xenophobia, and religious intolerance, which have always been prevalent in many societies, persist because most people cannot or will not get close enough to those they mistrust to get to know them better.

In my case, I had no choice. The vast majority see little to lose by choosing to keep a distance when faced with the "other."

When I look back on my life, what scares me most is that I would never have known what—and how much—I might have lost by making a different choice in each of those three instances.

CHAPTER 15

How to Be Lucky in Life

FOR MUCH OF MY CHILDHOOD in Ghana, I had poor self-esteem. I am not entirely sure where that feeling of inferiority originated. I had always been shy, but in elementary and middle schools I was not as easily intimidated, because everyone in the village was poor. That changed when I went to secondary school.

There were no specific experiences I can point to as the source of my inferiority complex. The students from Accra and some of the other larger towns just seemed happier and more confident. As an unsophisticated person from a poor village, I could not easily socialize with the vast majority of students. Those students in turn kept to their own social groups, and that sense of isolation fueled my insecurity.

Ghanaian society has always been hierarchical. When I was growing up, high levels of poverty and equally high levels of illiteracy exacerbated the country's class divisions. My parents were not only illiterate but also extremely poor, which put me in the bottom class of Ghanaian society.

In the several-month period after I suffered the terrible disappointment of losing my opportunity to attend Achimota Secondary School due to my family's poverty, whatever little self-confidence I possessed seemed to vanish. The other children I had met on the day of the interview appeared well fed and without a care in the world. I surmised that they were a different, better breed of human beings, and if that was indeed the case, there was no point in trying to play on the same field as them. I would have to find my rightful place in society, wherever it was, and do the best I could in that environment.

That lingering insecurity led me to do something that I have deeply regretted. One Saturday morning, during my time as a student at Achimota, I was in my room when a student came to inform me I had a visitor waiting in the lounge.

"Are you sure it's me the person is looking for?" I asked.

"Yes, he mentioned your name," he replied.

No one had ever visited me at Achimota, and I wasn't expecting anyone.

"Hello, Osei, it's great to see you!" my father said excitedly.

What's he doing here? I wondered nervously.

"Hello, Papa, I'm happy to see you as well. What brings you here?"

"I came to Accra to visit Daniel and Ebenezer, and thought I'd stop by and say a quick hello. I also thought you could show me the Achimota campus that your middle school teachers said so much about."

As he spoke, I grew increasingly nervous. What would my dormitory mates think when they saw him? My father wore traditional men's attire—a large piece of cloth, six yards long by two yards wide, wrapped around his body and draped over his left shoulder. On his feet were traditional men's sandals, a type of flip-flops made from local materials. Attired this way, he seemed completely out of place on that campus. I was certain no one had set foot on that campus in that type of traditional garb in the entire history of the school.

The fathers and male relatives of Achimota students who visited the campus were always either in suits or dress shirts and nice slacks, with dress shoes. To hide my poverty, I had kept a low profile ever since arriving on campus. Most students had multiple uniforms, so they could afford to change clothes daily. I had one set that I washed after school on Wednesdays and ironed on Thursday mornings to wear for the remainder of the week. On the surface, I looked like everyone else. And, because I had never said much about my family, no one knew how poor we were.

"Let's step outside," I said to my father. "I'll show you a couple of places and then I'll take you to where you can catch a taxi to Accra."

He hesitated for a second before following me. He seemed to expect a tour of the dormitory, but I needed to take him outside quickly before other students saw him. I was afraid that my true identity would be revealed if they saw my father. "Fortunately" for me, most students were still asleep on that weekend morning so only a couple of early risers saw us. The "damage" was thus limited.

I pointed out a few places to my father as we walked rather hurriedly toward the taxi stop.

"Unfortunately, I have a lot of homework this weekend, so I have to get back to the dormitory," I said as we came to the stop.

"I'm happy that I had the chance to see you, and a bit of the campus," he said as he entered the taxi.

I could see his disappointment. He hadn't seen as much as he wanted. By ushering him off the campus quickly, I'd denied him the chance to see the East Campus, which was the nicer part.

Years later, I realized the sheer stupidity of my actions on that day. I was ashamed to be seen with the very person who had made it possible for me to be on that elite campus. It is one of my biggest and lasting regrets.

My feelings of inferiority persisted well into adulthood. Only recently did I conquer it, and that process occurred gradually over time. Maturity, prolonged exposure to diverse cultures and ideas over many years, and hearing and reading about other people's struggles all helped me think differently about myself.

I have learned that one of the most important ingredients for success in life is self-confidence. In raising my two children, I have done my best to share the many lessons I have learned over the years about the issue of self-worth. I have encouraged them to pursue their goals and dreams rather than focus on perceived disadvantages.

In theory, all human beings come into this world on equal footing. We are all born with certain innate talents we must learn to access. Different people are born with different talents, but each person, at the very least, has something of value to harness. It could be argued that every child is given some opportunity to succeed in life. Having the means to seize that opportunity is a different matter altogether.

The sad reality is that the ability of some children to make productive use of their innate talents is constrained by external factors. Which part of the world a child is born in matters a great deal. For example, because there were no markets in Ghana for the talents of many of my classmates in Boadua, not every child had an equal opportunity to excel, especially in the fields of sports or entertainment. Children born in desperately poor or war-torn countries do not have the same educational opportunities, access to healthcare, and good nutrition that those born in richer, peaceful countries do. In some war-torn countries, education systems collapse completely for lengthy periods of time, depriving entire generations of a formal education.

In America and much of the developed world, the concept of "Equality of Opportunity" has been widely discussed as part of the broader debate about widening income inequality. The concept means different things to different people, depending on their ideological leanings. According to Peter Weston, a philosopher at Stanford University, opportunity is a three-way relationship between a person, some obstacles, and a desired goal. Something cannot be called an opportunity if the obstacles are insurmountable.

In that sense, I had an opportunity to gain admission to Achimota when I decided to apply to the school. My desired goal was the same as that of the kids from wealthy families. As applicants, we all had to overcome obstacles, although mine were vastly different from theirs. For me, the obstacles in many ways were not insurmountable. I was not disqualified from applying based on tribal affiliation, socio-economic background, or some other characteristic. I was competing against academic superstars, but the rules of the competition were fairly designed and evenly applied, so I at least had a chance to win one of the prizes. Ultimately, however, my opportunity turned out to be unequal because other factors came into play, which made it impossible for me to achieve my goal at first.

"Equality of Outcome" is another concept often discussed alongside equal opportunity. Some argue that there cannot be equality of opportunity without ensuring some measure of equality of outcome. In a 2011 *New York Times* article, economist Paul Krugman wrote that "[American] society does not, in fact, produce anything like equal opportunity (in part because it produces such unequal outcomes)." He argued in favor of transferring some income from the wealthy to the less fortunate. Krugman acknowledged that inequality of opportunity is not the only reason for inequality of outcomes. How much reward people receive for their work also depends on factors such as the degree of effort an individual or group puts in, as well as variations in talent.

Whenever Olympic gold medalist Usain Bolt took the field against his fellow runners in sprint races, the outcome was rarely equal, although the starting point and rules were the same for everyone. He simply had more ability than anyone else, so no one could argue with the outcomes. The superstars on an expensively assembled soccer team actually have to enter a game prepared to put in the effort required to win. If they fail to do so and lose to an average team with players who are less skilled but willing to work harder on the field, then the star players on the losing team have no one to blame but themselves.

I spent too many years worrying incessantly and unnecessarily about my self-worth. What I have ultimately learned, through careful observation of how the world works, is that life's playing field is not—and will never be—

level, and that many factors combine to keep it so. More importantly, I have learned that many of those factors have nothing to do with me as a person.

Luck is a critically important determinant of success in life. It can also be elusive—a point eloquently made by best-selling author Michael Lewis in his 2012 commencement speech at Princeton University. Lewis spoke about how he had graduated from the university thirty years earlier, unsure of what to do with his degree in art history—a major not highly valued in the job market. What he wanted most was to write for a living, but he did not have the standing to write about anything. He went to graduate school instead.

His big break came when, at a dinner one night, he sat next to the wife of a senior executive from Salomon Brothers, then a giant Wall Street investment bank. In Lewis' words, the woman "more or less forced her husband to give me a job at the bank." There, he was randomly assigned to a role that quickly made him the bank's expert on financial derivatives. That department, coincidentally, happened to be where all the action was. Before long, he was being paid hundreds of thousands of dollars to give advice on derivatives to professional investors. That expertise was what gave him the standing to write *Liar's Poker*, the book that made him the famous author he is today.

Lewis told that story to illustrate the importance luck plays in people's lives. Not many people get the chance to earn degrees from Princeton, so he had already been lucky at least once. Even then, it took that random seating assignment at that particular dinner for him to get the break that ultimately led him to where he really wanted to be in life. Without that lucky break, he could well have spent the rest of his days doing something he wasn't passionate about. That, in fact, is the fate that awaits most people.

I can't think of anything that should have suggested, when Francis and I were classmates in middle school, that I would one day have the chance to travel around the world, get all the education and experiences I have had, and live the life I have now, while he would be forever consigned to a life of poverty in the village where he was born. It is true that Francis could have joined me in taking the *common entrance* again during that last year of middle school. He declined, knowing his family could not afford to pay for his education. He quit playing before the referee's final whistle blew. I took the test again, despite my disappointment a year earlier, even though without the sheer luck of the cocoa farmer's scholarship, my top scores would have made no difference. Perhaps a scholarship could have been found for Francis, but perhaps not. Perhaps the experience would simply have broken his heart. Luck has played a serious part at every crossroads in my life. I cannot in good conscience look in any mirror and credit myself entirely for the things I have been able to do.

Ultimately, I was lucky to escape the village and go on to further my education. Sadly, no such opportunity presented itself for Francis. He has remained in Boadua all his life. With only a middle school education, his employment options are limited. With his wife and child, earning a sporadic income from occasional low-paying jobs, he is not much different from the millions of desperately poor Africans we see almost daily on our television screens in the Western world.

I have stayed in touch with Francis ever since I left Boadua forty-seven years ago. Whenever I return to Ghana for a visit and make it to Boadua, I hang out with him as much as I can. I wish I could have done more for him. The best I've been able to do is offer him periodic financial assistance, which he has always appreciated. He knows I have traveled the world and been fortunate to obtain advanced-level education from places that we could not have imagined in middle school.

My worldview has been, and forever will be, informed by how Francis' life has unfolded. Because of him, I am never quick to judge people at the bottom of the socio-economic ladder. With my naked eye, I can never tell who is poor and desperate because of bad life choices, and who is in that situation because, like Francis, despite doing everything asked of them, they were inhibited by too many factors beyond their control.

In most societies, downtrodden people are not given the same respect as those higher up on the socio-economic ladder. That is an unfortunate fact of life. Francis has probably been disrespected many times solely because he is poor. I sincerely hope that he has never, in those instances, been made to feel that his life is worth less than anyone else's.

Francis is often on my mind. He continues to read the newspaper to this day. He is one of those people who enjoys learning for learning's sake. He has remained the same disciplined person I knew in elementary and middle school and is always there to lend a hand to whoever needs it. To say that life has been unfair to a person of such upright character is a massive understatement.

"I really wish I could further my studies," Francis said to me one day.

It had been fifteen years since we left middle school, and I had returned to Ghana from the Soviet Union for a visit. Seeing how far education had taken me, Francis had realized how his own life might have been changed for the better. My heart sank.

"I wish I could help, but there's nothing I can do now to make it happen," I said regretfully.

As a scholarship student, I was incapable of providing the financial assistance he would need; moreover, he was too old for secondary school, and I wasn't sure what his other options would be. Although he hasn't brought up that issue again in my recent interactions with him, he will probably carry that regret his whole life.

Often, thinking of Francis, I have an intensely sad feeling that I believe to be a form of survivor's syndrome. He was by far the better student, and I cannot seem to get over the fact that such a brilliant person of such fine character could end up in his current situation.

Sometimes we have to make our own luck. On the surface, there was no path out of the remote village where we grew up. That accepted truth discouraged Francis from looking beyond middle school. Somehow I could not shake the burning desire to make it to places where, clearly, I did not belong. Pure blind faith led me to these once-unimaginable achievements.

I am extremely fortunate that those deep feelings of inferiority I harbored during my childhood and early adult years did not become a paralyzing force. Throughout that time, I somehow woke up each day, went wherever I needed to go, did the best I could with whatever tools I had, and let life take care of itself.

I allowed myself to be lucky.

EPILOGUE

Final Thoughts

TOWARD THE END OF MY secondary school years in Ghana, I noticed
a change in the attitude of some of my teachers. The teachers I had in
elementary and middle schools, as well as in the earlier years of secondary
school, had been dedicated people who arrived on time every day.
Collectively, their sole mission, as everyone in the country knew, was
to educate their students to be the best they could be. They set very high
standards that they expected every student to make the maximum effort to
meet.

When I was growing up in the 1960s and '70s, almost all the primary
and middle schools in Ghana were public institutions that did not charge
fees. There were only two or three private ones in the entire country. The
three universities Ghana had at the time were also public and tuition-free.
For some strange reason I never understood, students had to pay to attend
secondary school. This is what shut the door to advanced education for
thousands of village children like Francis, and those elsewhere from poor
families.

There was no such thing as after-school classes anywhere in Ghana,
as far as I knew, until a couple of my secondary-school teachers started
offering them. When they taught their regular classes during the school day,
they showed less diligence. As a result, they often did not get through all the
material. The after-school classes were meant to teach students the material
not covered during the school day. Those sessions were only available to
those who could pay the extra fees. My scholarship did not cover such non-
traditional classes.

Over time, these after-school tutoring sessions became a common feature in other top-tier secondary schools. Students who could not pay the fees fell behind. To make matters worse, these were difficult subjects—math and science—where a teacher was required. Effectively, students from poor families like mine had become a disadvantaged minority group within school environments that had previously been without any form of segregation. It was a classic case of economic inequality.

For many years after I left secondary school, I struggled to understand why that change occurred, and how the teachers involved got away with what they did. Although they pocketed the fees, they were conducting their after-school sessions in regular classrooms, using the teaching materials and resources available in those rooms. In essence, they were using public resources for private gain. My understanding is that school administrators knew what was going on but chose to do nothing about it. Clearly, it shouldn't have been allowed.

Although I left Ghana nearly four decades ago, I follow developments there closely because most of my siblings, nieces, and nephews still live there. I also make periodic visits, which allow me to see firsthand some of the social, economic, and cultural changes that have taken place in the country since I left. I now believe I have identified what caused the change in those teachers' attitudes. It seems to have been triggered by an alteration in the country's social complexion.

Ghana, formerly known as the Gold Coast, was a British colony from the mid nineteenth century until 1957, when it gained its independence. Kwame Nkrumah, who led the struggle for independence, became the country's first prime minister, and later, its first president.

When I started elementary school, Ghana had been an independent nation for only eight years. The national sense of patriotism was still strong. We proudly sang the national anthem in school each morning. In civics classes, we learned about the important responsibilities each of us had as citizens. Every indication was that the entire nation was working toward the common goal of helping to lay the strong foundations required for sustainable socio-economic development. Under Nkrumah's capable leadership in those early years, some of those basic foundations were created, and the country seemed to be headed in the right direction.

The national mood began to change for the worse shortly thereafter. Political divisions within the country, caused by a struggle between two factions that emerged almost immediately after independence, triggered the mood swing. One of the factions, led by Nkrumah, appeared to favor a socialist model. Nkrumah and the other leaders of his faction were accused by leaders of the other faction, which was pro-Western, of aligning themselves too closely with the Soviet Union. The pro-Western group feared that, if left unchecked, Nkrumah would ultimately turn the country into a communist dictatorship.

Those political divisions wound up splitting the country's population. The tensions were exacerbated by the overthrow of Nkrumah's regime in a military coup in 1966. That military government turned over power to a new civilian government in 1969, which was itself overthrown in another military coup in 1972. In the three-decade period after that, the country was ruled by a series of alternating military and civilian governments.

Amidst all that back and forth, Ghana seemed to lose its way. Much of the foundation built initially all but collapsed. Roads, ports, and water and electricity supply systems fell into disrepair. Schools, hospitals, and other soft infrastructure similarly began to collapse and, after a while, barely functioned. With government services increasingly nonexistent, ordinary citizens were forced to look elsewhere for solutions. Each individual family searched for private remedies to what were otherwise public problems.

Before then, Ghana's economy was almost entirely agrarian. The country's population was uniformly poor, so when I was growing up, there was little economic inequality. The overwhelming majority of Ghanaian children received basic education in public schools, people sought the healthcare they needed from government-run hospitals, and the police provided basic security services that kept the population safe. Life in the country was generally simple, but people seemed content to just get by.

Few Ghanaians had ever traveled overseas in those early years, and most people had no idea what life was like in other parts of the world. As government services continued to dwindle and families could not afford to pay for their basic needs, emigration became the next logical choice. People in Ghana had practically no avenues for earning enough income to sustain themselves and their families.

Emigration was a slow trickle initially because few could afford to pay for travel overseas. The first emigrants were mostly from Accra and other big towns where the few formal sector jobs paid well enough to cover travel expenses. In small towns and villages, it was rare to meet anyone who had traveled overseas. Initially, most emigrants went to Western European countries, but later people began to travel to far-flung places such as the U.S., Canada, and Australia.

There is one major difference between people who emigrate from Africa and those who do so from Europe and elsewhere. The typical African is born into a large family and usually has a strong extended family. African emigrants typically do not leave their countries permanently because they cannot afford to take their large families with them. Often, one family member is sent overseas to find employment so that they can send remittances to those left behind. Those strong family ties eventually pull most emigrants back home, after they have made enough money to take care of themselves and their families upon their return.

European immigrants to America do not generally have extended family networks and are often able to bring along their entire core families. For them, that pull factor is practically nonexistent. Their immigration therefore tends to be permanent.

When some of those first Ghanaian emigrants returned home, they not only helped their families financially but also imported their acquired tastes. They built houses fancier than anything the typical Ghanaian had ever seen. Initially, few Ghanaians owned vehicles, but as those people returned from overseas, many also brought along flashy cars. It didn't take long for the general population to realize that living the good life meant sending at least one family member overseas. What began as a trickle soon turned into a flood of people desperate to emigrate.

Even after all these years, it is difficult to emigrate from most parts of Africa. Not only is it expensive, but it is also not easy to get the required visas. Over time, those unable to emigrate turn to other means of finding the resources they need to pay for basic services. Bribery and corruption have always been a problem on the continent, but it has intensified since that gradual change in the complexion of Ghanaian society began.

This is why some of my teachers in secondary school were driven to change their attitude toward their work. Although they were among the lucky few to be formally employed, their salaries were no longer enough to get by. Ultimately, a few had decided that forcing their students into those private after-school classes was their only means of earning extra income. Despite putting the future well-being of their poorer students at risk, those teachers felt compelled to think of themselves and their families first.

* * *

COMING BACK TO THE ROLE luck plays in life outcomes, the timing of my birth turns out to have been extremely important. In Ghana, public elementary and middle schools currently exist in name only. They are so bad that few families send their children there. Even in remote villages, private schools have sprung up everywhere, and those are what most families patronize. All of them charge fees. While I was growing up, my family was so poor that we rarely had enough food to eat. If the education system then had been the way it is now, my parents would not have had the money to pay for even a basic education.

Children growing up in Boadua today in circumstances similar to mine have no better chance of succeeding in life compared to Black children born in urban American settings. I did feel I was better off in my youth than those students in Buffalo.

Because there is no such thing as government-provided school vouchers in Ghana, any child whose parents cannot afford to pay school fees is out of luck. For thousands of children in Ghana today, that is the case. Many are in schools where teachers don't bother to show up to teach them. The small amount of money the government allocates to those dysfunctional schools often gets stolen or mismanaged, and because the institutions that would ordinarily oversee accountability are weak or nonexistent, there appears to be little hope on the horizon for a poor child born in a Ghanaian village today.

Warren Buffett, the legendary American investor, is fond of saying that a child born in today's America is the luckiest in the world. Not everyone agrees. Some argue that, based on global indices that measure things such as life expectancy, happiness, and general satisfaction with life, Scandinavians, and citizens of other countries such as Switzerland and Australia are actually better off than their U.S. counterparts.

My own view is that Buffett makes a persuasive case. The strength of America's political and economic institutions is unparalleled, allowing the vast majority of the country's citizens to make use of their innate talents and therefore have decent standards of living. The systemic dysfunction that exists in Ghana today, which robs large sections of the population of the ability to rise above their dire living conditions, can largely be blamed on the absence of strong institutions. That is also the case in many developing nations.

United States citizens are blessed with political and economic institutions that empower them to have a say in how they are governed. U.S. politicians are held accountable by citizens and institutions. There is corruption in America, but politicians here cannot act with the same level of impunity I have observed in Africa and elsewhere. American institutions safeguard the integrity of financial, legal, and other governance systems and ensure civil, property, and other rights protections, thereby giving American citizens the peace of mind to make maximum use of their creative talents. The entire nation benefits as a result.

In my view, all Americans, regardless of their identity, should be thankful for their imperfect but functional socio-economic system. It is also a system that must be handled with care. If anything were to happen to cause the country's institutions to fail, there is no guarantee they could be fully restored. It cannot be taken for granted that the type of leadership that helped to build the system will be found again. That institutional failure, which would inevitably lead to a breakdown of law and order, would harm everyone, not just people of a particular race or socio-economic group.

* * *

IN DEALING WITH LIFE'S MANY challenges, the ability to put things into proper perspective is always helpful. Blacks like me who immigrate to America often arrive with very little money. Because of that, initially, we can afford to reside only in the same poor neighborhoods where a majority of African Americans live. There, we are confronted with many of the same problems associated with race that plague American-born Blacks.

However, because many of us left behind much worse conditions, we take a more pragmatic view of life here and try to make maximum use of any opportunities we can find. In doing so, many Black immigrants are able to make the leap into the middle—and sometimes upper—classes in America. We eventually move into better neighborhoods with better schools for our children who quite often go on to do even better than we did.

It is important to take a close look at what enables us to make the transition. Our sense that "things could be a lot worse" is always with us. It helps to keep us focused on our missions as we navigate the difficult terrain in an unfamiliar country and culture.

Most of us agree that African Americans carry a heavy psychological burden as a result of slavery and its legacy, as well as the persistent racial discrimination they face in American society. People who have been made to feel like lesser human beings relative to their fellow citizens from other racial groups since birth will naturally have an inferiority complex. African immigrants, on the contrary, do not have that psychological burden. Although there is tribalism on the continent, the racial homogeneity of Africa prevents that deep-seated feeling of inferiority within any ethnic group. Africans can therefore be seen as having a superiority complex compared to their African American cousins.

That is not to say that African immigrants carry no psychological burdens of their own. Living in crushing poverty, under highly corrupt and sometimes brutal dictatorships that deprive citizens of the most basic rights Americans take for granted, has been the norm in many parts of Africa for decades. Environments such as those do not nurture a superiority complex.

Children like Antoine and Jamal who grow up in poor urban areas should take some comfort in the knowledge that basic structures exist in most places in America for poor children to get a decent basic education. Even in the poorest school districts, students have access to textbooks and libraries. Most American K-12 schools provide free or subsidized lunches to students from families that qualify. Poor children, except in rare cases, generally have access to electric light to study after dark. If families are too poor to pay for utilities, many states offer discount programs.

Those basic structures exist because America's political system largely works, and the institutions that manage the affairs of the country fulfill their responsibilities effectively. Unlike in dysfunctional African countries— where education, healthcare, and security services have largely been privatized—in America, governments continue to provide those services. They can do this because of one of the most important institutions in the country, the Internal Revenue Service (IRS), which collects the tax revenues the federal government relies on to provide the myriad services that benefit everyone.

The poor certainly don't have the same comfortable lives the rich do, but through the tax system, America's upper and middle classes contribute to make the life of a poor American a lot more bearable than in places like Africa. The poor in America have access to many of the same beautiful highways rich people drive on. There are federally funded agencies, such as the Food and Drug Administration (FDA) and Environmental Protection Agency (EPA), which work to ensure that the foods and medicines Americans consume are safe and the air they breathe and the water they drink are clean. Because the administrative and judicial systems both work well, the funds allocated to schools in impoverished areas make it to their intended recipients. Most important, the protection the federal government provides against foreign aggression benefits all American citizens.

In theory, many African countries have tax systems similar to America's that fund government operations. These systems don't work nearly as well, for three main reasons.

First, the tax base in the typical African country is small, so not much is collected. Unlike in America, there are almost no corporations and other sizable private businesses to tax. Most Africans work in the informal sectors, and because of poor record-keeping, finding and taxing such people is nearly impossible.

Second, tax-collection systems in Africa are woefully ineffective. Civil servants in Africa don't apply themselves as their American counterparts do. There is little discipline and accountability nowadays at the top levels of government, so it is not surprising that lower-level bureaucrats bring negative attitudes to their workplaces.

Third, there is the familiar problem of theft. Much of whatever little is collected is stolen or misused.

* * *

SOCIO-ECONOMIC CONDITIONS ARE MUCH BETTER now for a good number of Ghanaians, compared to when I was growing up. That improvement, however, came at a great cost to other Ghanaians. The social landscape has become so severely distorted that for some children it is now all but impossible to escape the poverty they are born into. That is not necessarily the case in America. Would my improbable escape from the desolate environment I was born into have been possible if instead of being born in rural Ghana, I was born poor in today's urban America? I have contemplated this question frequently over the past two decades. Rather than being born now into the same family circumstances as in Boadua, I would certainly prefer to be born anywhere in this country.

All along I took more credit than I deserved for the good things that happened in my life. I came to this realization only recently.

My being the only one of approximately sixty children in my Ghanaian village middle school class to manage to go on to secondary school shows how unusual it is for any child in that environment to come as far as I have. I certainly worked exceptionally hard and made numerous sacrifices along the way. But other factors beyond my control played a critical role.

I struggled for years to understand why none of my classmates even considered taking the secondary school entrance examination. Their parents were poor, but mine were poorer. What made the difference for me was that my father looked at the world differently. The subliminal messages he sent, through incredible work ethic and optimism, encouraged me to take the initiative that ultimately got me out of the village. Without knowing it, I had a powerful role model.

A positive role model is what many of the students I taught in Buffalo lacked. The fatalistic culture that ruined the lives of so many of my classmates in Boadua is present in many minority communities in America.

Adults in those communities do indeed face monumental challenges in their daily lives, and those struggles can negatively impact anyone's ability to serve as a role model. Although external factors are mostly to blame for the deplorable living conditions in minority communities, the abdication of parental responsibility to motivate also contributes immensely to the perpetuation of the cycle of poverty.

The breakdown of traditional family structure bears substantial responsibility for the dysfunction in the nation's inner-city public schools. Increasingly large numbers of children are being raised in single-parent homes. And, in the case of Black children, fathers are often absent from their lives. The consequences can be tragic.

I wrote about the struggles of my own father who, although poor and illiterate, made unbelievable sacrifices to raise his fourteen children in the Ghanaian village. Through his sacrifices, my father created a platform for me to operate on. Many disadvantaged children in America have no such platform.

There is much talk in America about the role teachers in the K-12 education system should play in preparing disadvantaged students to succeed in life. The sad reality is that in many inner-city schools, large numbers of children go to school not fully prepared to learn. In such an environment, even a teacher with the best of intentions might throw up their hands. Opinions differ sharply as to who bears the responsibility for motivating children to work hard at school.

A well-qualified and highly dedicated teacher can make a significant positive impact on some children's lives. However, my experiences have convinced me that what happens outside of the school environment generally has a far greater bearing on children's life outcomes. The teachers in my village elementary school were some of the most dedicated educators I have encountered anywhere. They were very demanding, and they worked tirelessly to help every student succeed academically. Unfortunately, they were dealing mostly with children who, through no fault of their own, saw no clear purpose for education and hence did not respond appropriately to the teachers' demands.

In some parts of Africa and other developing nations where illiteracy rates are high, parents simply do not know enough about education to even begin to talk to their children about its importance. In America, every adult has had at least some exposure to the education system. I have heard many people in minority communities admit that it was their failure to focus on education that ruined their lives. Such parents must share this extremely important lesson with their children. It is a tragedy that so many parents are absent from their children's lives; thus this message is never delivered.

My extended family in Ghana could easily have become trapped in the never-ending cycle of poverty that thwarts so many people of color in America. In my case, it took one courageous person to take charge and break that cycle. That one selfless person is what every disadvantaged American child needs in life.

The good news is, there are various organizations, such as Boys & Girls Clubs of America, that offer free after-school and various mentoring programs to help disadvantaged children navigate the educational, professional, and other sectors of society. Children who lack proper nurturing environments in their homes should avail themselves of the opportunities these charitable organizations provide.

America's economic inequality has been well documented. It is clearly a major source of the country's myriad social problems, and therefore merits the intense focus it receives in today's policymaking and academic circles. The important thing to remember for disadvantaged children is that life's playing field has always been—and probably will be forever—tilted. The key is to learn to do the best one can with available resources.

Children like Jamal, even if they manage to graduate from high school, are poorly equipped for today's job market because they failed to acquire basic skills in school. Their ignorance invariably leads to chronic poverty and its attendant consequences in adulthood.

There is a consensus that the much-talked-about mass incarceration of Black men in America is a direct result of the environments that increasingly large numbers of Black children grow up in. The natural instinct of any crime victim is to seek retribution, so the tough-on-crime approach favored by some policymakers and segments of society is understandable. However, I have come to believe, based on what I observed in my classrooms in Buffalo, that the issue of agency is especially important in this national debate.

Many of the Black people currently in prison have suffered a double injury. Since childhood, they have survived under dire environmental conditions. Incarcerating them for years for actions that are a direct result of their upbringings is adding insult to injury.

Determining who or what is responsible for the plight of urban Black communities is a perennial American debate. Is it the failure of individuals in those communities to take responsibility for their own lives? Broken families? A collective failure? Dysfunctional public education systems?

Ineffective teachers? Slavery and its legacy? A racist society? Failure of government? Accusing fingers point in many directions.

The answer is all of the above and probably more. Slavery ended, but racial segregation and discrimination persist, trapping many Blacks in urban centers where there are no jobs because of offshoring, where public schools don't function properly, and where poor infrastructure and rampant crime add to the hardship.

Having lived in that type of environment when I first came to America, I am all too familiar with the challenges poor Blacks face in their daily lives. There are extremely powerful external forces that combine to make life miserable for a poor Black person living in an inner city. However, I believe—strongly—that there is an equally powerful internal negative force the Black community itself has a responsibility to confront: the culture that discourages learning.

From readings and news reports I have listened to over the years, I know that some schools in America's poorest communities are so dilapidated and staffed with such poorly qualified teachers that students hoping to receive an education are doomed from the start. The schools where I taught in Buffalo were certainly not dilapidated. Many of the teachers were trained professionals dedicated to their work. I am still convinced that those schools had everything children like Antoine and Jamal needed in order to obtain a good basic education. Something else got in the way.

* * *

BASED ON WHAT I KNOW now, I agree that the obstacles facing children from poor families in America's inner cities can indeed be daunting, especially when they enter the education system. The circumstances are so dire in some places that children cannot even get to school safely and in the right frame of mind to properly function as students. However, I also believe that many disadvantaged children have some platform to operate on. There isn't enough justification for so many to give up on education so quickly and so easily, in the manner I observed during my time as a teacher. Quite often, a person makes their own luck. One cannot know what is achievable until one tries.

The tilted-field phenomenon often exists even within families. My daughter Jennifer's life story to date is instructive. Because I somehow ended up in America, she has had opportunities her numerous cousins in Ghana can only dream of. She attended excellent American public schools and later went to Princeton. During the summer after her sophomore year, she studied at Cambridge University in England. After Princeton, she worked for two years before going to business school, graduating with her MBA from the University of Chicago at the tender age of twenty-five. Even by American standards, she reached top academic and professional levels at an astonishing speed.

Many of her cousins have attended universities in Ghana, but the quality of Jennifer's educational experiences and the professional opportunities now available to her in America are unquestionably much greater. While it is true that she made maximum use of her opportunities, she had a lucky draw in the birth lottery. From our numerous conversations over the years, this is a point she understands clearly. She also understands that although she must remain ambitious, she must never lose sight of the fact that the heavy dose of luck that made her achievements possible eludes most people. Many of the children she started school with in Akwatia did not make it beyond elementary school.

While Jennifer was at Cambridge that summer, Patricia, Patrick, and I went to visit her. Jennifer took us on an extensive tour of the campus. *This is the place I constantly dreamed about as a young boy,* I kept thinking as we walked around that magnificent campus. In a way, she had lived out my dream. We also traveled to Oxford University and spent a day touring its campus. The architecture on the Cambridge and Oxford campuses is simply stunning.

I saw the pride in my father's eyes as he watched my steady climb up the educational ladder. He took great consolation from the fact that one of his children had managed to do what he himself had always dreamed of. He would have been particularly proud to hear that I had obtained a graduate degree from Dartmouth, one of America's most elite institutions. I felt that same sense of fatherly pride on the day Jennifer got into Princeton, which is consistently ranked as the best undergraduate institution in America. Because Wyomissing is only a two-hour drive from Princeton, I visited Jennifer numerous times during her four years there. Sometimes, it was simply to spend a couple of hours strolling around with her on that gorgeous campus, modeled on the Oxford and Cambridge campuses.

This is the opportunity I stupidly denied my father on that Saturday morning in Achimota, I ruefully recalled as I walked with Jennifer. I couldn't stop admiring Princeton's impressive Gothic architecture. On Jennifer's graduation day, I proudly held her diploma in my hands, looked up at the sky, and dedicated it to my father. Without his many sacrifices, that monumental achievement would certainly not have been possible.

Some people are born lucky. The not-so-lucky ones must overcome many more hurdles to achieve their dreams, but many do so successfully. The absolute worst thing anyone can do is to dwell on some disadvantage they believe to be a permanent barrier to success.

Based on everything I have learned, I am convinced that in making that fatal mistake to disengage from the education system, few of my students had full agency. They had been bombarded with too many negative messages over lengthy periods of time, which led them to give up the fight even before it started. The adults who exposed them to those negative messages were part of the problem. In raising my two children, I am always reminded of the importance of protecting that precious childhood innocence.

Apart from being blessed with wonderful parents, I was also incredibly lucky to grow up in a place, and at a time, where and when it was possible for a child with my background to make something of himself out of almost nothing. The public elementary and middle schools in Ghana then had few resources, but they were functional. There were none of the disciplinary problems prevalent in inner-city American classrooms. I benefited from the full attention the teachers could devote to their lessons. And I never had to worry about being accused of "acting White."

One of the greatest tragedies of the dysfunction in the inner-city K-12 public education system is that children like Antoine—willing to work hard—are denied the educational benefits of their schools due to constant classroom disruptions. As a result, lives are ruined.

For many disadvantaged children growing up in America today, the problem is largely inequality of opportunity. In Ghana, there was a complete lack of opportunity. With no market for their talents, a life of perpetual poverty was inevitable. Ample evidence exists to show that such an outcome is not a foregone conclusion for poor children born in America. They at least have a fighting chance. Relative to their peers in poor countries, American children have a vast array of avenues through which they can make use of their innate talents. This is a useful perspective for disadvantaged American children. It might help them to know that although they live in an imperfect society, it is at least a functional one, and there are millions of other children around the world who would readily trade places with them because of worse conditions. That perspective has helped people like me navigate the complex American landscape.

Because I wasn't born and raised in this country, I will never be able to fully appreciate the entire range of feelings American-born people of color have during their daily interactions with broader society. I know that I risk sounding insensitive or naïve. That is partly why I waited more than twenty years to write this book. I wanted to ensure that I had a sufficient understanding of the issues.

Even then, I know the risk remains. Growing up in Ghana, I felt the hopelessness that prompted many of my students in Buffalo to disengage from the educational system. I was extremely fortunate to discover, purely by accident, a working formula I relied on to escape from that desolate environment. Remaining silent and failing to share that formula, as well as some of the valuable lessons I learned along the way, would be a far worse sin.

My journey began with the accidental discovery of an interesting piece of information on a discarded scrap of newspaper. That information triggered the series of events that ultimately took me on a magical journey around the world. I sincerely hope that disadvantaged children growing up in America's poor minority communities and elsewhere, in circumstances as hopeless as mine during my early years, will draw some inspiration from the lessons I have shared in this book.

Acknowledgments

THE PROMISE I MADE TO my father the first time I visited his grave was one of my main motivations for writing this book. I wanted to document his many heroic deeds to preserve his richly deserved place in the family's history for generations to come. Thank you, *Opanyin* Kwaku Asare, for everything you did for me and the extended family.

A big thank you to my mother, Augustina Mampomaa, for the crucial support she provided during those trying years. Having endured my own lengthy and painful separation from a woman I deeply loved, I can appreciate how it must have felt for my mother to have her beloved husband away from her for long periods of time, year after year, while he toiled alone in the jungle. Thank you, Mama, for your immense sacrifices, and for almost single-handedly raising us to become responsible adults. And of course much of that would not have been possible without the crucial support of Ernestina, whose generosity is boundless.

Thank you to Patricia, my beloved wife. On top of everything she endured for many years, she patiently allowed me to hijack many of our weekends and holidays these past few years. I spent what should have been precious family times working on this book, often in hiding. My sincere thanks to Jennifer, who read countless initial drafts of the manuscript and offered valuable suggestions.

I have never seen such a large group of children grow up together in the manner that Patrick Jr. and his friends in Wyomissing did. Thank you, Patrick, and your friends, for teaching me a few more life lessons about how to build and maintain strong relationships. You clearly took the people skills you developed here in Wyomissing to the University of Pittsburgh, where you are currently studying. Whenever I visit you on campus, I am awed by the large number of friends you've made there also. Enjoy the rest of your time at the university. Hail to Pitt!

I am exceedingly grateful to all the teachers, from kindergarten to graduate school, who helped transform me from a raw village kid to the educated professional I am today. Two deserve special mention: Mr. Vincent Kpatapka and Ms. Beatrice Kontoh. Mr. Kpatapka became so heavily invested in my effort to gain admission to Achimota that at times it felt as if he was my biological father. Ms. Kontoh similarly took me under her wings at secondary school in Oda, offering a level of love and support that one would normally expect only from a biological mother. It saddens me greatly that I am not able to share this book with the two of you because you both passed away. Thank you, angels. May your kind and beautiful souls rest in eternal peace.

Each of my thirteen siblings contributed in many ways toward helping me at various stages of my journey. Although I still think you could have shown me some sympathy at times in those early days in Boadua when I struggled to carry loads that were too large for my size, or was under constant duress combining chores and homework, your tough-love approach probably worked in my favor. It helped me grow up faster than I would have otherwise. I sincerely appreciate your love and guidance.

A special thank you to Francis, whose presence offered me the challenge I needed to make me a better student. Without him, I might have become complacent early on, and I'm not sure how that would have impacted me later in life. Wala Cosmas, another good friend of mine in elementary and middle schools in Boadua, was always there for me. In my latter years in secondary school and the period prior to my departure for the Soviet Union, he occasionally stepped in to provide some modest but crucial financial assistance. He did that despite having only odd jobs that did not pay much. Thank you, Wala, for your kindness.

I want to thank two very dear friends, Eric Antwi and Kate Asaah, for their invaluable support during my student days in the Soviet Union. Eric not only allowed me to stay with him in his tiny one-bedroom apartment in London three summers in a row, he also helped me find a job at the bakery where he worked at the time. The money I earned during those three summers was a vital supplement to my meager student stipend. On top of that, I had a lot of fun working at the factory and learned a great deal about breadmaking in the process.

Kate kept the door to her house in Utrecht open for me whenever I needed a place to stop and rest on that long train journey from Moscow to London. She accommodated me for an entire summer in Utrecht, which gave me an opportunity to thoroughly explore the Netherlands, one of my favorite countries in Europe. Thank you, Eric and Kate.

Much of what I have achieved in America over the past thirty years would not have happened without the vital assistance that Joe and Ernest provided early on in Buffalo. Being a cash-strapped student at the time, it was an incredible act of generosity for Ernest to not only host me in his apartment for so many months but also to share his meals with me. Thank you, Ernest, from the bottom of my heart. I am forever indebted to you.

I am immensely grateful to Brad Hall. A Tuck alum himself and a Wyomissing resident, he and his wife Barbara were tremendously helpful to us when we first moved to Wyomissing. They provided us with valuable information about school districts, ideal locations to live, and local doctors and dentists. They even babysat Patrick Jr. for a full day when Patricia and I traveled to Wyomissing one weekend from Vermont for apartment-hunting.

Brad was also one of the first people to suggest that I write a book about my personal story. He learned from one of our initial conversations that I had traveled from Ghana to the Soviet Union for college prior to coming to America and sensed there was something interesting in my background that would be worth writing about. I hope you enjoy the book, Brad.

My sincerest thanks to my two editors, Lara Asher and Catherine Treadgold. I worked on the manuscript first with Lara, who took a deep interest in the project right away. With her sharp eye for detail, she helped craft the story in a way only a great editor could. Working with her on the manuscript was a tremendous joy. Lara is not just an editor; she is a fantastic coach who has helped improve my writing considerably. Thank you, Lara, for helping to bring my story to life in such a vivid way.

Catherine later took the manuscript and made her own enhancements to it. I have learned a great deal about the mechanics of writing from working with her. Catherine, apart from being an editor, is a former publisher. She has graciously taught me a lot of important things about the publishing process. As a novice writer, I have found this knowledge to be particularly helpful. Thank you, Catherine, for your immense generosity. Catherine and Lara are both Princeton alums. Jennifer found them for me in the school's alumni database. I feel blessed to have had these three wonderful

Princetonians by my side as I worked on this project. Go, Tigers!

Lastly, it certainly would not have been possible for me to embark on that long and difficult journey from Boadua to America without the help of thousands of other people along the way. I want to say a big thank you to everyone who contributed in any way to make me who I am today. It's been quite a ride.

Patricia, Patrick Jr., Jennifer, and me at Jennifer's graduation from the University of Chicago Booth School of Business

My sister Christina, brother Ebenezer-and me at a social gathering in London

*Ernestina (second from right) on her seventieth birthday celebration;
my sister Beatrice is on the right.*

*My brothers Richard (left) and Daniel. Picture taken after
church service in Boadua*

My sister Gladys

Patricia, my sister Felicia (in chair), and my sister Charlotte at our house in Wyomissing

Me and Patrick Jr. in front of the Houses of Parliament in London

Me, Patrick Jr., and Jennifer, Cambridge

Patricia, Jennifer, and me at Jennifer's graduation from Princeton

Patrick Jr. and friends at his high school prom

My sister Comfort

My sister Matilda

Patrick Asare was born and raised in Ghana. After completing secondary school, he attended university in the former Soviet Union, studying electrical engineering at Donetsk National Technical University in the then Soviet republic of Ukraine. He graduated with a bachelor's degree in electrical engineering and also completed a certification program to become a Russian language teacher.

Patrick resided in the Soviet Union from 1985 to 1991, during the historic perestroika era, when President Mikhail Gorbachev introduced the reforms that ultimately led to the breakup of the Soviet Union. He traveled extensively throughout Eastern and Western Europe and became one of the few people with firsthand knowledge of ordinary life on both sides of the Iron Curtain.

After graduating from Donetsk, Patrick immigrated to America, where he initially taught Russian and math in public schools in Buffalo, New York. He earned a master's degree in electrical engineering from Purdue University in 1995 and an MBA from the Tuck School of Business at

Dartmouth College in 2003. Patrick is a principal at UGI Energy Services, LLC, a diversified energy services firm in Wyomissing, Pennsylvania, where he lives with his family. He previously worked as a senior electrical engineer at Caterpillar, Inc. in Lafayette, Indiana.

Patrick has written extensively on social, political, and energy policy topics. He is a Democracy and Development Fellow at the Ghana Center for Democratic Development, an Accra-based think-tank. Some of Patrick's energy policy articles have received attention worldwide.

For more information, go to www.patrickasareauthor.com.